Gordon Stables

Wild Adventures round the Pole

Gordon Stables

Wild Adventures round the Pole

ISBN/EAN: 9783337258528

Printed in Europe, USA, Canada, Australia, Japan

Cover: Foto ©Andreas Hilbeck / pixelio.de

More available books at **www.hansebooks.com**

"STAND BY, MEN! STAND BY!" [*Page* 43.

WILD ADVENTURES
ROUND THE POLE,

OR THE

Cruise of the 'Snowbird' Crew in the 'Arrandoon.'

BY

GORDON STABLES, M.D., R.N.

WITH EIGHT ILLUSTRATIONS.

New York:
A. C. ARMSTRONG & SON,
714 BROADWAY.
1885.

CONTENTS

CHAPTER I.

THE TWIN RIVERS—A BUSY SCENE—OLD FRIENDS WITH NEW FACES—THE BUILDING OF THE GREAT SHIP—PEOPLE'S OPINIONS—RALPH'S HIGHLAND HOME 1

CHAPTER II.

THE DINNER BY THE LAKE—RORY'S RUN ROUND AFRICA—THE RETURN OF THE WANDERERS . . 10

CHAPTER III.

RETROSPECTION—RALPH'S HOME IN ENGLAND—A HEARTY IF NOT POETIC WELCOME . . . 19

CHAPTER IV.

LIFE AT LEIGH HALL—THE LAUNCH OF THE "ARRANDOON"—TRIAL TRIPS—A ROW AND A FIGHT—"FREEZING POWDERS" 27

CHAPTER V.

DANGER ON THE DEEP—A FOREST OF WATERSPOUTS—THE "ARRANDOON" IS SWAMPED—THE WARNING 37

CHAPTER VI.

A LIFE ON THE OCEAN WAVE—ON THE ROCKS—MYSTERY—A HOME ON THE ROLLING DEEP. . 47

CHAPTER VII.

SANDIE McFLAIL, M.D.—"WHA WOULDNA' BE A SEA-BIRD?"—THE GIRL TELLS HER STRANGE ADVENTURES—NIGHTFALL ON THE SEA. . . . 56

CHAPTER VIII.

A GALE FROM THE MOUNTAINS—DAYBREAK IN ICELAND—THE GREAT BALLOON ASCENT—RORY'S YARN—THE SNOW-CLOUD—THE PIRATE IS SEEN . . 65

CHAPTER IX.

MOUNT HEKLA—THE GREAT GEYSER—A NARROW ESCAPE—THE SEARCH FOR THE PIRATE—McBAIN'S LITTLE "RUSE DE GUERRE"—THE BATTLE BEGUN 75

CHAPTER X.

"DOWN WITH THE RED FLAG AND UP WITH THE BLACK"—VICTORY—AN OLD ACQUAINTANCE—HIE, FOR THE NORTH 85

CHAPTER XI.

THE VOYAGE RESUMED—A PLEASANT EVENING—"THOSE RUSHING WINDS"—THE "ARRANDOON" GROWS SAUCY—THE DOCTOR SPREAD-EAGLED—A SCHOOL OF WHALES 94

Contents.

CHAPTER XII.

THE ISLE OF JAN MAYEN—RETROSPECTION—THE SEA OF ICE—THE DESERTED VILLAGE—CARRIED OFF BY A BEAR—DANCING FOR DEAR LIFE . . 105

CHAPTER XIII.

MORE ABOUT FREEZING POWDERS—PERSEVERANDO—DINING IN THE SKY—THE DESCENT OF THE CRATER 115

CHAPTER XIV.

ANXIOUS HOURS—EXPLORATION OF THE MOUNTAIN CAVERN—THE CAVE OF THE KING OF ICE AND GHOULS OF A THOUSAND WINTERS—TRANSFORMATION SCENES—SNOWBLIND—LOST . . . 125

CHAPTER XV.

THE "ARRANDOON" ANCHORS TO THE "FLOE"—THE VISIT TO THE "CANNY SCOTIA"—SILAS GRIG—A SAD SCENE—RORY RELIEVES HIS FEELINGS—STRANGERS COMING FROM THE FAR WEST . . 134

CHAPTER XVI.

SILAS GRIG'S DINNER-PARTY—A NEW MEMBER OF THE MALACOPTERYGII—THE STORM ON THE SEA OF ICE—BREAK-UP OF THE MAIN PACK—ROUGHING IT AT SEA 143

CHAPTER XVII.

THE STORM—THE "CANNY SCOTIA" IN DISTRESS—RUM, MUTINY, ANARCHY, AND DEATH—SAVED—ADVENTURE WITH A SHE-BEAR—CAPTURE OF THE YOUNG 153

CHAPTER XVIII.

A NEW ARRIVAL—THE DOGS—TRAPPER SETH BECOMES KENNEL-MAN—PREPARATIONS FOR A GREAT SEAL HUNT—THE GREENLAND BEAR 163

CHAPTER XIX.

"SILAS GRIG, HIS YARN"—THE WHITE WHALE—AFLOAT ON AN ICEBERG—A DREARY JOURNEY—BEAR ADVENTURES—"THE SEALS! THE SEALS!!" . . 172

CHAPTER XX.

SEAL-STALKING—A GLORIOUS DAY'S SPORT—PIPER PETER AND THE BEAR—A STRANGE DUET—THE SEAL-STALKERS' RETURN 182

CHAPTER XXI.

THE COMING FROST—SILAS WARNS THE "ARRANDOON" OF DANGER—FORGING THROUGH THE ICE—BESET—A STRANGE AND ALARMING ACCIDENT. . 191

CHAPTER XXII.

CAPTAIN COBB RETIRES—MORE TORPEDOING—THE GREAT ICE-HOLE—STRANGE SPORT—THE TERRIBLE ZUGÆNA—THE DEATH STRUGGLE. . . . 199

CHAPTER XXIII.

RORY'S REVERIE—SILAS ON THE SCYMNUS BOREALIS—THE BATTLE WITH THE SHARKS—RORY GETS IN FOR IT AGAIN—THROWN AMONG THE SHARKS . 209

Contents.

CHAPTER XXIV.

MAY-DAY IN THE ARCTIC REGIONS 219

CHAPTER XXV.

BREAKING-UP OF THE GREAT ICE PACK—IN THE NIPS—THE "CANNY SCOTIA" ON HER BEAM-ENDS—STAVING OF THE "ARRANDOON" . . . 229

CHAPTER XXVI.

AN ADVENTURE ON THE PACK—SEPARATED FROM THE SHIP—DESPAIR—THE DREAM OF HOME—UNDER WAY ONCE MORE 238

CHAPTER XXVII.

WORKING ALONG THE PACK EDGE—AMONG THE SEALS AGAIN—A BUMPER SHIP—ADVENTURES ON THE ICE—TED WILSON'S PROMOTION . . . 247

CHAPTER XXVIII.

A WONDERFUL YANK—ICE—"MAKING OFF" SKINS—PREPARING TO "BEAR UP"—THE SUMMER HOME OF THE GIANT WALRUS—THE SHIPS PART . . 257

CHAPTER XXIX.

NORTHWARD HO!—HOISTING BEACONS—THE WHITE FOG—THE GREAT SEA-SERPENT . . . 266

CHAPTER XXX.

LAND HO! THE ISLE OF DESOLATION—THE LAST BLINK OF SUNSHINE—THE AURORA BOREALIS—STRANGE ADVENTURE WITH A BEAR 274

CHAPTER XXXI.

A COUNCIL—PREPARING FOR WINTER QUARTERS—THE ISLE OF ALBA AND ITS MAMMOTH CAVES—MAGNUS' TALE—AT HIS BOY'S GRAVE 283

CHAPTER XXXII.

THE TERRIBLE SNOWSTORM—SOMETHING LIKE AN AQUARIUM—THE MAMMOTH CAVES AND THEIR STARTLING TREASURES—THE JOURNEY POLEWARDS—COLLAPSE OF THE BALLOON—"GOD SAVE THE QUEEN" 293

CHAPTER XXXIII.

ANOTHER WINTER AT THE POLE—CHRISTMAS DAY—THE CURTAIN RISES ON THE LAST ACT—SICKNESS—DEATH—DESPAIR 304

CHAPTER XXXIV.

A SAILOR'S COTTAGE—THE TELEGRAM—"SOMETHING'S IN THE WIND"—THE GOOD YACHT "POLAR STAR"—HOPE FOR THE WANDERERS . . . 314

CHAPTER XXXV.

THE RESCUE—HOMEWARD BOUND—ALL'S WELL THAT ENDS WELL 324

CHAPTER I.

THE TWIN RIVERS—A BUSY SCENE—OLD FRIENDS WITH NEW FACES—THE BUILDING OF THE GREAT SHIP—PEOPLE'S OPINIONS—RALPH'S HIGHLAND HOME.

WILDER scenery there is in abundance in Scotland, but hardly will you find any more picturesquely beautiful than that in which the two great rivers, the Clyde and the Tweed, first begin their journey seawards. It is a classic land, there is poetry in every breath you breathe, the very air seems redolent of romance. Here Coleridge, Scott, and Burns roved. Wilson loved it well, and on yonder hills Hogg, the Bard of Ettrick—he who "taught the wandering winds to sing"—fed his flocks. It is a land, too, not only of poetic memories, but one dear to all who can appreciate daring deeds done in a good cause, and who love the name of hero.

If the reader saw the rivers we have just named, as they roll their waters majestically into the ocean, the one at Greenock, the other near the quaint old town of Berwick, he would hardly believe that at the commencement of their course they are so small and narrow that ordinary-sized men can step across them, that bare-legged little boys wade through them, and thrust their arms under their green banks, bringing therefrom many a lusty trout. But so it is.

Both rise in the same district, within not very many miles of each other, and for a considerable distance they follow the same direction and flow north.

But soon the Tweed gets very faint-hearted indeed.

"The country is getting wilder and wilder," she says to

her companion, " we'll never be able to do it. I'm going south and east. It is easier."

"And I," says the bold Clyde, "am going northwards and west; it is more difficult, and therein lies the enjoyment. I will conquer every obstacle, I'll defy everything that comes against me, and thus I'll be a mightier river than you. I'll water great cities, and on my broad breast I will bear proud navies to the ocean, to do battle against wind and wave. 'Faint heart never won fair lady.' Farewell, friend Tweed, farewell."

And so they part.

This conversation between the two rivers is held fourteen hundred feet above the level of the sea, and five score miles and over have to be traversed before the Clyde can reach it. Yet, nothing daunted, merrily on she rolls, gaining many an accession of strength on the way from streams and burns.

"If you are going seaward," say these burns, "so are we, so we'll take the liberty of joining you."

"And right welcome you are," sings the Clyde; "in union lies strength."

In union lies strength; yes, and in union is happiness too, it would seem, for the Clyde, broader and stronger now, glides peacefully and silently onwards; or if not quite silently, it emits but a silvery murmur of content. Past green banks and wooded braes, through daisied fields where cattle feed, through lonely moorlands heather-clad, now hidden in forest depths, now out again into the broad light of day, sweeping past villages, cottages, mansions, and castles, homes of serf and feudal lord in times long past and gone, with many a sweep and many a curve it reaches the wildest part of its course. Here it must rush the rapids and go tumbling and roaring over the lynns, with a noise that may be heard for miles on a still night, with an impetuosity that shakes the earth for hundreds of yards on every side.

"I wonder how old Tweed is getting on?" thinks our brave river as soon as it has cleared the rocks and rapids and pauses for breath.

But the Clyde will soon be rewarded for its pluck and its daring, before long it will enter and sweep through the second city of the empire, the great metropolis of the west; but ere it does so, forgive it, if it lingers awhile at Bothwell, and if it seems sullen and sad as it dashes underneath the ancient bridge where, in days long gone, so fierce a fight took place that five hundred of the brave Covenanters lay dead on the field of battle. And pardon it when anon it makes a grand and splendid sweep round Bothwell Bank, as if loth to leave it. Yonder are the ruins of the ancient castle

> "Where once proud Murray held the festive board.
> * * * * *
> But where are now the festive board,
> The martial throng, and midnight song?
> Ah! ivy binds the mouldering walls,
> And ruin reigns in Bothwell's halls.
> O, deep and long have slumbered now
> The cares that knit the soldier's brow,
> The lovely grace, the manly power,
> In gilded hall and lady's bower;
> The tears that fell from beauty's eye,
> The broken heart, the bitter sigh,
> E'en deadly feuds have passed away,
> Still thou art lovely in decay."

But see, our river has left both beauty and romance far behind it. It has entered the city—the city of merchant princes, the city of a thousand palaces; it bears itself more steadily now, for hath not Queen Commerce deigned to welcome it, and entrusted to it the floating wealth of half a nation? The river is in no hurry to leave this fair city.

"My noble queen," it seems to say, "I am at your service. I come from the far-off hills to obey your high behests. My ambition is fulfilled, do with me as you will."

But soon as the bustle and din of the city are left behind, soon as the grand old hills begin to appear on the right, and glimpses of green on the southern banks, lo! the tide comes up to welcome the noble river; and so the Clyde falls silently and imperceptibly into the mighty Atlantic. Yet scarcely is the lurid and smoky atmosphere that hangs pall-like over the town exchanged for the purer, clearer air beyond, hardly have the waters from the distant mountains begun to mingle with ocean's brine, ere the noise of ten thousand hammers seems to rend the very sky.

Clang, clang, clang, clang—surely the ancient god Vulcan has reappeared, and taken up his abode by the banks of the river. Clang, clang, clang. See yonder is the *Iona*, churning the water into foam with her swift-revolving paddles. She has over a thousand passengers on board; they are bound for the Highlands, bent on pleasure. But this terrible noise and din of hammers—they will have three long miles of it before they can even converse in comfort. Clang, clang, clang—it is no music to them. Nay, but to many it is.

It is music to the merchant prince, for yonder lordly ship, when she is launched from the slips, will sail far over the sea, and bring him back wealth from many a foreign shore. It is music to the naval officer; it tells him his ship is preparing, that ere long she will be ready for sea, that his white flag will be unfurled to the breeze, and that he will walk her decks—her proud commander.

And it is music—merry music to the ears of two individuals at least, who are destined to play a very prominent part in this story. They are standing on the quarter-deck of a half-completed ship, while clang, clang, clang, go the hammers outside and inside.

The younger of the two—he can be but little over twenty-three—with folded arms, is leaning carelessly against the bulwarks. Although there is a thoughtful look upon his handsome face, there is a smile as well, a smile of pleasure.

He is taller by many inches than his companion, though by no means better "built," as sailors call it. This companion has a bold, brown, weather-beaten face, the lower half of it buried in a beard that is slightly tinged with grey; his eyes are clear and honest,—eyes that you can tell at a glance would not flinch to meet even death itself. He stands bold, erect, firm. Both are dressed well, but there is a marked difference in the style of their attire. The garments of the elder pronounce him at once just what he is,—one who has been "down to the sea in ships." The younger is dressed in the fashionable attire of an English gentleman. To say more were needless. A minute observer, however, might have noticed that there was a slight air of *negligé* about him, if only in the unbuttoned coat or the faultless hat pushed back off the brow.

"And so you tell me," said the younger, "that the work still goes bravely on?"

"Ay, that it does," said his companion; "there have been rumours of a strike for higher wages among the men of other yards, but none, I am proud to say, in this."

"And still," continued the former, "we pay but a fraction of wage more than other people, and then, of course, there is the extra weekly half-holiday."

"There is something more, Ralph—forgive me if I call you Ralph, in memory of dear old times. You will always be a boy to me, and I could no more call you Mr. Leigh than I could fly."

Ralph grasped his companion by the hand; the action was but momentary, but it showed a deal of kindly feeling. "Always call me Ralph," he said, "always, McBain, always. When we are back once more at sea I'll call you captain, not till then. But what is the something more that makes our men so happy?"

"Why, your kindly manner, Ralph boy. You mix with them, you talk with them, and take an interest in all their doings, and you positively seem to know every one of them by name. Mind you, that extra half-holiday isn't thrown away: they work all the harder, and they are happy. Why, listen to them now."

He paused, and held up one hand. From bows to stern of the vessel there arose the sound of industry, incessant, continual; but high over the clang of hammers and the grating noise of saws there arose the voice of song.

"They sing, you see," continued McBain; "but they don't put down their tools to sing. But here comes old Ap. What cheer, Mr. Ap Ewen?"

Those of my readers who knew Ap as he was two or three years ago[*]—the little stiff figure-head of a fellow—would be surprised to see him now. He is far more smartly dressed, he is more active looking, and more intelligent altogether. The truth is, McBain, seeing there was good in the man, had taken him in hand. He had caused him to study his trade of boat-builder in a far more scientific fashion, with the result that he was now, as our story opens, foreman over all the men employed on the ship in which Ralph Leigh stood.

Indeed, McBain himself, as well as Ap, were good examples of what earnest study can effect. There is hardly anything which either boy or man cannot learn if he applies his mind thereto.

"What cheer, Mr. Ap Ewen?" said McBain.

"More hands wanted, sir," said Ap, pulling out his snuff-box and taking a vigorous pinch.

"More hands, Ap?" exclaimed McBain.

"Ay, sir, ay; look you see," replied Ap, "you told me to hurry on, you see, and on Monday we shall want to begin the saloon bulkheads."

"Bravo! Ap, bravo! come to my office to-night at seven, and we'll put that all straight."

"Thank you, sir," said Ap, touching his hat and retiring.

Ralph Leigh was owner of the splendid composite steamship that was now fast nearing her completion.

[*] *Vide* "Cruise of the Snowbird." Same Author and Publishers.

She was not being built by contract, but privately, and McBain was head controller of every department, and for every department he had hired experts to carry on the work. The vessel was designed for special service, and therefore she must be a vessel of purity, a vessel of strength. There must not be a flaw in her, not a patch—all must be solid, all must be good. McBain had hired experts to examine everything ere it was purchased, but he made use of his own eyes and ears as well. The yard in which the ship was built was rented, and every bit of timber that entered it was tested first, whether it were oak or teak, pine, mahogany, or cedar; and the iron the same, and the bolts of copper and steel, so that Captain McBain's work was really no sinecure.

"Well, then," said Ralph, "I've been over all the ship; I'm extremely pleased with the way things are going on, so if you have nothing more to say to me I'm off. By the way, do the people still flock down on Friday afternoons to look over the ship?"

"They do," replied McBain; "and poor old Ap, I feel sorry for him. *He* gets no Friday half-holiday; he won't let me stop, but he insists upon remaining himself to show the people round."

"And the people enjoy it?"

"They do. They marvel at our engines, as well they may. The gear, so simple and strong, that Ap and I invented for the shipping and unshipping of the rudder, and the easy method we have for elevating the screw out of the water and reducing the vessel to a sailing ship, they think little short of miraculous. They are astonished, too, at the extraordinary strength of build of the ship. Indeed, they are highly complimentary to us in their general admiration. But," continued McBain, laughing aloud, "it would amuse you to hear the remarks of some of these good, innocent souls. The two 12-pounder Dalgrens are universal favourites. They pat them as if they loved them. One girl last Friday said 'they just looked for a' the warld like a couple o' big iron soda-water bottles.' They linger in the armoury; old Ap shows them our 'express' rifles, and our 'bone-crushers,' and the hardened and explosive bullets; then he takes them to the harpoon-room and shows them the harpoons, and the guns, and the electric apparatus, and all the other gear. They stare open-mouthed at the balloon-room and the sledge-lockers, but when they come to the door of the torpedo-chamber they simply hurry past with looks of awe. It is currently reported that we are bound for the very North Pole itself; I'm not sure we are not going to bring it back home with us. Anyhow, they say that as soon as we reach the ice, we are to fill our balloons, attaching one to each mast and funnel, and float away and away over the sea of ancient ice until we reach the Pole."

Ralph laughed right merrily, and next minute he was over the side, with his face set townwards, trudging steadily on to the railway-station. It was only a trifle over three miles; there were cabs to be had in abundance, but what young man would ride if he had time to walk?

Ralph was going home. Not to his fair English home far away in the south, for ever since, in the early spring-time—and now it was autumn—the keel of the ship—*his* ship—had been laid, Ralph had taken up his abode in a rustic cottage by the banks of a broad-bosomed lake in the Highlands of Argyll. Wild though the country was all around, it was but four miles from the railway, and this journey he used to accomplish twice or oftener every week, on the back of a daft-looking Welsh pony that he had bought for the purpose. Once on board the train, two hours took him to the city, and thence a brisk walk to the building-yard.

He had watched, week after week, the gradual progress of his ship towards completion, with an interest and a joy that were quite boyish. He dearly loved to see the men at work, and listen to their cheerful voices as they laboured.

RALPH'S HIGHLAND HOME.

[*Page* 8.

Even the smell of the pine or cedar shavings was perfume to Ralph, and the way he used to climb about and wander over and through the ship, when she was little more than ribs, knees, and beams, was quite amusing.

But he was nevertheless always happy to get back to his Highland home, his books, his boat, and his fishing-rod. She was a widow who owned the humble cottage, but she was kind and good, and Ralph's rooms, that looked away out over the lake, were always kept in a state of perfect cleanliness. The widow had one little daughter, a sweetly pretty and intelligent child, over whose fair wee head five summers had hardly rolled. Jeannie was her name, Jeannie Morrison, and she was an especial pet of Ralph's. She and the collie dog always came gleefully down the road to meet him on his return from the distant city, and you may be perfectly sure he always brought something nice in his pocket for the pair of them.

When tired of reading, Ralph used to romp with wee Jeannie, or take her on his knee and tell her wonderful stories, which made her blue eyes grow bigger and more earnest than ever as she listened.

In fact, Jeannie and Ralph were very fond of each other indeed, and every time he went to a romantic little island out in the lake to fish, he took Jeannie in the stern of the boat, and the time passed doubly quick.

"Oh, Mista Walph! Mista Walph!" cried Jeannie, bursting into Ralph's room one afternoon, clapping her hands with joy. "Mista McBain is coming; Capping McBain is coming."

"Yes," said Mistress Morrison, entering behind her little daughter. "I'm sure you'll be delighted, sir, and so am I, for the captain hasn't been here for a month."

Then Ralph got his hat, and, accompanied by the honest collie and his favourite Jeannie, went off down the road to meet McBain and bid him welcome to his Highland home.

CHAPTER II.

THE DINNER BY THE LAKE—RORY'S RUN ROUND AFRICA—THE RETURN OF THE WANDERERS.

"WHEN did you hear from Allan and Rory?" asked McBain that day, as they were seated at dinner in the little Highland cottage.

Mrs. Morrison had done her best to put something nice before them, and not without success either—so thought Ralph, and so, too, thought his guest. At all events, both of them did ample justice to that noble lake trout. Five pounds did he weigh, if he weighed an ounce, and as red was he in flesh as if he had been fed upon beet. The juicy joint of mountain mutton that followed was fit to grace the table of a prince—it was as fragrant and sweet as the blooming heather tops that had brought it to perfection. Nor was the cranberry tart to be despised. The berries of which it was composed had not come over the Atlantic in a barrel of questionable flavour—no, they had been culled on the dewy braelands that very morning by the fair young fingers of wee Jeannie Morrison herself. The widow did not forget to tell them that, and it did not detract from their enjoyment of the tart. For drink they had fragrant heather ale—home-brewed.

"When did I hear from Allan and Rory?" said Ralph, repeating McBain's question; "from the first, not for weeks—he is a lazy boy; from the latter, only yesterday morning."

"And what says Rory?" asked McBain.

"Oh!" replied Ralph, "his letter is beautiful. It is twelve pages long. He is loud in his praises of the behaviour of the yacht, as a matter of course; but in no single sentence of this lengthy epistle does he refer definitely to the health or welfare of anybody whatever."

"From which you infer——?"

"From which I infer," said Ralph, "that everybody is as well as Rory himself—that my dear father is well, and Allan, and his mother, and his sister Helen Edith. He is a queer boy, Rory, and he encloses me a couple of columns from a Cape of Good Hope paper, in which he has written an epitome of the whole voyage, since they first started in May last. He calls his yarn 'Right round Africa.' He commences at Suez, a place where even boy Rory, I should think, would fail to find much poetry and romance; but they must have enjoyed themselves at Alexandria, where Rory mounted on top of Pompey's Pillar, rode upon donkeys, and did all kinds of queer things. Well, they spent a week at Malta, with its streets of stairs, its bells, its priests, its convents, and its blood-oranges. Rory missed trees and shade, though; he says Malta is a capital place for lizards, or any animal, human or otherwise, that cares to spend the day basking on the top of a stone. He liked Tunis and Algiers better, and he quite enjoyed Teneriffe and Madeira. Then they crossed over to Sierra Leone, and he launches forth in praise of the awful forests—'primeval,' he calls them—and he says, in his own inimitable Irish way, that 'they are dark, bedad, even in broad daylight.' Then all down the strange savage West Coast they sailed; they even visited Ashantee, but he doesn't say whether or not they called on his sable majesty the king. Of course they didn't miss looking in at St. Helena, which he designates a paradise in mid-ocean, and not a lonely sea-girt rock, as old books call it. Ascension was their next place of resort. That is a rock, if you like, he says; but the sea-birds' eggs and the turtle are redeeming features. And so on to the Cape, and up the Mozambique, landing here and there at beautiful villages and towns, and in woods where they picked the oysters off the trees." *

"They really must be enjoying themselves," said McBain.

"That they are," Ralph replied, pulling out Rory's letter. "Just listen how charmingly he writes of the Indian Ocean—nobody else save our own poetic Rory could so write:—' My dear, honest, unsophisticated Ralph, —oh, you ought to have been with us as we rounded the Cape! That thunderstorm by night would have made even your somewhat torpid blood tingle in your veins. It was night, my Ralph; what little wind there was was dead off the ironbound coast, but the billows were mountains high. Yes, this is no figure of speech. I have never seen such waves before, and mayhap never will again. I have never seen such lightning, and never heard such thunder. We remained all night on deck; no one had the slightest wish to go below. As I write our yacht is bounding over a blue and rippling sea; the low, wooded shore on our lee is sleeping in the warm sunlight, and everything around us breathes peace and quiet, and yet I have but to clap my hand across my eyes, and once again the whole scene rises up before me. I see the lightning quivering on the dark waves, and flashing incessantly around us, with intervals of the blackest darkness. I see the good yacht clinging by the bows to the crest of the waves, or plunging arrowlike into the watery ravines; I see the wet and slippery decks and cordage, and the awe-struck men around the bulwarks; and I see the faces of my friends as I saw them then—Allan's knitted brow, his mother's looks of terror, and the pale features of poor

---

* Oysters growing on trees seems a strange paradox. They do so grow, however. The mangrove-trees are washed by the tide, and to their tortuous roots oysters adhere, which may be gathered at low water.

Helen Edith. There are nights, Ralph, in the life of a sailor that he is but little likely ever to forget; that was one in mine that will cling to my memory till I cease to breathe.'

"Don't you call that graphic?" said Ralph.

"I do," replied McBain; "give us one other extract, and then lend me the letter. I'll take it to town with me, and you can have it again when you come up."

"Well," said Ralph, "he describes Delagoa Bay and the scenery all round it so pleasantly, that if I hadn't an estate of my own in old England I would run off and take a farm there; right quaintly he talks of the curious Portuguese city of Mozambique; he is loud in the praises of the Comoro Islands, especially of Johanna, with its groves of citrons and limes, its feathery palm-trees, and its lofty mountains, tree-clad to the very summits; and he could write a lordly volume, he says, on the sultanic city of Zanzibar, where, it would seem, his adventures were not like angels' visits—few and far between. He has even fought with the wild Somali Indians, and assisted at a pitched battle between Arabs and a British cruiser. Then he describes his adventures in the woods and in the far-off hills and jungles, tiger-slaying; here is a serpent adventure: here is a butterfly hunt. Fancy butterflies as big as a lady's fan, and of plumage—yes, that is the very word Rory makes use of —'plumage' more bright than a noonday rainbow.

"Here again is a description of the great Johanna hornet, two inches long, blue-black in colour, and so dreaded by the natives that they will not approach within twenty yards of the tree these terrible insects inhabit. Here is a beetle as big as a fish, and as strong apparently as a man, for he seizes hold of the top of the big picklejar into which Rory wants to introduce him, and obstinately refuses to be drowned in spirits; and here is a centipede as long as an adder, green, transparent, deadly;

tarantulas as big as frogs, hairy and horrible; scorpions as big as crabs, green and dangerous as the centipedes themselves, that run from you, it is true, but threaten you as they run.

"It is pleasant," continued Ralph, "to turn from his descriptions of the awful African creepie-creepies, and read of the enchanting beauty of some parts of the Zanzibar woods, the mighty trees mango-laden, the patches of tempting pine-apples, through which one can hardly wade, the curious breadfruit-trees, the pomolos, the citrons, the oranges, and the guavas, that look and taste, says Rory, 'like strawberries smothered in cream.' He dilates, too, on the beauty of the wild flowers, and the brilliancy of the birds—birds that never sing, but flit sadly and silently from bough to bough in the golden sunlight. From the very centre of this beautiful wood Rory, with masterly pen, carries you right away to a lovely coral island in the Indian Ocean.

"'Although many, many miles in extent,' he tells us, although it is clothed in waving woods, although even the cocoa-nut palm waves high aloft its luscious fruit, it is not inhabited by man. Perhaps my boat was the first that ever rasped upon its shore of silvery sand, perhaps I was the first human being that ever lay under the shade of its mangrove-trees or bathed in the waters of its sunny lagune. My boat is a skiff—a tiny skiff; our yacht lies at anchor off Chak-Chak, and I have come all alone to visit this fairy-like island. I left the ship while the stars were still glittering in the heavens, long before the sun leapt up and turned the waters into blood; and now I have rested, bathed, and breakfasted, and am once more on board my indolent skiff. Here in this bay, even half a mile from the shore, you can see the bottom distinct and clear, for the water is as pellucid as crystal, and there isn't a ripple on the sea. And what do I gaze upon?—A submarine garden; and I gaze upon it like one enchanted, the while my boat

—impelled by the tide alone—glides slowly on and over it. Down yonder are flowers of every shape and hue, shrubs of every variety of foliage, coral bushes—pink, and white, and even black—rocks covered with medusæ of the most brilliant colours an artist could imagine, and patches of white sand, strewn with living shells, each one more lovely to look upon than another. And every bush and shrub and flower is all a-quiver with a strange, indescribable motion, which greatly heightens their magical beauty; and why? Because every bush and shrub and flower is composed of a thousand living things. But the larger creatures that creep and crawl or glide through this submarine garden are fantastic in the extreme. Monster crabs and crayfish, horny, abhorrent, and so strange in shape one cannot help thinking they were made to frighten each other; long transparent fishes, partly grayling partly eel; flat fishes that swim in all kinds of ridiculous ways; some fishes that seem all tail together, and others that are nothing but head. And among all the others a curious flat fish that swims on an even keel, and, by the very brilliancy of his colours and gorgeous array, seems to quite take the shine out of all the others. Both sides of this fish are painted alike; both sides of him are divided into five or six equal parts, and each part is of a different colour —one is a marigold yellow, another green, another brightest crimson, another steel grey, and so on. Him I dubbed the harlequin flounder. Yes, Ralph, Shakespeare was right when he said there are more things in heaven and earth than we dream of in our philosophy, and he might have added there are more things in ocean's depths, and stranger things, than any naturalist ever could imagine.'

"You see," said Ralph, folding Rory's funny letter, and handing it to McBain, "that our friends are enjoying themselves; but you won't fail to notice Rory's closing sentence, in which he says that, in the very midst of all the brightness and beauty so lavishly spread around him, he is ofttimes longing to visit once more the strange, mysterious regions around the Pole."

And you have never written a word to him about our new ship and our purposed voyage?" inquired McBain.

"Never a word," cried Ralph, laughing. "You see, I want to keep that a secret till the very last. Oh, fancy, McBain, how wild with glee both Rory and Allan will be when they find that the splendid ship is built and ready, and that we but wait for the return of spring to carry us once more away to the far north again."

"I'd like to see Rory's face," said McBain, smiling, "when you break the news to him."

* * * * *

Just six weeks after this quiet little *tête-à-tête* dinner on the bank of the Highland lake, a very important-looking and fussy little tug-boat come puff-puffing up the Clyde from seaward, towing in a large and pretty yacht; her sails were clewed, and her yards squared, and everything looked trig and trim, not only about her, but on board of her. The blue ensign floated proudly from her staff; her crew were dressed in true yachting rig, and her decks were white as the driven snow.

An elderly lady with snow-white hair paced slowly up and down the quarter-deck, leaning lightly on the arm of a tall and gentlemanly man of mature age. In a lounge chair right aft, and abreast of the binnacle, a fair young girl was reclining, book in lap, but not reading; she was engaged in pleasant conversation with a youth who sat on a camp-stool not far off, while another who leant upon the taffrail gazing shorewards frequently turned towards them, to put in his oar with a word or two. He was taller than the former and apparently a year or two older. He was probably more manly in appearance and build, but certainly not better-looking. Both were tanned with the tropical sun, and both were dressed alike in a kind of sailor uniform of navy blue.

"Yes, Rory," the girl was saying, "I must confess that I do feel glad to get back again to Scotland, much though I have enjoyed our cruise and all our strange adventures around that wild and beautiful coast. Oh! I do not wonder at your being fond of the sea. If I were a man I feel sure I would be a sailor."

"And here we are," replied Rory, with pleasure beaming from his bright, laughing eyes, "within three miles of Glasgow. And, you know, Ralph is here; how delighted he will be to meet us all again! I really wonder he did not come with us."

But Ralph was very much nearer to them at that moment than they had any idea of.

"Helen Edith," cried Allan at that moment, "and you, Rory, do come and have a look at this beautiful steam barque on the stocks."

Both Helen and Rory were by his side in a moment.

"She is a beauty indeed," said Rory, enthusiastically. "There are lines for you! There is shape! Fancy that craft in the water! Look at the beautiful rake that even her funnel has! But is she a man-o'-war, I wonder?"

"More like a despatch boat, I should say," said Allan. "Look, she is pierced for guns."

Allan was right about the guns, for just as he spoke a balloon-shaped cloud of white smoke rose slowly up from her side, and almost simultaneously the roar of a big gun came over the water and died away in a hundred echoes among the rocks and hills. Another and another followed in slow and measured succession, until they had counted fourteen.

"It is saluting they are," said Allan; "but they surely cannot be saluting us; and yet there is no other craft of any consequence coming up the water."

"But I feel sure," said Helen, "it is some one bidding us welcome. And see, they dip the flag."

The yacht's flag was now dipped in return, but still the mystery remained unravelled.

But it does not remain so long.

For see, the yacht is now almost abreast of the new ship, and the decks of the latter are crowded with wildly cheering men. Ay, and yonder, beside the flagstaff, is Ralph himself, with McBain by his side, waving their hats in the air.

The good people on the yacht are for a minute rendered dumb with astonishment, but only for a minute; then the air is rent with their shouts as they give back cheer for cheer.

"Och! deed in troth," cried Rory, losing all control of his English accent, "it's myself that is bothered entoirely. Is it my head or my heels that I'm standing on? for never a morsel of me knows! Is it dreaming I am? Allan, boy, can't you tell me? Just look at the name on the stern of the beautiful craft."

Allan himself was dumb with astonishment to behold, in broad letters of gold the words, "THE ARRANDOON."

CHAPTER III.

RETROSPECTION—RALPH'S HOME IN ENGLAND—A HEARTY IF NOT POETIC WELCOME.

MANY of my readers have met with the heroes of this tale before,* but doubtless some have not; and as it is always well to know at least a little of the *dramatis personæ* of a story beforehand, the many must in the present instance give place to the few. They must either, therefore, listen politely to a little epitomized repetition, or sit quietly aside with their fingers in their ears for the space of five minutes. But, levity apart, I shall be as brief as brevity itself.

Which of our heroes shall we start with first? Allan? Yes, simply because his initial letter stands first on the alphabetic list.

Allan McGregor is a worthy Scot.

We met him for the first time several years prior to the date of this tale; met him in the company of his foster-father, met him in a wildly picturesque Highland glen, called Glentruim, at the castle of Arrandoon. It was midwinter; the young man's southern friends, Ralph Leigh and Rory Elphinston, were coming to see him and live with him for a time, and right welcomely were they received, all the more in that they had narrowly escaped losing their lives in the snow.

Allan was—and so remains—the chieftain of his clan,

* In the "Cruise of the Snowbird," by the same Author and Publishers.

his father having died years before, sword in hand, on a bloodstained redoubt in India, leaving to his only son's care an encumbered estate, a mother and one daughter, Edith, or Helen Edith.

The young chief was poor and proud, but he dearly loved his widowed mother, his beautiful sister, the romantic old castle, and the glen that had reared him from his boyhood; and how he wished and longed to be able to better the position of the former and the condition of the latter, none but he could tell or say. Allan was brave—his clan is proverbially so; his soul was deeply imbued with the spirit of religion, and, it must be added, just slightly tinged with superstition—a superstition born of the mountain mists and the stern, romantic scenery, where he had lived for the greater part of his lifetime.

Ralph Leigh was the son of a once wealthy baronet, and had just finished his education.

Rory Elphinston was an orphan, who owned estates in the west of Ireland, from which property, however, he seldom realised the rents. Like Ralph, Rory was fond of adventure, and ready and willing to do anything honest and worthy to earn that needful dross called gold; and when, one evening, McBain hinted at the wealth that lay ungathered in the inhospitable lands around the Pole, and of the many wild adventures to be met with in those regions, the relation fired the youthful blood of the trio. The boys clubbed together, as most boys might, and bought a small yacht. Small as she was, however, in her, under the able tuition of McBain, they were taught seamanship and discipline, and they became enamoured of the sea and longed to possess a larger ship, in which they might go in quest of adventures in far-off foreign lands.

Now Ralph's father, poor though he was, was very fond —and perhaps even a little proud—of his son; he would, therefore, not refuse him anything in reason he could afford. He rejoiced to see him happy. The good yacht *Snow-*

bird was therefore bought, and in it our brave boys sailed away to the far north. The narrative of their adventures by sea and land is duly recorded in "The Cruise of the Snowbird." You may seek for them there if you wish to read of them; if not, there is little harm done.

The *Snowbird* returned at last, if not really rich, yet with what sailors call an excellent general cargo, quite sufficient for each of them to realise a tolerably large sum of money from. Every shilling of his share Allan had expended in improving the glen, with its cottages and sheep farms, and the dear old castle itself. But, meanwhile, Ralph had fallen into a large fortune, and found himself possessed of rich estates, and a splendid old mansion in ——shire, England. He might have married now, and settled quietly down for life as a country squire, enjoying to the full all the pleasures and luxuries that health combined with wealth are capable of bringing to their possessors. Ah! but then the spirit of the rover had entered into him; he had learned to love adventure for the sake of itself, and to love a life on the ocean wave.

Loving a life on the ocean wave, he might, had he so chosen, have had a very pleasant cruise with his friends, had he gone with them in their run round Africa, alluded to in the last chapter of this tale; but, as would be gleaned from the conversation recorded therein, he did not so choose. He and McBain had their little secret, which they kept well. They were determined to turn explorers, so Ralph built a ship, built a noble ship—built it without acquainting any one what service it was intended for, and even his dear friends Ralph and Rory were to know nothing about her until they returned from their cruise in the tropics. Ralph meant it all as a kindly and a glad surprise to them, for well did he know how their hearts would bound with joy at the very thoughts of sailing once more in quest of adventures. Nor, as the sequel will show, was he in one whit disappointed.

In character, disposition, and appearance my four principal heroes may be thus summed up—I have already told you about Allan's:—

McBain—Captain McBain—was a hardy, fear-nothing, daring man, his mind imbued with a sense of duty and with piety, both of which he had learned at the maternal knee.

Ralph was a young Englishman in every sense of the word—tall, broad, shapely, somewhat slow in action, with difficulty aroused, but a very lion when he did march out of his den intent on a purpose.

Somewhat more youthful was Rory, smaller as to person, poetic as to temperament, fond of the beautiful, an artist and a musician. And if you were to ask me, "Was he, too, brave?" I should answer, "Are not poets and Irishmen always brave? Does not Sir Walter Scott tell us that they laugh in their ranks as they go forward to battle—that they

"Move to death with military glee"?

Sir Walter, I may also remind those who live in the land o' cakes, says in the same poem :

"But ne'er in battlefield throbbed heart more brave
Than that which beats beneath the Scottish plaid."

* * * * *

So now we are back again at the place where we left off in the last chapter, with the yacht being towed slowly past good Ralph's ship on the stocks, and lusty cheers being exchanged from one vessel to the other.

Rory and Allan exchanged glances. The faces of each were at that moment a study for a physiognomist, but the uppermost feeling visible in either was one of astonishment—not blank astonishment, mind you, for there was something in the eyes of each, and in the smile that flickered round their lips, that would have told you in a moment that Ralph's nicely-kept secret was a secret no more. Rory, as usual with natives of green Erin, was the first to break the silence.

"Depend upon it," he said, nodding his head mirthfully, "it is all some mighty fine joke of Ralph's, and he means giving us a pleasant surprise."

"The same thought struck me," replied Allan, "as soon as I clapped eyes on the word '*Arrandoon*.'"

"Oh!" chimed in Helen Edith, with her sweet, musical voice; "that is the reason your friend would not come with us on our delightful voyage."

"That *was* the reason," said Allan, emphatically, "because he was building a ship of his own, the sly dog."

"But wherever do you think he means cruising to at all, at all?" added Rory, with puzzled face.

"That's what I should like to know," said Allan.

And this thought occupied their minds all the way up to Glasgow; but once there, and the ladies seen safely to their hotels, Rory and Allan sped off without delay to visit this big, mysterious yacht; and they had not been half an hour on board ere, as Rory expressed it, in language more forcible than elegant,

"The secret was out entirely, the cat flew out of the bag, and every drop of milk got out of the cocoa-nut."

Poor Ralph was delighted at the return of his friends from their long cruise; and now that he had their company he had no longer any wish or desire to remain in the vicinity of the *Arrandoon;* so giving up his pretty Highland cottage, bidding a kindly adieu to the widow, kissing wee weeping Jeannie, and promising to be sure o return some day, the trio hurried them southwards, to spend most of their time at Ralph's pleasant home, until the ship should be ready to launch.

Leigh Hall was a lordly mansion, possessing no very great pretensions to architectural splendour, but beautifully situated among its woods and parks on a high braeland that overlooked one of England's fairest lakes. For miles you approached the house from behind by a road which, with many a devious turning, wound through a rich but rolling country. Past many a rural hamlet; past many a picturesque cottage, their gables and fronts charmingly painted and tinted by the hands of the magic artist Time; past stately farms, where sleek cattle seemed to low kindly welcome to our heroes as their carriage came rolling onwards, with here a wood and there a field, and yonder a great stretch of common where cows waded shoulder deep in ferns and furze, daintily cropping the green and tender tops of the trailing bramble; and here a broad, rushy moor, on which flocks of snowy geese wandered.

Alluding to the latter, says Rory, "Don't these geese come out prettily against the patches of green grass, and how soft and easy it must be for the feet of them!"

"They're preparing for Christmas," said Ralph.

Poet Rory gave him a look—one of Rory's looks. "There's never a bit of poetry nor romance in the soul of you," he said.

"Except the romance and poetry of a well-spread table," said Allan, laughing.

"And, 'deed, indeed," replied Rory, "there is little to choose betwixt the pair of you; so what can I do but be sorry for you both?"

It was on a beautiful autumn afternoon that the three young men were now approaching the manor of Leigh. The trees that had been once of a tender green, whose leaves in the gentle breath of spring had rustled with a kind of silken *frou-frou*, were green now only when the sun shone upon them; all the rest was black by contrast. Feathery seedlings floated here and there on the breeze that blew from the north. This breeze went rushing through the woods with a sound that made Rory, at all events, think of waves breaking in mid-ocean, and even the fields of ripe and waving grain had, to his mind, a strange resemblance to the sea. The rooks that floated high in air seemed to glory in the wind, for they screamed with delight, baffled though at times they were—taken aback you might say, and hurled yards out of their course.

It was only a plain farmer's autumn wind after all, but it made these youthful sailors think of something else than baffled rooks and fields of ripening grain.

Now up through a dark oak copse, and they come all at once to one of the old park gates. Grey is it with very age, and so is the quaintly-gabled lodge; its stones are crumbling to pieces. And well suited for such a dwelling is the bent but kindly-faced old crone who totters out on her staff to open the ponderous gates. She nods and smiles a welcome, to which bows and smiles are returned, and the carriage rolls on. A great square old house; they come to it at last, so big and square that it did not even look tall at a distance. They drove up to what really appeared the back of this mansion, with its stairs and pillars and verandahs, the door opening from which led into the hall proper, which ran straight through the manor, and opened by other doors on to broad green terraces, with ribbon gardens and fountains, and then the braelike park, with its ancient trees, and so on, downwards to the beautiful lake, with the hills beyond.

Right respectfully and loyally was Ralph greeted by his servants and retainers. All this may be imagined better than I can describe it.

While Rory was marching through the long line of servants I believe he felt just a little awed; and if, as soon as they found themselves alone, Ralph had addressed himself to his guests in some such speech as follows, he would not have been very much astonished. If Ralph had said, "Welcome, Ronald Elphinston, and you, my lord of Arrandoon, to the ancient home of the Leighs!" Rory would have thought it quite in keeping with the poetry of the place.

Ralph did nothing of the kind, however; he pitched

his hat and gloves rather unceremoniously on a chair, and said, all in one breath and one tone of voice, "Now, boys, here we are at last; I'm sure you'll make yourselves at home. We'll have fine times for a few weeks, anyhow. Would you like to wash your hands?"

Well, if it was not a very poetic welcome, it was a very hearty one nevertheless.

CHAPTER IV.

LIFE AT LEIGH HALL—THE LAUNCH OF THE "ARRANDOON"—TRIAL TRIPS—A ROW AND A FIGHT—"FREEZING POWDERS."

AS the owner of a large house, the head of a county family, and a landed proprietor, there were many duties devolved upon Ralph Leigh when at home, from which he never for a moment thought of shrinking. Though a great part of the day was spent in shooting, rowing, or fishing, the mornings were never his own, nor the evenings either. He had a knack of giving nice dinners, and young though he was, he also possessed the happy knack of making all his guests feel perfectly at home, so that when carriages drew round, and it was time to start for their various homes, everybody was astonished at the speed with which the evening had sped away; and that was proof positive it had passed most pleasantly.

They kept early hours at Leigh Hall, and so they did at every house all over the quiet, romantic country, and no doubt they were all the better for it, and all the more healthy.

But our heroes must be forgiven, if after the last guest had gone, after the lights were out in the banqueting hall, and the doors closed for the night, they assembled in a cosy, fire-brightened room upstairs, all by their three selves, for a quiet confab and talk, a little exchange of ideas, a little conversation about the days o' auld lang syne, and their hopes of adventures in the far north, whither they were so soon to sail.

About once a fortnight, McBain, whom we may as well call Captain McBain now—Captain McBain, of the steam yacht *Arrandoon*—used to run down to Leigh Hall to report progress; the "social hour," as Rory called it, was then doubly dear to them all, and I'm not at all sure that they did not upon these occasions steal half an hour at least from midnight. You see they were very happy: they were happy with the happiness of anticipation. They never dreamt of failure in the expedition on which they were about to embark.

> "In the lexicon of youth, which fate reserves
> For a great manhood, there is no such word as—fail."

True, but had they known the dangers they were to encounter, the trials they would have to come through, brave as they undoubtedly were, their hearts might have throbbed less joyfully. They had, however, the most perfect confidence in each other, just as brothers might have. The friendship, begun long ago between them, cemented, during the cruise of the *Snowbird*, in many an hour of difficulty and danger—for had they not come through fire and death together?—was strengthened during their residence at Leigh Hall. Indeed, it would not be too much to say that their affection for each other was brotherly to a degree. Dissimilar in character in many ways they were, but this same dissimilarity seemed but to increase their mutual regard and esteem. Faults each one of them had—who on this earth has not?—and each could see those of the other, if he did not always notice his own. Says Burns—

> "O would some power the giftie gie us,
> To see ourselves as others see us,
> It would from mony a fautie free us."

Probably, individually they did not forget these lines, and so the one was most careful in guarding against anything that might hurt the feelings of the others. Is not this true friendship?

But as to what is called "chaff," they had all learned long ago to be proof against that—I'm not sure they did not even like it; Rory did, I know; he said so one day; and on Allan asking him his reason, "My reason is it?" says Rory; "sure enough, boys, chaffing metres with laughing; where you find the chaff you find the laugh, and laughing is better to a man than cod-liver oil. And that's my reason!"

And Rory's romantic sayings and doings were oftentimes the subject of a considerable deal of chaff and fun; so, too, was what the young Irishman was pleased to call Ralph's English "stolidity" and Allan's Scottish fire and intensity of patriotism; but never did the blood of one of our boys get hot, never did their lips tighten in anger or their cheeks pale with vexation.

Just on one occasion—which I now record lest I forget it—was boy Rory, as he was still affectionately called, very nearly losing his temper under a rattling fire of chaff from Allan and Ralph, who were in extra good spirits. It happened months after they had sailed in the *Arrandoon*. All at once that day Rory grew suddenly quiet, and the smile that still remained on his face was only round the lips, and didn't ripple round the eyes. It was a sad kind of a smile; then he jumped up and ran away from the table.

"We've offended him," said Allan, looking quite serious.

"I hope not," said Ralph, growing serious in turn.

"I'll go and look him up;" this from Allan.

"No, that you won't!" put in McBain. "Leave boy Rory alone; he'll come to presently."

Meanwhile, ridiculous as it may seem, Rory had sped away forward to the dispensary, where he found the doctor. "Doctor, dear," cried Rory, "give me a blue pill at once—a couple of them, if you like, for sure it isn't well I am!"

"Oh!" said the surgeon, "liver a bit out of order, eh?"

"Liver!" cried Rory; "I know by the nasty temper that's on me that there isn't a bit of liver left in me worth mentioning! There now, give me the pills."

The doctor laughed, but Rory had his bolus; then he came aft again, smiling, confessing to his comrades what a ninny he had very nearly been making of himself. Just like Rory!

The bearing of our young heroes towards Captain McBain was invariably respectful and affectionate; they both loved and admired him, and, indeed, he was worthy of all their esteem. In wealth there is power, but in wisdom worth, and Ralph, Rory, and Allan felt this truth if they never expressed it. McBain had really raised himself to the position he now held; he was a living proof that—

"Whate'er a man dares he can do."

I will not deny, however that McBain possessed a little genius to begin with; but here is old Ap, once but a poor boat-builder, with never a spark of genius in him, superintending the construction of a noble ship. In him we have an example of industry and perseverance pure and simple.

The *Arrandoon* made speedy progress on the stocks, and the anxious day was near at hand when she would leave her native timbers, and slide gracefully and auspiciously it was to be hoped, into the smooth waters of the Clyde.

That day came at last, and with it came thousands to view the launch. With it came Mrs. McGregor and Allan's sister; and the latter was to break the tiny phial of wine and name the ship.

On the platform beneath, and closely adjoining the bows of the *Arrandoon*, were numerous gentlemen and ladies; conspicuous among the former was Rory. He was full of earnest and pleasant excitement. Conspicuous among the latter was Helen Edith. She certainly never looked more lovely than she did now. The ceremony she was about to engage in, in which, indeed, she was chief actress, was just a trifle too much for her delicate nerves, and as she stood, bouquet in hand, with a slight flush on her cheek and a sparkle in her eye, with head slightly bent, she looked like a bride at the altar. Rory stood near her; perhaps his vicinity comforted her, as did his remarks, to which, however, he met with but little response.

I am beginning to think that Rory loved this sweet child; if he did it was a love that was purely Platonic, and it needed be none the less sincere for all that. As for Helen Edith —but hark! A gun rings out from the deck of the *Arrandoon* causing every window in the vicinity to rattle again, and the steeples to nod. The gallant ship moves off down the slip slowly—slowly—slowly, yes, slowly but steadily, swerving neither to starboard nor larboard, quicker now faster still. Will she float? Our heroes' hearts stand still. McBain is pale and breathes not. She slows, she almost stops, now she is over the hitch and on again, on—on—and on—and into the water. Hurrah! You should have heard that cheer, and Rory shakes hands with Helen Edith, and compliments her, and positively there are tears in the foolish boy's eyes. There was a deal of hand-shaking, I can assure you, after the launch, and a deal of joy expressed, and if the truth be told, more than one prayer breathed for the future safety of the *Arrandoon* and her gallant crew. There was lunch after launch in the saloon of the new yacht, at which Allan's mother presided with the same quiet dignity she was wont to maintain at the castle that gave the ship its name.

McBain made a speech, and a good one, too, after Ralph had spoken a few words. Poor Ralph! speaking was certainly not his strong point. But there was no hesitancy about McBain, and no nervousness either, and during its delivery he stood bolt upright in his place, as straight as an arrow, and his words were manly and straightforward. Allan felt proud of his foster-father. But Rory came next. For once in his life he hadn't the slightest intention of making anybody laugh. But because he tried not to, he did; and when Irish bull after Irish bull came rattling out, "Och!" thinks Rory to himself, "seriousness isn't my forte after all;" then he simply gave himself rein, and expressed himself so comically that there was not a dry eye in the room, for tears come with laughing as well as weeping.

There was a deal to be done to the *Arrandoon*—in her, on her, and around her—after she was launched, before she was ready; but it would serve no good purpose and only waste time to describe her completion, for we long to be "steam up" and away to sea *en route* for the starry north.

She was a gallant sight, the *Arrandoon*, as she stood away out to sea, past the rocky shores of Bute, bound south on her trial trip by the measured mile. Fifteen hundred tons burden was she, with tall and tapering masts: lower, main, topgallant, and royal; not one higher; no star-gazers, sky-scrapers, or moon-rakers; she wouldn't have to rake much for the wind in the stormy seas they were going to. Then there was the funnel, such a funnel as a man with an eye in his head likes to see, not a mere pipe of a thing, but a great wide armful of a funnel, with the tiniest bit of rake on it; so too had the masts, though the *Arrandoon* did not look half so saucy as the *Snowbird*. The *Arrandoon* had more solidity about her, and more soberness and staidness, as became her—a ship about to be pitted against dangers unknown.

Her figure-head was the bust of a fair and beautiful girl.

That day, on her trial trip, the ladies were on board; and Rory made this remark to Helen Edith:

"The fair image on our bows, Helen, will soon be gazing wistfully north."

"Ah! you seem to long for that," said Helen, "but," she added archly, "mamma and I look forward to the time when she will be gazing just as wistfully south again."

Rory laughed, and the conversation assumed a livelier tone.

Steamers, I always think, are very similar in one way to colts, they require a certain amount of breaking in, they seldom do well on their trial trip. The *Arrandoon* was no exception; she promised well at first, and fulfilled that promise for twenty good miles and two; then she intimated to the engineers in charge that she had had enough of it. Well, this was a good opportunity of trying her sailing qualities, and in these she exceeded all expectations.

McBain rubbed his hands with delight, for no yacht at Cowes ever sailed more close to the wind, came round on shorter length, or made more knots an hour. He promised himself a treat, and that treat was to run out some day with her in half a gale of wind, when there were no ladies on board. He would then see what the *Arrandoon* could do under sail, and what she couldn't. He did this; and the very next day after he came back he made the journey to Leigh Hall, and stopped there for a whole week. That was proof enough that the captain was pleased with his ship.

Early in the month of the succeeding February, the *Arrandoon* lay at the Broomielaw, with the blue-peter unfurled, steam up, all hands on board, and even the pilot. That very morning they were to begin their adventurous voyage. Ralph, Allan, and Rory would be picked up at Oban, and the vessel now only awaited the arrival of McBain before casting off and dropping down stream.

The Broomielaw didn't look pretty that morning, nor very comfortable. Although the hills all around Glasgow were white with snow, over the city itself hung the smoke like a murky pall. There was mud under feet, and a Scotch mist held possession of the air. Here was nothing cheering to look at, slop-shops and pawn-shops, and Jack-frequented dram-shops, bales of wet merchandise on the quay, and eave-dripping dock-houses; nor were the people pleasant to be among; the only human beings that did seem to enjoy themselves were the ragged urchins who had taken shelter in the empty barrels that lined the back of the warehouses; they had shelter, and sugar to eat. McBain thought he wouldn't be sorry when he was safely round the Mull of Cantyre.

"Come on, Jack," cried one of these tiny gutter-snipes, rushing out of his tub; "come on, here's a row."

There was a row; apparently a fight was going on, for a ring had formed a little way down the street; and simply out of curiosity McBain went to have a peep over the shoulders of the mob. As usual, the policemen were very busy in some other part of the street.

Only a poor little itinerant nigger boy lying on the ground, being savagely kicked by a burly and half-drunken street porter.

"Oh!" the little fellow was shrieking; "what for you kickee my shins so? Oh!"

McBain entered the ring in a very businesslike fashion indeed; he begged for room; he told the mob he meant thrashing the ruffian if he did not apologise to the poor lad. Then he intimated as much to the ruffian himself.

"Come on," was the defiant reply, as the fellow threw himself into a fighting attitude. "Man, your mither'll no ken ye when you gang home the nicht."

"We'll see," said McBain, quietly.

For the next three minutes this ruffianly porter's movements were confined to a series of beautiful falls, that would have brought down the house in a circus. When he rose the last time it was merely to assume a sitting position.

"Gie us your hand," he said to McBain. "You're the first chiel that ever dang Jock the Wraggler. I admire ye, man—I admire ye."

"Come with me, my little fellow," said McBain to the nigger boy; and he took him kindly by the hand. Meanwhile a woman who had been standing by placed a curious-looking bundle in the lad's hand, and bade him be a good boy, and keep out of Jock the Wraggler's way next time.

"I'll see you a little way home, Jim," continued McBain, when they were clear of the crowd. "Jim is what they call you, isn't it?"

"Jim," said the blackamoor, "is what dey are good enough to call me. But, sah, Jim has no home."

"And where do you sleep at night, Jim?"

"Anywhere, sah. Jim ain't pertikler; some time it is a sugar barrel, an oder time a door-step."

A low, sneering laugh was at this moment heard from the mysterious bundle Jim carried. McBain started.

"Don't be afeared, sah," said Jim; "it's only de cockatoo, sah!"

"Have you any money, Jim?" asked McBain.

"Only de cockatoo, sah," replied Jim; "but la!" he added, "I'se a puffuk gemlam (gentleman), sah—I'se got a heart as high as de steeple, sah!"

"Well, Jim," said McBain, laughing, "would you like to sail in a big ship with me, and—and—black my boots?"

"Golly! yes, sah; dat would suit Jim all to nuffin."

"But suppose, Jim, we went far away—as far as the North Pole?"

"Don't care, sah," said Jim, emphatically; "der never was a pole yet as Jim couldn't climb."

'Have you a surname, Jim?"

"No, sah," replied poor Jim; "I'se got no belongings but de cockatoo."

"I mean, Jim, have you a second name?"

"La! no, sir," said Jim; "one name plenty good enough for a nigga boy. Only—yes now I 'members, in de ship dat bring me from Sierra Leone last summer de cap'n never call me nuffin else but Freezin' Powders."

McBain did not take long to make up his mind about anything; he determined to take this strange boy with him, so he took him to a shop and bought him a cage for the cockatoo, and then the two marched on board together, talking away as if they had known each other for years.

Freezing Powders was sent below to be washed and dressed and made decent. The ship was passing Inellan when he came on deck again. Jim was thunderstruck; he had never seen snow before.

"La! sah," he cried, pointing with outstretched arm towards the hills; "look, sah, look; dey never like dat before. De Great Massa has been and painted dem all white."

CHAPTER V.

DANGER ON THE DEEP—A FOREST OF WATERSPOUTS—THE "ARRANDOON" IS SWAMPED—THE WARNING.

"'LA lă lăy lēē-āh, lāy lā lĕ lō-O." So went the song on deck—a song without words, short, and interrupted at every bar, as the men hauled cheerily on tack and sheet.

Such a thing would not be allowed for a single moment on board a British man-o'-war, as the watch singing while they obeyed the orders of the bo'sw'n's pipe, taking in sail, squaring yards, or doing any other duty required of them. And yet, with all due respect for my own flag, methinks there are times when, as practised in merchant or passenger ships, that strange, weird, wordless song is not at all an unpleasant sound to listen to. By night, for instance, after you have turned in to your little narrow bed—the cradle of the deep, in which you are nightly rocked—to hear it rising and falling, and ending in long-drawn cadence, gives one an indescribable feeling of peace and security. Your bark is all alone—so your thoughts may run—on a wild world of waters. There may not be another ship within hundreds of miles; the wind may be rising or the wind may be falling—what do you care? What need you care? There are watchful eyes on deck, there are good men and true overhead, and they seem to sing your cradle hymn, "Lā lă leē-āh," and before it is done you are wrapt in that sweetest, that dreamless slumber that landsmen seldom know.

There was one man at least in every watch on board the *Arrandoon*, who usually led the song that accompanied the hauling on a rope, with a sweet, clear tenor voice; you could not have been angry with these men had you been twenty times a man-o'-war's man.

It was about an hour after breakfast, and our boys were lazing below. For some time previous to the working song, there had been perfect silence on board—a silence broken only now and then by a short word of command, a footstep on deck, or the ominous flapping of the canvas aloft, as it shivered for a moment, then filled and swelled out again.

Had you been down below, one sign alone would have told you that something was going to happen—that some change was about to take place. It was this: when everything is going on all right, you hear the almost constant tramp, tramp of the officer of the watch up and down the quarter-deck, but this was absent now, and you would have known without seeing him that he was standing, probably, by the binnacle, his eyes now bent aloft, and now sweeping the horizon, and now and then glancing at the compass.

Then came a word or two of command, given in a quiet, ordinary tone of voice—there was no occasion to howl on this particular morning. And after this a rush of feet, and next the song, and the bo'sw'n's pipe. Thus:—

Song.—" Lā lă lēē āh, lāy lā lĕ lō-O."

Spoken.—" Hoy!"

Boatswain's Pipe.—" Whēē-ē, wĕet wĕet wĕet, wēē-ē."

Song.—" Lā lă lāy lă, lā lō-O."

Spoken.—" Belay!"

Boatswain's Pipe.—" Wēē wēē weet weet weet weet, wēē ē."

Spoken.—" Now lads."

Song.—" Lŏ āh ō ĕĕ."

Pipe.—" Weet weet!"

Then a hurry-scurrying away forward, a trampling of feet enough to awaken Rip van Winkle, then the bo'sw'n's pipe *encore*.

Allan straightens his back in his easy-chair—he has been bending over the table, reading the " Noctes Ambrosianæ " —straightens his back, stretches his arms, and says " Heigho ! " Rory is busy arranging some beautiful transparent specimens of animalculæ, not bigger than midges, on a piece of black cardboard; he had caught them overnight in a gauze net dragged astern. He doesn't look up. Ralph is lying " tandem " on a sofa, reading " Ivanhoe." He won't take his eyes off the book, nor move as much as one drowsy eyelid, but he manages to say,

" What are they about on deck, Rory ? "

" Don't know even a tiny bit," says Rory.

" Rory," continues Ralph, in a slightly louder key; " you're a young man ; run up and see."

" Rory won't then," says Rory, intent on his work ; " fag for yourself, my lazy boy."

" Oh ! " says Ralph, " won't you have your ears pulled when I do get up ! "

" Ha ! ha ! " laughed Rory, " you'll have forgotten all about it long before then."

" Freezing Powders ! " roared Ralph.

The bright-faced though bullet-headed nigger boy introduced in last chapter appeared instantly. He was dressed in white flannel, braided with blue. Had he been a sprite, or a djin, he couldn't have popped up with more startling rapidity. Truth is, the young rascal had been asleep under the table.

" Off on deck with you, Freezing Powders, and see what's up."

Freezing Powders was down again in a moment.

" Take in all sail, sah ! and square de yard ; no wind, sah ! nebber a puff."

It was just as Freezing Powders said, but there was noise

enough presently, and puffing too, for steam was got up, and the great screw was churning the waters of the dark northern ocean into creamish foam, as the vessel went steadily ahead at about ten knots an hour. There was no occasion to hurry. When Rory and Allan went on deck, they found the captain in consultation with the mates, Mitchell and Stevenson.

"I must admit," McBain was remarking, "that I can't make it out at all."

"No more can we," said Stevenson with a puzzled smile. "The wind has failed us all at once, and the sea gone down, and the glass seems to have taken leave of its senses entirely. It is up one moment high enough for anything, and down the next to 28 deg. There, just look at that sea and look at that sky."

There was certainly something most appalling in the appearance of both. The ocean was calm and unruffled as glass, with only a long low heave on it; not a ripple on it big enough to swamp a fly; but over it all a strange, glassy lustre that—so you would have thought—could have been skimmed off. The sky was one mass of dark purple-black clouds in masses. It seemed no distance overhead, and the horizon looked hardly a mile away on either side. Only in the north it was one unbroken bluish black, as dark seemingly as night, from the midst of which every now and then, and every here and there, would come quickly a little puff of cloud of a lightish grey colour, as if a gun had been fired. Only there was no sound.

There was something awe-inspiring in the strange, ominous look of sea and sky, and in the silence broken only by the grind and gride of screw and engine.

"No," said McBain, "I don't know what we are going to have. Perhaps a tornado. Anyhow, Mr. Stevenson, let us be ready. Get down topgallant masts, it will be a bit of exercise for the men; let us have all the steam we can command, and——"

"Batten down, sir?"

"Yes, Mr. Stevenson, batten down, and lash the boats inboard."

The good ship *Arrandoon* was at the time of which I write about fifty miles south of the Faroes, and a long way to the east. The weather had been dark and somewhat gloomy, from the very time they lost sight of the snow-clad hills around Oban, but it now seemed to culminate in a darkness that could be felt.

The men were well drilled on board this steam-yacht. McBain delighted to have them smart, and it was with surprising celerity that the topgallant masts were lowered, the hatches battened down, and the good ship prepared for any emergency. None too soon; the darkness grew more intense, especially did the clouds look threatening ahead of them. And now here and there all round them the sea began to get ruffled with small whirlwinds, that sent the water wheeling round and round like miniature maelstroms, and raised it up into cones in the centre.

"How is the glass now, Mr. Stevenson?" asked McBain.

"Stands very low, sir," was the reply, "but keeps steadily down."

"All right," said McBain; "now get two guns loaded with ball cartridge; have no more hands on deck than we want. No idlers, d'ye hear?"

"Ay, ay, sir."

"Send Magnus Bolt here."

"Now, Magnus, old man," continued McBain, "d'ye mind the time, some years ago in the *Snowbird*, when you rid us of that troublesome pirate?"

"Ay, that I do right well, sir," said this little old weasened specimen of humanity, rubbing his hands with delight. "It were a fine shot that. He! he! he! Mercy on us, to see his masts and sails come toppling down, sir, —he! he! he!"

"Well, I want you again, Magnus; I'd rather trust to your old eye in an emergency than to any in the ship."

" But where is the foe, sir?"

" Look ahead, Magnus."

Magnus did as he was told; it was a strange, and to one who understood it, a dreadful sight. Apparently a thousand balloons were afloat in the blue, murky air, each one trailing its car in the sea, balloons of terrible size, flat as to their tops, which seemed to join or merge into one another, forming a black and ominous cloud. The cars that trailed on the sea were snowy white.

"Heaven help us!" said Magnus, clasping his hands for just a moment, while his cheeks assumed an ashen hue. "Heaven help us, sir; this is worse than the pirate."

" They are all coming this way," said McBain; "fire only at those that threaten us, and fire while they are still some distance ahead."

Meanwhile Ralph had come on deck, and joined his companions. I do not think that through all the long terrible hour that followed, either of them spoke one word; although there was no sea on, and for the most part no motion, they clutched with one hand rigging or shroud, and gazed terror-struck at the awful scene ahead and around them.

They were soon in the very centre of what appeared an interminable forest of waterspouts. Few indeed have ever seen such a sight or encountered so pressing a danger and lived to tell it.

The balloon-shaped heads of these waterspouts looked dark as midnight; their shafts, I can call them nothing else, were immense pillars rising out of gigantic feet of seething foam. So close did they pass to some of these that the yardarms seemed almost to touch them. Our heroes noticed then, and they marvelled at it afterwards, the strange monotonous roaring sound they emitted,—a sound that drowned even the noise of the troubled waters around their shafts.*

Old Magnus made good use of his guns on those that threatened the good ship with destruction; one shot broke always one, and sometimes more, probably with the vibration; but the thundering sound of the falling waters, and the turmoil of the sea that followed, what pen can describe?

But, good shot as he is, Magnus is not infallible, else McBain would not now have to grasp his speaking-trumpet and shout,

"Stand by, men, stand by."

A waterspout had wholly, or partially at least, broken on board of them. It was as though the splendid ship had suddenly been blown to atoms by a terrible explosion, and every timber of her engulfed in the ocean!

For long moments thus, then her crew, half drowned, half dead, could once more look around. The *Arrandoon* was afloat, but her decks were swept. Hundreds of tons of water still filled her decks, and poured out into the sea in cataracts through her broken bulwarks; ay, and it poured below too, at the fore and main hatchways, which had been smashed open with the violence and force of the deluge. The main yard had come down, and one whaler was smashed into matchwood. I wish I could say this was all, but two poor fellows lost for ever the number of their mess. One was seen floating about dead and unwounded on the deck ere the water got clear; the other, with sadly splintered brow, was still clutching in a death-grasp a rope that had bound a tarpaulin over a grating.

But away ahead appeared a long yellowish streak of clear sky, close to the horizon. The danger had passed.

All hands were now called to clear away the wreck and

* Such a phenomenon as this has rarely been witnessed in the Northern Ocean. It is somewhat strange that on the selfsame year this happened, an earthquake was felt in Ireland, and shocks even near Perth, in Scotland.

make good repairs. The pumps, too, had to be set to work, and as soon as the wind came down on them from the clear of the horizon, sail was set, for the fires had been drowned out.

The wind increased to a gale, and there was nothing for it but to lay to. And so they did all that night and all next day; then the weather moderated, and the wind coming more easterly they were able to show more canvas, and to resume their course with something akin to comfort.

The bodies of the two poor fellows who had met with so sad a fate were committed to the deep—the sailor's grave.

"Earth to earth and dust to dust."

There was more than one moist eye while those words were uttered, for the men had both been great favourites with their messmates.

Rory was sitting that evening with his elbows resting on the saloon table, his chin on his hands, and a book in front of him that he was not looking at, when McBain came below.

"You're quieter than usual," said McBain, placing a kindly hand on his shoulder.

Rory smiled, forced a laugh even, as one does who wants to shake off an incubus.

"I was thinking," he said, "of that awful black forest of waterspouts. I'll never get it out of my head."

"Oh! yes you will, boy Rory," said McBain; "it was a new sensation, that's all."

"New sensation!" said Allan, laughing in earnest; "well, captain, I must say that is a mild way of putting it. *I* don't want any more such sensations. Steward, bring some nice hot coffee."

"Ay!" cried Ralph, "that's the style, Allan. Some coffee, steward—and, steward, bring the cold pork and fowls, and make some toast, and bring the butter and the Chili vinegar."

Poor Irish Rory! Like every one with a poetic temperament, he was easily cast down, and just as easily raised again. Ralph's wondrous appetite always amused him.

"Oh, you true Saxon!" said Rory—"you hungry Englishman!" But, ten minutes afterwards, he felt himself constrained to join the party at the supper-table.

You see, reader mine, a sailor's life is like an April day —sunshine now and showers anon.

"How now, Stevenson?" said McBain, as the mate entered with a kind of a puzzled look on his face.

"Well, sir, we are, as you said, off the Faroes. The night is precious dark, but I can see the lights of a village in here, and the lights of a vessel of some size, evidently lying at anchor."

"Then, mate," said the captain, "as we don't know exactly where we are, I don't think we can do wrong to steam in and drop anchor alongside this craft. We can then board her and find out. How is the weather?"

"A bit thick, sir, and seems inclined to blow a little from the east-south-east."

"Let it, Stevenson—let it. If the other vessel can ride it out I don't think the *Arrandoon* is likely to lose her anchors. Hullo! Mitchell," he continued, as the second mate next entered hat in hand, "what's in the wind now, man?"

"Why, sir," said Mitchell, "I'm all ashore like, you see; I can't make it out. But here is a boat just been a-hailing of us, and the passenger—there is only one, a comely lass enough—has just come on board, and wants to see you at once. Seems a bit cranky. Here she be, sir;" and Mitchell retired.

A young girl. She was probably not over seventeen, fair-faced, and with wild blue eyes, and yellow hair, dripping with dew, floating over her shoulders.

"Stop the ship!" she cried, seizing McBain by the arm. "Go no farther, or her ribs will be scattered over the waves, and your bones will bleach on the cliffs of the rocks."

"Poor thing!" muttered McBain.

"Oh, you heed me not!" continued the girl, wringing her hands in despair. "It will be too late—it will be too late! I tell you here is no harbour, here is no ship. The lights you see are placed there to lure your vessel on shore. They are wreckers, I tell you; they will——"

"By the deep three!" sung the man in the chains.

Then there was a shout from the man at the foretop.

"Breakers ahead!" Then,

"Stand by both anchors. Ready about."

CHAPTER VI.

A LIFE ON THE OCEAN WAVE—ON THE ROCKS—MYSTERY
—A HOME ON THE ROLLING DEEP.

HAS the reader ever been to sea? The first feeling that a landsman objects to at sea is that of the heaving motion of the ship; to your true sailor the cessation of that motion, or its absence under circumstances, is disagreeable in the extreme. To me there is always a certain air of romance about the old ocean, and about a ship at sea; but what can be less romantic than lying in a harbour or dull wet dock, with no more life nor motion in your craft than there is in the slopshop round the corner? To lie thus and probably have to listen to the grating voices and pointless jokes of semi-inebriated stevedores, as they load or unload, soiling, as they do, your beautiful decks with their dreadful boots, is very far from pleasant. In a case like this how one wishes to be away out on the blue water once more, and to feel life in the good ship once again—to feel, as it were, her very heart throb beneath one's feet!

But disagreeable as the sensation is of lying lifeless in harbour or dock, still more so is it to feel your vessel, that one moment before was sailing peacefully over the sea, suddenly rasp on a rock beneath you, then stop dead. Nothing in the world will wake a sailor sooner, even should he be in the deepest of slumber, than this sudden cessation of motion. I remember on one particular occasion being awakened thus. No crew ever went to sleep with a greater feeling of security than we had done, for the night was fine and the ship went well. But all at once, about four bells in the middle watch,

Kurr—r—r—r! that was the noise we heard proceeding from our keel, then all was steady, all was still. And every man sprang from his hammock, every officer from his cot.

We were in the middle of the Indian Ocean, or rather the Mozambique Channel, with no land in sight, and we were hard and fast on the dreaded Lyra reef. A beautiful night it was, just enough wind to make a ripple on the water for the broad moon's beams to dance in, a cloudless sky, and countless stars. We took all this in at the first glance. Safe enough we were—for the time; *but* if the wind rose there was the certainty of our being broken up, even as the war-ship *Lyra* was, that gave its name to the reef.

At the first shout from the man on the outlook in the *Arrandoon*, McBain rushed on deck.

"Stand by both anchors. Ready about."

But these orders are, alas! too late.

Kurr—r—r—r! The stately *Arrandoon* is hard and fast on the rocky bottom.

The ship was under easy sail, for although there was hardly any wind, what little there was gave evident signs of shifting. It might come on to blow, and blow pretty hard, too, from the south-east or east-south-east, and Mr. Stevenson was hardly the man to be caught in a trap, to find himself on a lee shore or a rock-bound coast, with a crowd of canvas. Well for our people it was that there was but little sail on her and little wind, or, speedily as everything was let go, the masts—some of them at least—would have gone by the board.

Half an hour after she struck, the *Arrandoon* was under bare poles and steam was up.

The order had been given to get up steam with all speed.

Both the engineer and his two assistants were brawny Scots.

"Man!" said the former, " it'll take ye a whole hour to get up steam if you bother wi' coals and cinders alone. But do your best wi' what ye hae till I come back."

He wasn't gone long ere he came staggering down the ladder again, carrying a sack.

"It's American hams," he said; " they're hardly fit for anything else but fuel, so here goes."

And he popped a couple into the fire.

"That's the style," he said, as they began to frizzle and blaze. "Look, lads, the kettle'll be boilin' in twa seconds."

"Thank you, Stuart," said McBain, when the engineer went on the bridge to report everything ready; "you are a valuable servant; now stand by to receive orders."

All hands had been called, and there was certainly plenty for them to do.

It wanted several hours to high-water, and McBain determined to make the best of his time.

"By the blessing of Providence on our own exertions, Stevenson," the captain said, "we'll get her off all right. Had it been high-water, though, when we ran on shore, eh!"

Stevenson laughed a grim laugh. "We'd leave her bones here," he said, "that would be all."

The men were now getting their big guns over the side into the boats. This would lighten her a little. But as the tide was flowing, anchors were sent out astern, to prevent the ship from being carried still farther on to the reef.

"Go astern at full speed."

The screws revolved and kept on revolving, the ship still stuck fast. The night was very dark, so that everything had to be done by the weird light of lanterns. Never mind, the work went cheerily on, and the men sang as they laboured.

"High-water about half-past two, isn't it, Stevenson?" asked Captain McBain.

"Yes, sir," the mate replied, "that's about the time, sir."

"Ah! well," the captain said, "she is sure to float then, and there are no signs of your storm coming."

"There is hardly a breath of wind now, sir, but you never know in these latitudes where it may come on to blow from next."

The cheerful way in which McBain talked reassured our heroes, and towards eleven o'clock English Ralph spoke as follows,

"Look here, boys——"

"There isn't a bit of good looking in the dark, is there?" said Allan.

"Well," continued Ralph, "figuratively speaking, look here; I don't see the good of sticking up on deck in the cold. We're not doing an atom of good; let us go below and finish our supper."

"Right," said Allan; "and mind you, that poor girl is below there all this time. She may want some refreshment."

When they entered the saloon they found it empty, deserted as far as human beings were concerned. Polly the cockatoo was there, no one else.

"Well?" said the bird, inquiringly, as she helped herself to an enormous mouthful of hemp-seed. "Well?"

"What have you done with the young lady?" asked Allan.

"The proof o' the pudding——"

Polly was too busy eating to say more. Peter the steward entered just then, overhearing the question as he came.

"That strange girl, sir," he replied, "went over the side and away in her boat as soon as the ship struck."

"Well, I call that a pity," said Allan; "the poor girl comes here to warn us of danger and never stops for thanks. It is wonderful."

"From this date," remarked Ralph, "I cease to wonder at anything. Steward, you know we were only half done with supper, and we're all as hungry as hunters, and——"

But Peter was off, and in a few minutes our boys were supping as quietly and contentedly as if they had been in the Coffee-room of the Queen's Hotel, Glasgow, instead of being on a lee shore, with the certainty that if it came on to blow not a timber of the good ship *Arrandoon* that would not be smashed into matchwood.

But hark! the noise on deck recommences, the men are heaving on the winch, the engines are once more at work, and the great screw is revolving. Then there is a shout from the men forward.

"She moves!"

"Hurrah!* then, boys, hurrah!" cried McBain; "heave, and she goes."

The men burst into song—tune a wild, uncouth sailor's melody, words extempore, one man singing one line, another metreing it with a second, with a chorus between each line, in which all joined, with all their strength of voice to the tune, with all the power of their brawny muscles to the winch. Mere doggerel, but it did the turn better, perhaps, than more refined music would have done.

<pre>
        In San Domingo I was born,
            Chorus—Hurrah! lads, hurrah!
        And reared among the yellow corn.
                Heave, boys, and away we go.
        Our bold McBain is a captain nice,
            Chorus—Hurrah! lads, hurrah!
        The mainbrace he is sure to splice.
                Heave, boys, and away we go.
        The Faroe Isles are not our goal,
                Oh! no, lads, no!
        We'll reach the North, and we'll bag the Pole,
                Heave, boys, and away we go,
                        Hurrah!
</pre>

"We're off," cried Stevenson, excitedly. "Hurrah! men. Hurrah! hurrah! hurrah!"

* The word "hurrah" in the parlance of North Sea sailors means "do your utmost" or "make all speed."

The men needed but little encouragement now, though. Round went the winch right merrily, and in a quarter of an hour the bows were abreast of the anchors.

"Now, steward," said the captain, "splice the mainbrace."

The ration was brought and served, Ted Wilson, who was a moving spirit in the 'tween decks, giving a toast, which every man re echoed ere he raised the basin to his head,

"Success to the saucy *Arrandoon*, and our bold skipper, Captain McBain."

The vessel's head was now turned seawards, and presently the anchors that had been taken in were let go again, and fires banked. The long night wore away, and the dismal dawn came. McBain had lain down for a short time, with orders to be roused on the first appearance of daylight. Rory, anxious to see how the land looked, was on deck nearly as soon as the captain.

A grey mist was lifting up from off the sea, and from off the shore, revealing black, beetling crags, hundreds of feet high at the water's edge, a sheer beetling cliff around which thousands of strange sea-birds were wheeling and screaming, their white wings relieved against the black of the rocks, on which rows on rows of solemn-looking guillemots sat, and lines of those strange old-fashion-faced birds, the puffins.

The cliffs were snow-clad, the hills above were terraced with rocks almost to their summits. Between the ship and this inhospitable shore lay a long, dangerous-looking reef of rocks.

"Ah! Rory," said McBain, "there was a merciful Providence watching over us last night. Yonder is where we lay; had it come on to blow, not one of us would be alive this morning to see the sun rise."

Rory could hardly help shuddering as he thought of the narrow escape they had had from so terrible a fate.

When steam was got up they went round the island—it was one of the most southerly of the Faroes; but except around one little bay, where boats might land with difficulty, it seemed impossible that human beings could exist in such a place. What, then, was the mystery of the previous evening, of the fair-haired girl, of the lights inside the reef that simulated those of a broad-beamed ship, of the lights like those of a village that twinkled on shore? The whole affair seemed strange, inexplicable. Now that it was broad daylight the events of the preceding night, with its dangers and its darkness, had more the similitude of some dreadful dream than a stern reality.

This same evening the anchor was let go in the Bay of Thorshaven, the capital—city, shall I say?—of the Faroe Islands. I am writing a tale of adventure, not a narrative of travel, else would I willingly devote a whole chapter to a description of this quaint and primitive wee, wee town. Our heroes saw it at its very worst, its very bleakest, for winter still held it in thrall; the turf-clad roofs of its cottages, that in summer are green with grass and redolent of wild thyme, were now clad with snow; its streets, difficult to climb even in July, were now stairs of glass; its fort looked frozen out; and its little chapel, where Sunday after Sunday the hardy and brave inhabitants, who never move abroad without their lives in their hands, worship God in all humility—this little chapel stood up black and bold against its background of snow.

Although the streamlets were all frozen, although ice was afloat in the bay, and a grey and leaden sky overhead, our boys were not sorry to land and have a look around. To say that they were hospitably received would be hardly doing the Faroese justice, for hospitality really seems a part and parcel of the people's religion. The viands they placed before them were well cooked, but curious, to say the least of it. Steak of young whale, stew of young seal's liver, roast guillemot and baked auk; these may sound queer as dinner dishes, but as they were cooked by the ancient Faroese gentleman who entertained our heroes at his house, each and all of them were brave eating.

Couldn't they stop a month? this gentleman, who looked like a true descendant of some ancient viking, asked McBain. Well then, a fortnight? well, surely one short week?

But, "Nay, nay, nay," the captain answered, kindly and smilingly, to all his entreaties; they must hurry on to the far north ere spring and summer came.

The Faroese could give them no clue to the mystery that shrouded the previous night. They had never heard of either wreckers or pirates in these peaceful islands.

"But," said the old viking, "we are willing to turn out to a man; we are one thousand inhabitants in all—including the women; but even they will go; and we have ten brave, real soldiers in the fort, they too will go, and we will make search, and if we find them we will hang them on—on——" the old man hesitated.

"On the nearest tree," suggested Rory with a mischievous smile.

The viking laughed grimly at the joke.

"Well," he said, "we will hang them anyhow, trees or no trees."

But McBain could not be induced to deviate from his set purpose, and bidding these simple folk a friendly farewell, they steamed once more out of the bay, passed many a strange, fantastic island, passed rocks pierced with caves, and bird-haunted, and so, with the vessel's prow pointing to the northward and west, they left the Faroes far behind them.

Tremendous seas rolled in from the broad Atlantic all that night and all next day, little wind though, and no broken water. In the evening, in the dog watch, the waves seemed to increase in size; they were miles long, mountains high; when down in the trough of the sea you had to look up to their crests as you would to the summer's sun at noontide. Indeed, those waves made the brave ship *Arrandoon* look wondrous small.

McBain, somewhat to Stevenson's astonishment, made the man at the wheel steer directly north.

"We're out of our course, sir," said the mate.

"Pardon me for a minute or two," replied the captain, half apologetically, "we are now broadside on to these seas, I just want to test her stability."

"Well, everything is pretty fast, sir," said the mate, quietly; "but if the ship goes on her beam ends don't blame me."

"Perhaps, Mr. Stevenson, there wouldn't be much time to blame any one; but I can trust my ship, I think. Wo! my beauty."

The beauty didn't seem a bit inclined to "wo!" however. She positively rolled her ports under, and Rory confessed that the doldrums were nothing to this.

Presently up comes Rory from below.

"Och! captain dear," he says, "my gun-case has burst my fiddle-case, and I'm not sure that the fiddle herself is safe, the darling."

Next up comes Stevenson. "Please captain," he says, "the steward says his crockery is all going to smithereens, and the cook can't keep the fire in the galley range, and Freezing Powders has broken the tureen and spilt the soup, and——"

"Enough, enough," cried McBain, laughing; "take charge, mate, and do as you like with her, I'm satisfied."

So down below dived the captain, the ship's head was once more turned north-west, and a bit of canvas clapped on to steady her.

CHAPTER VII.

SANDIE MCFLAIL, M.D—"WHA WOULDNA' BE A SEA-BIRD?"—THE GIRL TELLS HER STRANGE ADVENTURES—NIGHTFALL ON THE SEA.

THERE is one member of the mess whom I have not yet introduced, but a very worthy member he is, our youthful doctor. Poor fellow! never before had he been to sea, and so he suffered accordingly. Oh! right bravely had he tried to keep up for all that. He was the boldest mariner afloat while coming down the Clyde; he disappeared as the ship began to round the stormy Mull. He appeared again for a short time at Oban, but vanished when the anchor was weighed. At Lerwick, where they called in to take old Magnus Bolt on board, and ship a dozen stalwart Shetlanders, the doctor was once more seen on deck; and it was currently reported that when the vessel lay helpless on the reef, a ghostly form bearing a strong resemblance to the bold surgeon was seen flitting about in the darkness, and a quavering voice was heard to put this solemn question more than once, "Any danger, men? Men, are we in danger?" This was the last that had been seen of the medico; but Rory found a slate in the dispensary, into which sanctum, by the way, he had no right to pop even his nose. He brought this slate aft, the young rascal, and read what was written thereon to Allan and Ralph, from which it was quite evident that Sandie McFlail, M.D., of Aberdeen, had made a most intrepid attempt to keep a diary. The entries were short, and ran somewhat thus:—

"February 9th.—Dropped away from the Broomielaw and steamed down the beautiful Clyde. Charming day, though cold, and the hills on each side the river clothed in virgin snow. Felt sad and sorrowful at leaving my native land. I wonder will ever we return, or will the great sea swallow us up? Would rather it didn't. I wonder if *she* will think of me and pray for her mariner bold when the wind blows high at night, when the cold rain beats against the window-panes of her little cot, and the storm spirit roars around the old chimneys. I feel a sailor already all over, and I tread the decks with pride.

"Feb. 10th.—At sea. The ocean getting rough. Passed some seagulls.

"Feb. 11th.—Sea rougher. Passed a ship.

"Feb. 12th.—Sea still rough. Passed some seaweed.

"Feb. 13th.—Sea mountains high. Passed——"

"And here," says Rory, "the diary breaks off all of a sudden like; and all of a sudden the entries close; so, really, there is no saying what the doctor passed on the 13th. But just about this time, the mate tells me, he was seen leaning languidly over the side, so——"

"Ho, ho!" cried McBain, close at his ear.

The captain had entered the saloon unperceived by boy Rory, and had been standing behind him all the time he was reading. Ralph and Allan saw him well enough, but they, of course, said nothing, although they could not refrain from laughing.

"Ho, ho, Rory, my boy!" says McBain; "ho, ho, boy Rory! so you're fairly caught!"

"And indeed then," says Rory, jumping up and looking as guilty as any schoolboy, "I didn't know you were there at all at all."

"Of that I am perfectly sure," McBain says, laughing, "else you wouldn't have been reading the poor doctor's private diary. What shall we do with him, Ralph? What shall he be done to, Allan?"

"Oh!" said Ralph, mischievously; "send him to the masthead for a couple of hours. Into the foretop, mind, where he'll get plenty of air about him."

"No," said Allan, grinning; "give him a seat for three hours on the end of the bowsprit. Of course, Captain McBain, you'll let him have a bottle of hot water at his feet, and a blanket or two about him. He is only a little one, you know."

"But now that I think of it," said McBain, "you are all the same, boys; there isn't one of you a whit better than the other."

"Sure and you're right, captain," Rory put in, "for if I was reading, they were listening, most intently, too."

"Well then, boys, I'll tell you how you can make amends to the honest doctor. Off you go, the three of you, and see if you can't rouse him out. Get him to come on deck and breathe the fresh air. He'll soon get round."

And off our three heroes went, joyfully, on their mission of mercy.

They found the worthy doctor in bed in his cabin, and forthwith set about kindly but firmly rousing him out. They had even brought Freezing Powders with them, to carry a pint of moselle.

"I feel vera limp," said Sandie, as soon as he got dressed, "vera limp indeed. Well, as you say, the moselle may do me good, but I'm a teetotaler as a rule."

"We never touch any wine," said Ralph, "nor care to; but this, my dear doctor, is medicine."

Sandie confessed himself better immediately when he got on deck. With Allan on one side of him and big Ralph on the other, he was marched up and down the deck for half an hour and more.

"Man! gentlemen!" he remarked, "I thought I could

walk finely, but I'm just now for a' the world like a silly drunken body."

"We were just the same," said Allan, "when we came first to sea—couldn't walk a bit; but we soon got our sea legs, and we've never lost them yet."

The doctor was struck with wonder at the might and majesty of the waves, and also at the multitude of birds that were everywhere about and around them. Kittiwakes, solons, gulls, guillemots, auks, and puffins, they whirled and wheeled around the ship in hundreds, screaming and shrieking and laughing. They floated on the water, they swam on its surface, and dived down into its dark depths, and no fear had they of human beings, nor of the steamer itself.

"How happy they all seem!" said Rory; "if I was one of the lower animals, as we call them, sure there is nothing in the wide world I'd like better to be than a sea-bird."

"True for you," said Allan; "it's a wild, free life they lead."

"And they seem to have no care," said the doctor. "Their meat is bound to their heads; at any rate, they never have far to go to seek it. When tired they can rest; when rested they can fly again. Then look at the warm and beautiful coats they wear. There is no wetting them to the skin; the water glides off o' them like the rain from a duck's back. Then think o' the pleasure o' possessin' a pair o' wings that can cleave the air like an arrow from a bowstring; that in a few short days, independent o' wind or waves or weather, can carry them from the cauld north far, far awa' to the saft and sunny south. Wha wouldna' be a sea-bird?"

"Yes," reiterated Rory, stopping in front of the doctor; "as you say, doctor, 'Wha wouldna' be a sea-bird?' But pardon me, sir, for in you I recognise a kindred spirit, a lover of nature, a lover of the beautiful. You and I will be friends, doctor—fast friends. There, shake hands."

"As for Ralph and Allan," he added, with a mischievous grin, "'deed in troth, doctor dear, there isn't a bit of poetry in their nature, and they would any day far sooner see a couple of eider ducks roasted and flanked with apple sauce, than the same wildly beautiful birds happy and alive and afloat on the dark, heaving breast of the ocean. It's the truth I'm telling ye, doctor. D'ye play at all? Have you any favourite instrument?"

"Weel, sir," the doctor replied, "I canna say that I'm vera much o' a musician, but I just can manage to toot a wee bit on the flute."

"And I've no doubt," said Rory, "that you 'toot' well, too."

The conversation never slackened for a couple of hours, and so well did the doctor feel, that of his own free will he volunteered joining them at dinner in the saloon. McBain was as much surprised as delighted when he came below to dine, and found that their new messmate, Sandie McFlail, had at long last put in an appearance at table.

The swell on the sea was much less next morning; the wind had slightly increased, and more sail had been spread, so that the ship was moderately steady. The rugged coast and strange, fantastic rocks of the outlying islands of Iceland were in sight, and, half-buried in misty clouds, the distant mountains could be dimly descried.

"Yonder," said the mate, advancing towards Captain McBain, glass in hand,—"yonder is a small boat, sir, with a bit of a sail on her; she has just rounded the needle rocks, and seems standing in for the mainland."

"Well," said the captain, "let us over-haul her, anyhow. There can be no harm in that, and it may secure us a fresh fish or two for dinner."

"A SMALL BOAT, SIR, WITH A BIT OF A SAIL ON HER."

[*Page* 60.

In less than an hour the *Arrandoon* had come up with this strange sail, which at first sight had seemed a mere speck on the ocean, seen at one moment and hidden the next behind some mountain roller. The surprise of our heroes may be better imagined than described, to find afloat in this cockle-shell of a boat, with an oar shipped as a mast and a tartan plaid as a main-sail, none other than the heroine of the wreckers' reef. Seeing that she was in the power of the big ship, she made no further attempt to get away, but, dropping her sail, she seized the oars, paddled quietly and cooly alongside, and next moment stood on the quarter-deck, with bowed head and modest mien, before Captain McBain.

The captain took her kindly by the hand, smiling as he said, " Do not be afraid, my girl ; consider yourself among friends—among those, indeed, who would do anything in their power to serve you, even if they were not already deeply in your debt, and deeply grateful."

"Ah!" she said, mournfully, "my warning came all too late to save you. But, praised be God ! you are safe now, and not in the power of those terrible men, who would have spared not a single life of those the waves did not engulf."

"But tell us," continued McBain, "all about it—all about yourself. There is some strange mystery about the matter, which we would fain have solved. But stay—not here, and not yet. You must be very tired and weary ; you must first have rest and refreshment, after which you can tell us your tale. Stevenson, see the little boat hauled up ; and, doctor, I place this young lady under your care ; to-night I hope to land her safely in Reikjavik ; meanwhile my cabin is at her disposal."

"Come, lassie," said the good surgeon, laconically, leading the way down the companion.

Merely dropping a queenly curtsey to McBain and our young heroes, she followed the doctor without a word.

Peter the steward placed before her the most tempting viands in the ship, yet she seemed to have but little appetite.

"I am tired," she said at length, "I fain would rest. Long weary weeks of sorrow have been mine. But they are past and gone at last."

Then she retired, this strange ocean waif and stray, and so the day wore gradually to a close, and they saw no more of her until the sun, fierce, fiery, and red, began to disappear behind the distant snow-clad hills; then they found her once more in their midst.

She had gathered the folds of her plaid around her, her long yellow hair still floated over her shoulders, and her dreamy blue eyes were shyly raised to McBain's face as she began to speak.

"I owe you some explanation," she said. "My strange conduct must appear almost inexplicable to you. My appearance among you two nights ago was intended to save you from the destruction that awaited you—from the destruction that had been prepared for you by the Danish wreckers."

"Sir," she continued, after a pause, "I am myself a Dane. My father was parish minister in the little village of Elmdene. Alas! I fear he is now no more. Afflictions gathered and thickened around us in our once happy little home, and the only way we could see out of them was to leave our native land and cross the ocean. In America we have many friends who had kindly offered us an asylum, until happier days should come again. Our vessel was a brig, our crew all told only twenty hands, and we, my brother, father, and myself—for mother has long since gone Up Beyond—were the only passengers.

"All went well until we were off the northern Shetlands, when at the dark, starry hour of midnight our ship was boarded and carried by pirates. Every one in the ship was put to the sword, saving my father and myself. My poor dear brave brother was slain before my eyes, but he died as the Danes die—with his face to the foe. My father was promised his life if he would perform the ceremony of marriage between myself and the pirate captain, who is a Russian, a daring, fearless fellow, but a strange compound of superstition and vice—a man who will go to prayers before scuttling a ship! The object of this pirate was to seize your vessel; he would have met and fought you at sea, but the easier plan for him was to try to wreck you. Fortune seemed to favour this bold design of his. The lights placed on shore, to represent a vessel of large size, were part and parcel of his vile scheme. But the darkness of the night enabled me to escape and come towards you. Then I feared to return; but, alas! alas! I now tremble lest my dear father has had to pay the penalty of my rashness with his life." *

"But the ship—this pirate?" said McBain. "We sailed around the island next day but saw no signs of him?"

"Then," said the girl, "he must have escaped in the darkness, immediately after discovering the entire failure of his scheme."

"And whither were you bound for when we overtook you, my poor girl?" asked McBain.

"At Reikjavik," she replied "I have an uncle, a minister. He it was who taught me all I know, while he was still at home in Elmdene—taught me among other things the beautiful language of your country, which I speak, but speak so indifferently."

"Can this be," said McBain, "the self-same pirate that attacked the *Snowbird*?"

"The very same thought," answered Ralph, "was passing through my own mind."

"And yet how strange that a pirate should cruise in these far northern seas!"

"She has less chance of being caught, at all events," Allan said.

* The story of the pirate is founded on fact.

"Ha!" exclaimed McBain, with a kind of grim, exultant laugh, "if she comes across the *Arrandoon*, that chance will indeed be a small one. She'll find us a different kind of a craft from the *Snowbird*."

The vessel was now heading directly for the south-east coast of Iceland. Somewhere in there, though at present hidden by points of land and rocky islets, lay the capital of Iceland, which they hoped to reach ere midnight.

A more lovely land and seascape than that which was now stretched out before them, it would indeed be difficult to conceive. The sun had gone down behind the western end of a long line of snow-clad mountains, serrated, jagged, and peaked, but their tops were all rose-tipped with his parting beams. Above them the sky was clear, with just one speck of crimson cloud; the lower land between was bathed in a purple mist, through which the icebound rocks could dimly be discerned, while the mantle of night had already been spread over the ocean.

It was "nightfall on the sea."

CHAPTER VIII.

A GALE FROM THE MOUNTAINS—DAYBREAK IN ICELAND—THE GREAT BALLOON ASCENT—RORY'S YARN—THE SNOW-CLOUD—THE PIRATE IS SEEN.

A WHOLE week has elapsed since the events transpired which I have related in last chapter,—a week most interestingly if not always quite pleasantly spent. The *Arrandoon* is lying before the quaint, fantastical old town of Reikjavik, surrounded almost in every direction by mountains bold and wild, the peaked summits and even the sides of which are now covered with ice and snow. For spring has not yet arrived to unrivet stern winter's chains, to swell the rivers into roaring torrents, and finally to carpet the earth with beauty. The streams are still frozen, the bay in which the good ship lies at her anchors twain, is filled with broken pancake-ice, which makes communication with the shore by means of boat a matter of no little difficulty, for oars have to be had in-board or used as pressing poles, and boat-hooks are in constant requisition.

Winter it is, and the country all around might be called dreary, were it not for the ever-varying shades of colour that, as the sun shines out, or anon hides his head behind a cloud, spread themselves over hill and dale and rugged glen. Oh! the splendour of those sunrises and sunsets, the rose tints, the purples, the emerald greens and cool greys, that blaze and blend, grow faint and fade as they chase each other among mountains and ravines! What a poor morsel of steel my pen feels as I attempt to describe them! Yet have they a beauty peculiarly their own,—a beauty which never can be forgotten by those whose eyes have once rested thereon.

The fair-haired Danish girl has been landed, and for a time has found shelter and peace in the humble home of her uncle the clergyman. Our heroes have been on shore studying the manners and customs of the primitive but hospitable people they find themselves among.

Several city worthies have been off to see the ship and to dine. But to-night our heroes are all by themselves in the saloon. Dinner is finished, nuts and fruit and fragrant coffee are on the table, at the head of which sits the captain, on his right the doctor and Ralph, on his left Allan and Rory. Freezing Powders, neatly dressed, is hovering near, and Peter, the steward, is not far off, while the cockatoo is busy as usual, helping himself to tremendous billfuls of hemp-seed, but nevertheless putting in his oar every minute, with a "Well, duckie?" or a long-drawn "Dea-ah me!"

I cannot say that all is peace, though, beyond the wooden walls of the *Arrandoon*, for a storm is raging with almost hurricane violence, sweeping down from the hills with ever-varying force, and threatening to tear the vessel from her anchorage. Steam is up, the screw revolves, and it taxes all the engineer's skill to keep up to the anchors so as to avert the strain from them.

But our boys are used to danger by this time, and there is hardly a moment's lull in the conversation. Even Sandie McFlail, M.D. o' Aberdeen, has already forgotten all the horrors of *mal-de-mer*; he even believes he has found his sea-legs, and feels all over as good a sailor as anybody.

"Reikjavik!" says Ralph; "isn't it a queer break-jaw kind of a name. It puts one in mind of a mouthful of exceedingly tough beefsteak."

"A gastronomic simile," says Rory; "though maybe neither poetical nor elegant, sure, but truly Saxon."

"Ah! weel," the doctor says, in his quiet, thoughtful, canny way, "I dinna know now. Some o' the vera best poetry of all ages bears reference to the pleesures o' the table. Witness Horace's Odes, for instance."

"Hear! hear!" from Allan; and "Horace was a brick!" from honest English Ralph; but Rory murmurs "Moore!"

"But," continues the doctor, "to my ear there is nothing vera harsh in the language that these islanders speak. They pronounce the 'ch' hard, like the Scotch; their 'j's' soft, like the Spanish; and turn their 'w's' into 'v's.' They pronounce church—kurk; and the 'j' is a 'y,' or next thing to it. 'Reik' or 'reyk' means smoke, you know, as it is in Scotch 'reek;' and 'wik,' or 'wich,' or 'vik' means a bay, as in the English 'Woolwich,' 'Sandwich,' etc., so that Reikjavik is simply 'the bay of smoke,' or 'the smoking bay;' but whether with reference to the smoke that hangs over the town, or the spray that rises mist-like from the seething billows when the wind blows, I cannot say—probably the former; and it is worthy of note, gentlemen, that some savage races far, far away from here—the aborigines of Australia, for example—designate towns by the term 'the big smoke.'"

"How profoundly erudite you are, doctor!" says Rory. "Now, wouldn't it have been much better for your heirs and assigns and the world at large, if you had accepted a Professorship of Antiquity in the University of Aberdeen, instead of coming away with us, to cool the toes of you at the North Pole, and maybe leave your bones to bleach beneath the Aurora Borealis, eh?"

"Ha! there I have you," cries Sandie, smiling good-humouredly, for by this time he was quite used to Rory's bantering ways,—"there I have you, boy Rory; and it is with the profoundest awe and respect for everything sacred, that I remind you that the Aurora Borealis never bleached any bones; and those poor unfortunates who, in their devotion for science, have wandered towards the mystery land around the Pole, and there laid down their lives, will never, never moulder into dust, but, entombed in the green, salt ice, with the virgin snow as their winding-sheet, their bodies will rest in peace, and rest intact until the trumpet sounds."

There was a lull in the conversation at this point, but no lull in the storm; the waves dashed wildly over the ship, the wind roared through the rigging, the brave vessel quivered from stem to stern, as if in constant fear she might be hurled from the protection afforded by anchor and cable, and cast helpless upon the rock-bound shore.

A lull, broken presently by a deep sigh from Freezing Powders.

"Well, duckie?" said Polly, in sympathising tones.

"Well, Freezing Powders," said McBain, "and pray what are you sighing about?"

"What for I sigh?" repeated Freezing Powders. "Am you not afraid you'se'f, sah! You not hear de wild winds roar, and de wave make too much bobbery? 'Tis a'most enuff, sah, to make a gem'lam turn pale, sah!"

"Ha! ha!" laughed Rory; "really, it'll take a mighty big storm, Freezing Powders, to make you turn pale. But, doctor," he continued, "what say you to some music?"

"If you'll play," said the surgeon, "I'll toot."

And so the concert was begun; and the shriek of the storm-spirit was drowned in mirth and melody, or, as the doctor, quoting Burns, expressed it,—

> "The storm without might roar and rustle,
> They didna mind the storm a whustle."

But after this night of storm and tempest, what a wonderful morning it was! The sun shot up amidst the encrimsoned mountain peaks, and shone brightly down from a sky of cloudless blue. The snow was everywhere dazzling in its whiteness, and there was not a sigh of wind to raise so much as a ripple on the waters of the bay, from which every bit of ice had been blown far to sea. Wild birds screamed with joy as they wheeled in hundreds around the ship, while out in the bay a shoal of porpoises were disporting themselves, leaping high in air from out of the sparkling waters, and shrieking—or, as the doctor called it, "whustling"—for very joy.

Every one on board the *Arrandoon* was early astir—up, indeed, before the sun himself—for there were to be great doings on shore to-day. The first great experimental balloon ascent and flight was about to be made. Every one on shore was early astir, too; in fact, the greatest excitement prevailed, and on the table-land to the right of, and some little distance from, the town, from which the balloon was to ascend, the people had assembled from an early hour, even the ladies of Reikjavik turning out dressed in their gayest attire, no small proportion of which consisted of fur and feathers.

The aëronaut was a professional, Monsieur De Vere by name. McBain had gone all the way to Paris especially to engage his services. Nor had he hired him at random, for this canny captain of ours had not only satisfied himself that De Vere was in a scientific point of view a clever man, but he had accompanied him in several ascents, and could thus vouch for his being a really practical aëronaut.

Who would go with De Vere in this first great trip over the regions of perpetual snow? The doctor stepped forward as a volunteer, and by his side was Rory. Perhaps Allan and Ralph were rather lazy for any such aërial exploit; anyhow, they were content to stay at home.

"We'll look on, you know," said Ralph, "as long as we can see you; and when you return—that is, if ever you do return—you can tell us all about it."

When all was ready the ropes were cast loose, and, with

a ringing cheer from the assembled multitude, up arose the mighty balloon, straight as arrow from bow, into the blue, sunny sky. Like the eagle that soars from the peak of Benrinnes, she seemed to seek the very sun itself.

Rory and the surgeon, who had never been in a balloon before—nor even, for the matter of that, down in a coal-pit—at first hardly relished their sudden elevation, but they soon got used to it.

Not the slightest motion was there; Rory could hardly credit the fact that he was moving, and when at last he did muster up sufficient courage to peep earthwards over the side of the car.

"Oh, look, doctor dear!" he cried; "sure, look for yourself; the world is moving away from us altogether!"

And this was precisely the sensation they experienced. Both the doctor and Rory were inclined to clutch nervously and tremulously the sides of the car in the first part of their ascent; but though the former was not much of a sailor, somewhat to his surprise he experienced none of those giddy feelings common to the landsman when gazing from an immense height. He could look beneath him and around him, and enjoy to the full the strange bird's-eye landscape and seascape that every moment seemed to broaden and widen, until a great portion of the northern island, with its mountains, its lakes, its frozen torrents, its gulfs and bays and islands, and the great blue southern ocean, even to the far-off Faroe Isles, lay like a beautifully portrayed map beneath their feet. The grandeur of the scene kept them silent for long minutes; it impressed them, it awed them. It did more than even this, for it caused them to feel their own littleness, and the might of the Majesty that made the world.

De Vere himself seldom vouchsafed a single glance landwards; he seemed to busy himself wholly and solely with the many strange instruments with which he was surrounded. He was hardly a moment idle. The intense cold, that soon began to benumb the senses of Sandie, seemed to have no deterrent effect on his efforts.

"I must confess I do fell sleepy," said the worthy medico, "and I meant to assist you, Mr. De Vere."

"Here," cried the scientist, pouring something out of a phial, and handing it to him, "drink that quick."

"I feel double the individual," cried Sandie, brightly, as soon as he had swallowed the draught.

"Come," said Rory—"come, monsieur, *I* want to feel double the individual, too."

"No, no, sir," said De Vere, smiling, "an Irishman no want etherism; you are already—pardon me—too ethereal."

Sandie was gazing skywards.

> "It is the moon,"—he was saying—"I ken her horn,
>   She's blinkin' in the lift sae hie;
> She smiles, the jade! to wile us hame,
>   But, 'deed, I doubt, she'll wait a wee."

"Happy thought!" cried Rory; "let us go to the moon."

"No," laughed the doctor; "nobody ever got that length yet."

"Oh, you forget, Mr. Surgeon," said Rory,—"you forget entirely all about Danny O'Rourke."

"Tell us, then, Rory."

"Troth, then," began Rory, in his richest brogue, "it was just like this same. Danny was a dacint boy enough, who lived entoirely alone with Biddy his wife, and the pig, close to a big bog in old Oireland. Sitting on a stone in the midst of this bog was Danny, one foine summer's evening, when who should fly down but an aigle. 'Foine noight,' says the aigle. 'The same to you,' says Danny, 'and many of them.' 'But,' says the aigle, 'don't you see that it is sinking you are?' 'Och! sure,' cries Danny, 'and so it is. I'll be swallowed up in the bog, and poor Biddy and the pig will nivir set eyes on me again. Och! och! what'll I do?' 'Git on to me back, troth,' says the aigle, 'and I'll fly you sthraight to your Biddy's door.' 'And the blessings av the O'Rourkes be wid ye 'thin,' says Danny, putting his arms round the aigle's neck, 'for you are the sinsible bird, and whatever I'd have done widout ye, ne'er a bit o' me knows. But isn't it high enough you are now, aroon? Yonder is my cottage just down there.' For," continued Rory, "you must know that by this time the aigle had mounted fully a mile high with poor Danny. 'Be quiet wid ye,' says the aigle, 'or I'll shake ye off me back entoirely. Don't ye remember robbing my nest last year? *I* do. And it's niver a cottage you'll ever see again, nor Biddy, nor the pig either. It's right up to the moon I'm flying wid ye.' 'What!' cries Danny, 'to that bit av a thing like a raping-hook? Och! and och! what'll become av me at all at all?' But the moon got bigger the nearer they came to it, and they found it a dacint size enough when they got there entirely. 'Catch a howld av the end av the raping-hook,' says the aigle, 'or by this and by that I'll shake ye off me shoulder.' And so poor Danny had no ho' but just to do as he was told, and away flew the aigle and left him. While he was wondering what he should do now, a stern voice behind him says, 'Let go—let go the end of the raping-hook, and be off wid ye back to your own counthry.' 'It's hardly civil av you,' says Danny, 'to ask me sich a thing. Sure it is few ever come to call on you anyhow.' 'Let go,' thundered the man o' the moon; and he gave Danny just one kick, and off went the poor boy flying into the air. 'It's killed I'll be,' says he to himself, 'killed entoirely wid the fall, and what'll become o' me wife Biddy and the pig is more'n I can tell.' But he fell, and he fell, and he fell, and he never seemed to stop falling, till plump he alights right in the middle o' the sea, and there he lay on the broad back av him, till a big lump av a whale came and splashed him all over wid his tail. But sure enough the sea was only his bed, and the big whale turned out to be

Biddy herself, with the watering-pot, telling him to get up, for a lazy ould boy, and feed the pig, and troth it was nothing but a dream after all.

"But where in the name of wonder are we now?" he continued, gazing around.

It was a very natural question. It had got suddenly dark. They were enveloped in a snow-cloud. The brave balloon seemed to struggle through it.

Ballast was thrown over, and up and out into the sunshine she rose again, but what a change had come over her appearance—every rope and length of her and the car itself and our bold aëronauts were covered white with virgin snow.

"Monsieurs," said De Vere, "this is more than I bargained for. We must descend. You see she has lost all life. De lofely soul dat was in de balloon seems to have gone. We will descend."

Indeed the huge balloon was already moving slowly earthwards, and in a minute more they were again passing through the snow-cloud. Once clear of this a breeze sprang up, or, to speak more correctly, they entered a current of air, that carried them directly inland for many miles. Tired of this direction, the valve was opened, out roared the gas, and the descent became more rapid, until the wind ceased to blow—they were beneath the adverse current. More ballast was thrown out, and her "way" was stopped.

But see, what aileth our hero, boy Rory? For some minutes he has been gazing southwards over the sea, so intensely indeed that his looks almost frighten the honest doctor.

"The glass, the glass," he hisses, holding round his hand, but not taking his glance for a moment off the southern horizon.

The glass is handed to him, he adjusts it to his eye, and takes one long, fixed look; and when he turns once more towards the doctor his face is radiant with joy and excitement.

"It is she," he cried, "it is *she*, it is SHE!"

The doctor really looked scared.

"Man!" he said, "are ye takin' leave o' your wuts? There, tak' a hold o' my hand and dinna try to frighten folk. There's never a 'she' near ye."

"It is *she*, I tell you," cried Rory again; "take the glass and look in under the land yonder, and heading for Stromsoe. It is the pirate herself,—the pirate we fought in the *Snowbird*. Hurrah! hurrah!!"

CHAPTER IX.

MOUNT HEKLA—THE GREAT GEYSER—A NARROW ESCAPE—THE SEARCH FOR THE PIRATE—MCBAIN'S LITTLE "RUSE DE GUERRE"—THE BATTLE BEGUN.

"THAT puts quite another complexion on the matter," said Dr. Sandy McFlail, with a sigh of relief, when Rory explained to him that he had spied the pirate, "quite another complexion, though, for the time bein' ye glowered sae like a warlock that I did think ye had lost your reason; so give me the glass, and I'll e'en take a look at her mysel'.

"Eh! sirs," he continued, with the telescope at his eye, "but she is a big ship, and a bonnie ship. But, Rory boy, just catch a hold o' my coat-tails, and I'll feel more secure like. I wouldn't wish to go heels o'er head out o' the car. A fine big ship indeed—square-rigged forward and schooner-rigged aft; a vera judeecious arrangement."

"Now," cried Rory, "the sooner we are landed on old mother earth the better. Bend on to the valve halyards, De Vere. Down with her."

"Sirs! sirs!" cried the doctor, in great alarm; "pray don't be rash. Be judeecious, gentlemen, be judeecious."

De Vere looked from one to the other, then laughed aloud. He was amused at the impetuosity of the Irishman and at the canniness of the Scot.

A very pleasant little man was this De Vere to look at, black as to hair and moustache, dark as to eyes; thoughtful-looking as a rule were these eyes, yet oft lit up with fun. He never spoke much, perhaps he cogitated the more; he seldom made a joke himself, but he had a high appreciation of humour in others. Taking him all and all he gave you the impression of one who would be little likely to lose his presence of mind in a time of danger.

"Gentlemen," he said, quietly, "you will leave the descent in my hands, if you please. We are now, by my calculation, some ninety miles from the city of Reikjavik. You see beneat' you wild mountains, ice-bound plains, frozen lakes, rivers and waterfalls, deep ravines and gorges, but no sign of smoke, no life. Shall I make my descent here? Shall I pull vat Monsieur Rory call de valve halyard? Shall I land in de regions of desolation?"

"Dinna think o't," cried Sandy. "Never mind Rory; he is only a laddie."

"It's yourself that's complimentary," quoth Rory.

"Ah! ver' well," said De Vere; "I will go on, for since you have been gazing on de ship, de current have change, and we once more get nearer home."

An hour went slowly by. Both the doctor and Rory were gazing at the far-off mountain, Hekla, that lay to the south and east, though distant many miles. The vast hill looked a king among the other mountains; a king, but a dead king, being still and quiet in the sunshine, enrobed in a shroud of snow.

Sandy was doubly engaged—he was talking musingly, and aloud; but at the same time he was doing ample justice to the venison pie that lay so confidingly on his knee, for Sandy was a bit of a philosopher in his own quiet way.

"Mount Hekla," he was saying; "is it any wonder that these Norsemen, these superstitious sons of the ancient Vikings, look upon it as the entrance-gate to the terrible abode of fire and brimstone, gloom and woe, where are confined the souls of the unhappy dead? Hekla, round thy snow-capped summit the thunders never cease to roll——"

"Hark," said Rory, holding up his hand; "talk about thunder, list to that."

Both leant over the car and looked earthwards. What could it mean, that low, deep, long-continued thunder-peal? Was a storm raging beneath them? Yes, but not of the kind they at first imagined. For see, from where yonder hill starts abruptly from the glen, rise immense clouds of silvery white, and roll slowly adown the valley. The balloon hangs suspended right above the great *geyser*, which is now in full eruption.

"It is as I thought," said De Vere; "let us descend a little way;" and he opened the valve as he spoke.

The balloon made a downward rush as he did so, as if she meant to plunge herself and all her occupants into the very midst of the boiling cauldron. The steam from the geyser had almost reached their feet; the car thrilled beneath them, while the never-ceasing thunder pealed louder and louder.

"My conscience!" roared honest Sandy, losing all control over himself; "we'll be boiled alive like so many partans!" *

De Vere coolly threw overboard a bag or two of sand, and the balloon mounted again like a skylark. And not too soon either, for, awful to relate, in his sudden terror Sandy had made a grab at the valve-rope, as if to check her downward speed. Had not Rory speedily pulled him back, the consequences would have been too dreadful to think of.

De Vere only laughed; but he held up one finger by way of admonishing the doctor as he said, "Neever catch hold of de reins ven anoder man is driving."

"But," said Rory, "didn't you go a trifle too near that time, Mister de Vere?"

"A leetle," said the Frenchman, coolly. "It was noding."

* Partans : Scottish, crabs.

"Ach! sure no," says Rory; "it was nothing at all; and yet, Mister de Vere, it isn't the pleasantest thing in the world to imagine yourself being played at pitch and toss with on the top of a mighty geyser, for all the world like a nut-gall on the top of a twopenny fountain!"

Sandy resumed the dissection of his venison pie. He would have a long entry for his diary to-night, he thought.

Luck does not always attend the aëronaut, albeit fortune favours the brave, and the current of air that was carrying the balloonists so merrily back to Reikjavik, ceased entirely when they were still within ten miles of that quaint wee place. It was determined, therefore, to make a descent. Happily, they were over a glen. Close by the sea and around the bay were many small farms, and so adroitly did De Vere manage to attach an anchor to the roof of an old barn, that descent was easy in the extreme.

Perhaps the happiest man in the universe at the moment Sandy McFail's feet touched mother earth again was Sandy himself. "Man!" he cried to Rory, rubbing his hands and laughing with glee, "I thought gettin' out meant a broken leg at the vera least, and I haven't even bled my nose."

There was some commotion, I can tell you, among the feathered inmates of the barnyard when the balloonists popped down among them; as for the farm folks, they had shut themselves up in the dwelling-house. The geese were particularly noisy. Geese, reader, always remind me of those people we call sceptics: they are sure to gabble their loudest at things they can't understand.

But convinced at last that the aëronauts were neither evil spirits nor inhabitants of the moon, the good farmer made them heartily welcome at his fireside, and assisted them to pack, so that, by the aid of men and ponies, they found themselves late that evening safely on board the *Arrandoon;* and right glad were their comrades to see them again, you may be sure, and to listen to a narration by Rory of all their adventures, interlarded by Sandy's queer, dry remarks, which only served to render it all the more funny.

But before they sat down to the ample supper that Peter had prepared for them, Rory reported to the captain his great discovery.

McBain's eyes sparkled like live coals as he heard of it, but he said little. He sent quietly for the engineer and the mate. "How soon," he asked the former, "can you get up steam?"

"In an hour, sir—easy."

'That will do," said the captain. "Mr. Stevenson, when will the moon rise?"

"She is rising now, sir."

"All right, Mr. Stevenson. Have all ready to weigh anchor in two hours' time."

"Ay, ay, sir!"

The engineer still lingered. "I *could* get up steam in twenty minutes," he said; "those American hams, sir——"

"Oh, bother the hams!" said the captain, laughing. "No, no; we may be glad of those yet when frozen in at the Pole. Bear-and-ham pie, engineer; how will that eat, eh?" and he bowed him kindly out.

*   *   *   *   *

By two bells in the middle watch the good ship *Arrandoon* was off the needle rocks of the Portland Huck. They stood up out of the water like tall sheeted ghosts, with the moonlight and starlight shimmering from their shoulders. The sea was calm, with only a gentle heave on it; and there were but a few snowy clouds in the sky skirting the southern horizon, so the vessel ploughed along as beautifully as any sailor could wish, with a steady, contented throb of engine and gride of screw, leaving in her wake a long silvery line for the moonbeams to dance in. Save the noise of the ship's working there was not another sound to be heard, only occasionally a gull would float past overhead emitting a strange and mournful cry. What makes the sea-birds, I have wondered, sometimes leave the rocks at the midnight hour, and go skimming alone through the darkling air, emitting that weird and plaintive wail of theirs? It is a wail that goes directly to one's heart, and you cannot help thinking they must be bereaved ones mourning for their dead.

Our heroes walked long on deck that night, talking quietly, as became the hour, of the prospects of their having a brush with the pirate. But they got weary at last, and turned in. Next morning they found the decks wet and slippery, more clouds in the sky, a fair beam wind blowing, and a trifle of canvas displayed.

After breakfast McBain called all hands aft. In calm, dispassionate language he told them the story of the poor girl who had risked her life on their account, of her murdered brother and captive father, and of the pirate he was about to try to find and capture. Then he paused; and as he did so every one of the crew turned eyes on Ted Wilson, who strode forward.

"Captain," said Ted, firmly, "we didn't sign articles to fight, did we, mates?"

"No," from all hands.

"*But*," continued Ted, "for such a captain as you be, and in such a cause, we *will* fight, every man Jack of us, as long as the saucy *Arrandoon* has a timber above the water. Am I right, mates?"

A ringing cheer was all the reply, and Ted retired.

Now, reader, were I a landsman novelist I would very likely here make my captain give the orders to "splice the mainbrace," but I'm a sailor, and I tell you this, boys, that British seamen never yet needed Dutch courage to make them do their duty.

Captain McBain only waved a hand and said, "Pipe down."

An hour afterwards the crow's-nest was rigged and hoisted at the main-truck, and either the mate or the captain was in it off and on the whole day. But no pirate appeared that day nor the next. In the evening, however, some fishermen boarded the *Arrandoon*, and reported having seen a large barque, answering to the description of the suspected craft, that same morning lying at anchor off Suddersöe, with boats passing to and fro 'twixt ship and shore.

"It is my precious opinion, captain," said old Magnus Bolt, "that this craft does a bit o' smuggling 'tween here and Shetland."

"And it is my precious opinion, my dear Magnus," said McBain, "that the rascal doesn't care what he does so long as he lands the cash."

The *Arrandoon* was now kept away for the island named by the honest fishermen. Not straight, however; McBain gave it a wide berth, and passed it far to the west, and held on his course until many miles to the southward. In the morning it was "'bout ship" and stand away north and by east again. They sighted the island about seven bells in the morning watch. Suddenly there was a hail from the crow's-nest. It was the captain's voice.

"Come up here, Magnus Bolt, if your old bones will let you, and see what you shall see."

Magnus sprang up the rigging somewhat after the fashion of an antiquated monkey, but with an agility no one would have given him credit for.

"It is she!" he shouted, after he had had a look through the long glass in towards the iron-bound shores of the islands; "it is she! it is she! Ha! ha! ha!" and he positively danced and chuckled with delight.

6

"You'll fight? you'll fight?" he gasped.

"Rather," replied McBain; "but we'll run first. She shall fire the first shot, and, Magnus, you shall fire the second."

Half an hour afterwards, when our heroes came on deck to have their morning look around, they stared at each other in blank astonishment. The *Arrandoon* looked as if she had just come out of a tornado and had been dreadfully handled. The foretop-gallant mast was down, the jibboom in board, the screw was hoisted up, the funnel itself had been unshipped and was lashed to the deck, and the flag was flying at half-mast, as if the vessel were in distress, or had death on board.

Now let me, with one touch of the fairy wand the storyteller wields, waft my readers on board the pirate herself. Fear not, for we will stay there but a brief space of time indeed. The tall and by no means unprepossessing form of the captain, armed *cap-à-pie*, is leaning against the rudder-wheel, one spoke of which he holds. His mate is by his side, glass in hand, examining the *Arrandoon*, now only a few miles off.

"Ha! ha!" says the latter; "it is the same big craft we tried to strand; and she's had dirty weather, too—foretop-gallant mast and jibboom both gone. She is flying a signal of distress."

"Distress? Eh? Ha! ha! ha!" laughed the pirate. "Isn't it funny? She'll have more of it; won't she, matie mine?"

The mate laughed and commenced to sing—

> "'Won't you walk into my parlour?'
> Said the spider to the fly?"

"She's evidently a whaler, crow's-nest and all," he said.

"Well," said the captain, "we'll w(h)ale her;" and he laughed at his own stupid joke.

"I say there, old lantern-jaws," he bawled down the companion.

"I reckon," said a Yankee voice, "you alludes to this child."

"I do," cried the captain; "and look ye here. We are going to fight and so forth. If we're like to be bested, scupper the old man at once. D'ye hear?"

"Well, I guess I ain't deaf."

"Very well, then. Obey, or a short shrift yours will be."

"Why, captain," said the mate, "she knows us. She has put about, and is bearing away to the nor'-nor'-west."

"Then hands up-anchor," cried his superior. "Crowd all sail; she can't escape us in her crippled condition."

"Ah! captain," the mate remarked, "had you taken my advice and given that pretty but sly minx the *sack*, ere she gave you the *slip*, that whaler would have been ours before now."

"Silence," roared the captain. "On that subject I will not hear a word. She shall be mine yet—or her father dies."

With the exception of the few sentences bawled down the companion, all this was said in Danish, and my translation is a free one.

And so the chase commenced, and seawards before the pirate, in an apparently crippled condition, staggered the *Arrandoon*.

"How far do you intend to bring her out?" asked Allan.

"Ten miles clear of these islands, anyhow," replied McBain, "then she won't be able to play any pranks with us. Boys," continued McBain, a few minutes afterwards, "I'm going to write letters—home."

There was nothing very unusual in the tone of his voice as he spoke these words, but there was a meaning in them, nevertheless, that was perfectly understood by our young heroes. They were not long, then, before they were each and all of them seated by the saloon table, inditing, it might or might not be, the last communications to the loved ones at home they *ever* would pen. They were performing a duty—a sad one, perhaps, but still a duty; they were about to fight in a good cause, doubtless, but the result of the battle was uncertain. The *Maelsturm*, for that was the name of the pirate, was better—or rather, I should say, more copiously—manned than the *Arrandoon*, and though not so large a ship, she had more guns; her crew too fought with halters round their necks, and would therefore doubtless fight to the bitter end. The only advantage —and it was a great one—possessed by the *Arrandoon* was steam-power. Hours went by, and the chase was still kept up. It was six bells in the forenoon watch, and the *Maelsturm* was hardly a mile astern. Our men had already had dinner, and were all in readiness—waiting, when, borne towards them over the wind-rippled waters from the pirate ship, came the quick, sharp rattle of a kettledrum. One roll, two rolls, three.

"At last," said McBain, "they are beating to quarters."

A puff of smoke from the bow of the pirate, the roar of a gun, and almost immediately after a round shot ricocheted past the quarter of the *Arrandoon*.

The battle was begun.

CHAPTER X.

"DOWN WITH THE RED FLAG AND UP WITH THE BLACK!"—VICTORY—AN OLD ACQUAINTANCE—HIE, FOR THE NORTH.

IF the crew of the *Arrandoon* needed any stimulus to fight the pirate, beyond the short speech that their captain had made them, it certainly was given them when the order was issued on board the latter craft, "Down with the red flag and up with the black!" and the broad, white-crossed ensign of merchant Denmark gave place to the hideous skull and cross-bones flown by sea marauders of all nations. She had rounded, too, in order to fire her broadside guns, or this would hardly have been visible. Perhaps the pirates imagined it would strike sudden fear into the hearts of those they had elected to consider their foes. Hatred and loathing it certainly inspired, but as to fear—well, in the matter of scaring, British sailors are perhaps the most unsatisfactory class of beings in the world.

For the next quarter of an hour the doings on board the *Arrandoon*, as seen from the pirate's poop, must have considerably astonished—not to say puzzled—the officers of that ship, for in that short space of time what had appeared to be a sadly disabled vessel in distress, had hoisted a funnel, lowered a screw, and, while sail was being taken in, moved slowly away beyond reach of her guns. Not for long was she gone, however. She rounded almost on her own length; then, bows on, back she came, black and grim, athirst for vengeance. But the pirate was no coward, and broadside after broadside was poured into the advancing ship, without eliciting a single shot save one.

This was the shot—the second shot—that McBain had promised Magnus. It went roaring through the air, crashed through the *Maelsturm's* bulwarks midships, and smashed a boat to flinders.

Magnus Bolt, or "Green," as he was better known, old as he was, was by far the best shot in the ship. He and Mitchell, the mate, a man of eagle eye and firm of nerve, were the gunners proper, and fired every gun in the fight that followed the second shot. If it were a starboard broadside they were there; if a port, they but crossed the deck to take deadly aim and fire it.

"Remember, gunners," cried McBain, "we've got to take that ship, and not to sink her; so waste not a shot between wind and water!"

On came the vessels, bow to bow, as arrow might meet arrow, and when within two hundred yards of each other, the *Maelsturm* heading north and west, the *Arrandoon* going full speed south and east, the pirate delivered her broadside, and immediately luffed up and commenced firing with her bow guns. She could get no nearer the wind, however. To go on the other tack would be but to hasten the inevitable.

"Hard a port! Ease her a little! Steady as you go!" were the orders from the quarter-deck of the *Arrandoon*. "Small-arm men to fire wherever head or hand is visible."

Now the *Arrandoon* delivers her broadside as she again comes parallel with the *Maelsturm*, whose sails are all a-shiver. This just by way of confusing her a little. There is worse to come, for the order is now given to double-shot the port Dalgrens with canister. Away steams the *Arrandoon*, and round goes the *Maelsturm*. Ah! well he knows what the foe intends, but he will try to outmanœuvre her if he can. But see! the *Arrandoon* is round again;

there will be no escaping her this time. Fire your bow guns, Mr. Pirate; fire your broadside, you cannot elicit a reply.

"Sta'board!" cries the captain; "starboard!" he signals, with his calm, uplifted arm. "Starboard still! steady now!" Then, in a voice of thunder, as they rounded the port quarter of the pirate, and, in spite of all good handling, got momentarily broadside on to her stern, "Stand to your guns—*Fire!*"

When the *Arrandoon* forged ahead clear of the smoke, it was evident from the confusion on board the *Maelsturm*, and the dishevelment of running and standing rigging, that the havoc on her decks must have been terrible. She was not beaten, though, as a gun from her broadside soon told.

"We'll end this," said the captain to Rory, by his side, who had constituted himself clerk, and was coolly taking notes in the very thick of the fight, while shot roared through the ship's rigging and sides, men fell on all hands, and splinters filled the air. "We'll end it in the good old fashion, Rory. Stand by to grapple with ice-anchors! Prepare to board!" Now Allan and Ralph, who had been below assisting the surgeon, heard that word of command, and, just as the sides of the two ships had grated together, after firing their last broadsides, they were both, sword in hand, by their captain's side.

McBain and our heroes were the very first to leap on to the blood-slippery decks of the pirate. The crew of that doomed ship fought for a time like furies—for a time, but only for a time. In less than five minutes every pirate on board was either disarmed or driven below, and the *Maelsturm* was the prize of the gallant *Arrandoon*, and her captain himself lay bound on the quarter-deck.

But the commander of this pirate ship was the very last man on board of her to yield. Even when the battle was virtually ended, as fiercely as a lion at bay he fought on his own quarter-deck, McBain himself being his antagonist. The latter could have shot him down had he been so minded, but he was not the man to take a mean advantage of a foe. The pirate was taller than McBain, but not so well built nor so muscular. They were thus pretty well matched, and as they fought, round and round the quarter-deck, a more beautiful display of swordsmanship was perhaps never witnessed. Once the pirate tripped and fell, McBain lowered his weapon until he had regained his feet, then swords clashed again and sparks flew. But see, the captain of the *Arrandoon* clasps his claymore double-handed; he uses it hatchet fashion almost. He looks in his brawny might as if he could fell trees. The pirate cannot withstand the shock of the terrible onslaught, but he makes up in agility what he lacks in strength. He is borne backward and backward round the companion, McBain "showering his blows like wintry rain;" and now at last victory is his, the pirate's sword flies into flinders, our captain drops his claymore and springs empty-handed on his adversary, and next moment dashes him to the deck, where he lies stunned and bleeding, and before he can recover consciousness he is bound and helpless.

Ralph, Allan, and Rory, none of whom, as providence so willed it, are wounded, and who had been silent spectators of the duel, now crowd around their captain, and shake his willing hand.

"Heaven," says McBain, "has given the enemy into our hands, boys, but there is now much to be done. Let us buckle to it without a moment's delay. The wounded are to be seen to, both our own and the pirate's, the decks cleared, and everything made ship-shape, and, if all goes well, we'll anchor with our prize to-morrow at Reikjavik."

"And the clergyman, captain, the clergyman, the poor girl's father?" exclaimed Rory.

"Ay, ay, boy Rory," said McBain; "he is doubtless on the vessel. We will proceed at once to search for him."

If fiends ever laugh, reader, it must be with some such sound as that which now proceeded from the larynx of the pirate captain ; if fiends ever smile, it must be with the same sardonic expression that now spread itself over his features. All eyes were instantly turned towards him. He had raised himself to the sitting position.

" Ha ! ha ! ha ! " he chuckled, while, manacled though his wrists were, he drew his right forefinger rapidly across his throat, uttering, as he did so, these words, " Your padre ; ha ! ha ! dead—dead—dead."

His listeners were horrified. What McBain's reply would have been none can say. It was not needed, for at that very moment, ere the exultant grin had vanished from the wretch's face, there sprang on deck from the companion a figure, tall and gaunt, clad from top to toe in skins. He knelt on the deck in front of the pirate, the better to confront him.

With forefinger raised, " he held him with his glittering eye," while he addressed him as follows :

" Look here, Mister Pirate, I was going to use strong language, but I won't, though I guess and calculate mild words are wasted on sich as you. The parson ain't dead ; ne'er a hair on his reverend head. Ye thought I'd scupper him, didn't you, soon's the ship was taken ? Ye thought this child was your slave, didn't ye ? Ha ! ha ! though, he has rounded on ye at last, and if that bit of black rag weren't enough to hang you and your wretched crew of cut-throats, here in front o' ye kneels one witness o' your dirty deeds, and the other will be on deck in a minute in the person o' the parson you thought dead. How d'ye like it, eh ? " and the speaker once more stood erect, and confronted our heroes.

" Seth ! " they ejaculated, in one voice.

" Seth ! by all that is marvellous ! " said McBain, clutching the old man by the right hand, while Rory seized his left, and Allan and Ralph got hold of an arm each.

"Ah! gentlemen," said honest Seth—and there was positively a tear in his eye as he spoke—" it's on occasions like these that one wishes he had four hands,—a hand for every friend. Yes, I reckon it is Seth himself, and nary a one else. You may well say wonders will never cease. You may well ask me how on earth I came here. It war Providence, gentlemen, and nuthin' else, that I knows on. It war Providence sent that cut-throat skipper to the land where you left me on the *Snowbird*, though I didn't think so at the time, when they burned and pillaged my hut and killed poor old Plunkett, nor when they carried me a prisoner on board the *Maelsturm*. They meant to scupper old Seth. They did talk o' bilin' his old bones in whale oil, but they soon found out he could heal a hole in a hide as well as make one, and so, gentlemen, I've been surgeon-in-chief to this craft for nine months and over. Yes, it war Providence and nuthin' else, and I knew it war as soon as I saw your ship heave in sight, the day they guessed they'd wreck ye. The parson's daughter, poor little Dunette, war on board then. I sent her to save ye; and when I heard your voice, Captain McBain, on the reef, I felt sure it war Providence then, and I kind o' prayed in my rough way that He might spare ye. Shake hands, gentlemen, again. Bother these old eyes o' mine; they will keep watering."

And Seth drew his sleeve rapidly across his face as he spoke.

* * * *

Rory was a proud—boy, ahem! well, *man*, then, if you will have it so, when that same afternoon he was put on board the *Maelsturm*, as captain of her, with a picked crew from the *Arrandoon*, and with orders to make all sail for Reikjavik. McBain's last words to him were these,—

"Keep your weather eye lifting, Captain Roderick

Elphinstone. Clap two sentries on those ruffianly prisoners of yours, and let your men sleep with their cutlasses by their sides and their revolvers under their heads."

"Ay, ay, sir!" said Rory.

Rory allowed his crew to sleep, but he himself paced the deck all the livelong night. Occasionally he could see the lights of the *Arrandoon* far on ahead; but towards morning the weather got thick and somewhat squally, and at daylight the *Maelsturm* seemed alone on the ocean. Sail was taken in, but the ship kept her course, and just in the even-glome Rory ran into the Bay of Reikjavik, and dropped anchor, and shortly after a boat came off from the *Arrandoon* with both Allan and Ralph in it, to congratulate the boy-captain on the success of his first voyage as skipper-commandant.

Next day both the pirate vessel and her captor were show-ships for the people—all the *élite* and beauty of Reikjavik crowded off from the shore in dozens to see them. The dilapidated condition of the *Maelsturm*, her broken bulwarks, rent rigging, and shivered spars, showed how fierce the fight had been. Nor were evidences of the struggle wanting on board the *Arrandoon*, albeit the men had been hard at work all the day making good repairs.

The dead were buried at sea; the wounded were mostly sent on shore. Five poor fellows belonging to McBain's ship would never fight again, and many more were placed for a time *hors de combat*.

As to the prisoners, they were transferred to a French ship that lay at Reikjavik, and that in the course of a week sailed with them for Denmark. Seth and the officers of the *Arrandoon* made and signed depositions; and in addition to this, as evidence against the pirates, the old clergyman and his daughter Dunette, now joyfully reunited, went along with the Frenchman, while, with a crew from shore, the *Maelsturm* left some days after. The black flag had never been lowered, nor was it until the day the pirate captain and many of his crew expiated their long list of crimes on the scaffold at the Holms of Copenhagen.

Poor Dunette, the tears fell unheeded from her sad blue eyes as she bade farewell to our heroes on the deck of the *Arrandoon*. She did not say good-bye to the surgeon, however—at least not there. He had begged for a boat, and accompanied her on board the vessel in which she was to sail. Have they a secret, we wonder? Is it possible that our quiet surgeon has won the heart of this beautiful fair-haired Danish maiden? These are questions we must not seek answer to now, but time may tell.

Not until the pirate ship had left the bay, and the wounded were so far convalescent as to be brought once more on board, did the old peace and quiet settle down upon the good ship *Arrandoon*. And now once more all was bustle and stir; in a day or two they would start for the far north, and bid adieu to civilisation—a long but not, they hoped, a last adieu.

The very evening before they sailed, a farewell party was given on board the *Arrandoon*. The decks were tented over with canvas lined with flags, and the whole scene was gay and festive in the extreme. Poetic Rory could not have believed that there was so much female youth and loveliness in this primitive little town of Reikjavik. No wonder that day was dawning in the east ere the last boat of laughing and merry guests left for the shore.

Many and many a time afterwards, when surrounded by dangers innumerable, when beset in ice, when engulfed in darkness and storm, in the mysterious regions of the Pole, did they look back with pleasure to that last happy night spent in the bay of Reikjavik.

But see, it is twelve o'clock by the sun. Flags are floating gaily on the fort, on the little church tower, and on every eminence in or near the town, and the beach and snow-clad rocks are lined with an excited crowd. Hands and handkerchiefs are waved, and with the farewell cheers the far-off hills resound. Then our brave fellows man the rigging and waft them back cheer for cheer, as the noble vessel cleaves the waters of the bay, and stands away for the Northern Ocean.

CHAPTER XI.

THE VOYAGE RESUMED—A PLEASANT EVENING—"THOSE RUSHING WINDS"—THE "ARRANDOON" GROWS SAUCY—THE DOCTOR SPREAD-EAGLED—A SCHOOL OF WHALES.

ERE the day had worn to a close, before the sun went down in a golden haze, leaving one long line of crimson cloud, as earnest of a bright to-morrow, the *Arrandoon*, steaming twelve knots to the hour, was once more far away at sea, and the rugged mountains of Iceland could hardly be descried. As night fell a breeze sprang up, and as there was little doubt it would freshen ere long —for it blew from the east-south-east, and the glass had slightly gone down, with the mercury still concave at top —Captain McBain gave orders for the fires to be banked, and as much canvas spread as she could comfortably carry.

"Just make her snug, you know, Mr. Stevenson," said McBain, "for the night will be dark, and we may have more wind before the middle watch."

"And troth," said Rory to his companions, "if the ship is to be made snug, I don't see why we shouldn't make ourselves snug for the night too."

Ralph was gazing down through the skylight at the brilliantly-lighted saloon, where Peter, with the aid of the assistant-steward and Freezing Powders, was busy laying the cloth for dinner.

"I've just come from forward," replied Ralph, in raptures, "where I've been sniffing the roast beef and the boiled potatoes; and now just look below, Rory,—look how Peter's face beams with intelligent delight; see how radiant Freezing Powders is; behold how merrily the flames dance on that fire of fires in the stove, and how the coloured crystal shimmers, and the bright silver shines on that cloth of spotless snow! Yes, Rory, you're right, boy—let us make ourselves snug for the night. So down we go, and dress our smartest—for, mind, boys, there is going to be company to-night."

Yes, there was going to be company; five were all that as a rule sat down to table in the grand saloon, but to-night the covers were laid for five more, namely Stevenson, Seth, old Magnus, and Ap, and last, though not least, De Vere, the French aëronaut.

The cook of the *Arrandoon* had been chosen specially by Ralph himself. Need I say, then, that he was an artist? and to-night he had done his best to outshine himself, and, I think, succeeded. I think, too, that when Peter went forward, some time after the great joints had been put on the table, and told him that everything was going on "as merrily as marriage bells," and that the gentlemen were loud in their praises of Ralph's cook, that that cook was about the happiest man in the ship. Peter had not exaggerated a bit either, for everything did go off well at this little dinner-party. It would have done your heart good to have seen the beaming countenances of little Ap, old man Magnus, and honest trapper Seth; and to have noticed how often they passed their plates for another help would have made you open your eyes with wonder—that is, if you never had been to Greenland; but had you made the voyage North Pole-wards even once, you would have known that of all countries in the world that is just the place to give man or boy a healthy appetite.

When the cloth was removed and dessert placed upon the table they seemed happier than ever, if that were possible, and smiles and jokes and jocund yarns were the order of the evening. After every good story the cockatoo helped himself to an immense mouthful of hemp-seed, and cried,

"Dea-ah me! Well, well, but go on, *go on*—next."

And as to Freezing Powders, he was so amazed at many things he heard, that more than a dozen times in one hour he had to refresh himself by standing on his head in a corner of the saloon.

"Well, well, well!" said McBain, taking the advantage of a mere momentary lull in this feast of reason and flow of soul, "and what a strange mixture of nationalities we are, to be sure! Here is our bold, quiet Ralph, English to the spine——"

"And I," said Rory, "I'm Oirish to the chine."

"That you are," assented McBain; "and Allan and myself here are Scotch; and if you look farther along the table there is Wales represented in the form of cool, calculating, mathematical Ap; Shetland in the shape of our brave gunner Magnus; France in the form of friend De Vere; and the mightiest republic in the world in Seth's six feet and odd inches; to say nothing of Africa standing on its head beside Polly's cage. Freezing Powders, you young rascal, drop on to your other end; don't you see you're making Polly believe the world is upside down? look at her hanging by the feet with her head down!"

"Dat cockatoo not a fool, sah," said Freezing Powders; "he know putty well what he am about, sah!"

"D'ye know," said Ralph, looking smilingly towards Seth, "it is quite like old times to see Seth once more in the midst of us?"

"And oh!" said Seth, rubbing his hands, while a modest smile stole over his wiry face, "mebbe this old trapper ain't a bit pleased to meet ye all again. Gentlemen, Seth and civilisation hain't been 'cquaintances very long; skins seem to suit this child better'n the fine toggery ye've rigged him out in. But ye've made him feel a deal younger, and he guesses and calculates he may die 'pectable yet."

I fear it was pretty far into the middle watch ere our friends parted and betook themselves to their berths. Two bells had gone—"the wee short hoor ayont the twal"—when McBain rose from the table, this being a signal for general good-nights.

"I'm going part of the way home with you, old man," he said to Magnus, and with his arm placed kindly over his shoulder he left the saloon with the brave wee Shetlander. "Two turns on the deck, Magnus," he continued, "and then you can turn in. And so, you say, in all your experience—and it has been very vast, hasn't it, my friend?"

"That it has, sir," replied Magnus. "I may say I was born in these seas, for the first thing I remember—when our ship went down under us in the pack north of Jan Mayen—is my father, bless him! putting me in a carpetbag for safety, to carry me on to the ice with him. Yes, sir, yes."

"And in all your experience," McBain went on, "you don't remember a season likely to have been more favourable for our expedition to the North Pole than the present?"

"I don't, sir—I don't," said little Magnus, "Look, see, sir, the frost has been extreme all over the north. In the Arctic regions the ice has been all of a heap like. It isn't yet loosened. We haven't met a berg yet. Funny, ain't it, sir?—queer, isn't it, cap'n?"

"It is strange," said McBain; "and from this what do you anticipate?"

"Anticipate isn't the word, cap'n," cried Magnus, fixing McBain by the right arm, stopping his way, and emphasising his words with wildfire glints from his warlock eyes. "Anticipate?—bah! cap'n—bah! I'm old enough to be your grandfather. Ask me rather what I *augur*? And I answer this, I augur a glorious summer. Ice loosened before May Day. Fierce heat south of England, and consequently rarefication of the atmosphere, and rushing winds from the far north to fill up the heated vacuum—rushing winds to trundle the icebergs south before them—rushing winds to split the packs, and rend the floes, and open up a passage for this brave ship to the far-off Isle of Alba."

"Bless you, Magnus! Give us your hand, my old sea-dad. You always gave me comfort, even when I was a boy in the wilds of Spitzbergen. You taught me to splice, and reef, and steer. Bless you, Magnus! I couldn't have sailed without you."

"But stay, my son, stay," continued this weird little man, holding up a warning finger; "those rushing winds——"

"Yes, Magnus?"

"They will bring danger on their wings."

"I'll welcome it, Magnus," laughed McBain.

"Those rushing winds will tear down on us, hurricane-high, tempest-strong. The great bergs, impelled by force of wind and might of wave, will dash each other to atoms."

"All the better for us, Daddy Magnus," said the captain.

"Were your voice as loud as cannon's roar you will be as one dumb amid the turmoil."

"Then I'll steer by signs," said McBain.

"Should our ship escape destruction, we will be enveloped by fogs, encircled by a darkness that will be felt."

"Then we'll heave-to and wait till they evaporate. But there, my good Magnus, you see I'm not afraid of anything. I'd be unworthy of such a sea-dad as you if I were; so no more tragic airs, please. Thou mindest me, old Magnus, of the scene between Lochiel and the Wizard.

"'Lochiel, Lochiel, beware of the day
When the Lowlands shall meet you in battle array,'

says the Wizard, and so on and so forth.

"'False wizard, avaunt!' replies Lochiel, and all the rest of it, you know. But, beloved Magnus, I don't say 'avaunt!' to you. But just see how the cold spray is dashing inboard. So, not to put too poetic a point on it, I simply say, 'Go down below, old man, and don't get wet, else your joints will ache in the morning with the rheumatiz.'"

The morning broke beautifully fine and clear, the reefs were shaken out of the topsails, topgallant-sails and royals were set, and, indeed, all the square cloth she could carry, and away went the *Arrandoon* before the wind, as happy, to all appearance, as the malleys and gulls that seemed to play at hide-and-seek with her, behind the comb-crested seas of olive-green.

Ralph and Allan, arm-in-arm, were marching rapidly up and down one side of the quarter-deck, Rory and McFlail on the other, and ever and anon a merry laugh from some one of them rang out bright and joyously on the fresh frosty air.

Towards noon stunsails were set, and the *Arrandoon* looked more like a sea-bird than ever; she even seemed to sing to herself—so thought Rory and so thought the doctor—as she went nodding and curtseying along over the waves, with now a bend to starboard, and now a lean to port; now lowering her bows till the seas ahead looked mountains high, and anon giving a dip waterwards till her waist was wet with the seething spray, and her lower stunsail-booms seemed to tickle the very breast of old mother ocean.

The wind was increasing, and there were times when our boys had to pause in their walk and grapple the mizzen rigging, laughing at each other as they did so.

"Wo ho, my beauty!" said McBain. "Mr. Mitchell, I daresay we must take in sail."

"I'm afraid so, sir," replies Mitchell; "but—" and here he eyes the bellowing canvas—"it do seem a pity, sir, don't it?"

But here "my beauty" gives a vicious plunge forwards,

elevating herself aft like a kicking mare, and shipping tons of water over her bows.

"I don't want to be wicked," the ship seems to say, "and I don't want to lose a spar, though I *could* kick one off as easy as a daddy-longlegs gets rid of a limb; but if you don't ease me a bit I'll——"

A bigger and more decided plunge into the sea, followed by a rising of her jibboom zenithwards, and the water comes roaring aft in one great bore, which seeks exit by the quarter-deck scupper-holes, and goes tumbling down the companion ladder, to the indignation of Peter and the disgust of Freezing Powders, who is standing on his head in an attitude of contemplation, and ships a green sea down his nostrils. Our heroes leap in time on to the top of the skylight, and there sit grinning delightedly as the waters go roaring past them, and floating thereon evidence enough that the men had been preparing dinner when Neptune boarded them, for yonder float potatoes and turnips and cabbages, to say nothing of a leg of Highland mutton and a six-pound piece of bacon.

"Hands, shorten sail!"

But next day—so changeable is a sailor's life—the wind had all got bottled up again or gone back to its cave; the sea was smooth as glass, and steam was up, but the sky was still clear, and the sun undimmed by the slightest haze.

Just before lunch came the first signs that ice was not far ahead. The *Arrandoon* encountered a great " stream," as it is called, of deep, snowy slush—I do not know what else to call it. It stretched away eastwards to westwards, as far as the eye from the crow's-nest could reach, and it was probably nine or ten miles wide. It lessened the good ship's way considerably, you may be sure. Her bows clove through it with a brushing sound; her screw revolved in it with a noise like dead leaves stirred by autumn winds.

"Losh!" cried Sandy, the surgeon, looking curiously

overboard, "what's this noo? Wonders will never cease!"

"Och, sure!" replied Rory, mischievously, "you know well enough what it is; it's only speaking for speaking's sake you are."

"The ne'er a bone o' ma knows, I do assure ye," said Sandy.

"Well, doctor dear," said Rory, "it is simply the belt, or zone, that geographers call the 'Arctic circle.'"

But Sandy looked at him with a pitying smile. "Man—Rory!" he said, "I'm no' so sea-green as you tak me to be. I've a right good mind to pu' your lugs. Young men, sir, dinna enter Aberdeen University stirks and come out cuddies!"

"Mon!" cried Rory, imitating Sandy's brogue, "if ye want to pu' my lugs you'll hae to catch me first;" and off he went round the deck, with the doctor after him. But Ralph caught him, if Sandy couldn't, and handed him over to justice.

"Now," cried the surgeon, catching him by the ear, "whistle, and I'll let you free."

It is no easy matter to whistle when you want to laugh, but when Rory at long last did manage to emit a labial note that passed muster as a whistle, the doctor was as good as his word, and Rory was free.

Luncheon was barely finished, when down from the crow's-nest rang the welcome hail, "Ice ahead!"

Our heroes rushed on deck, McBain was there before them, and when they stepped on to the "lid" of the ship, as Sandy once called the deck, they found the captain half way up to the nest.

There wasn't a bit of ice to be seen from the deck.

"Hurrah for the foretop!" cried Rory, laying hold of a stay. "Who's coming?"

"I will!" cried Allan.

"I'm going below to finish lunch," said Ralph.

"I'll be safer on deck, I think," said the canny doctor.

But when Rory on the foretop struck an attitude of wonderment, and pointing away ahead, exclaimed, in rapture, "Oh, boys, what a scene is here!" the doctor thought he would give anything for a peep, so he summoned up his courage and began to ascend the rigging, slowly, and with about as much grace in his actions as a mud turtle would exhibit under the like circumstances.

Allan roared, "Good doctor! good! Bravo, old man! Heave round like a brick! Don't look down."

Rory was in a fit of merriment, and trying to stifle himself with his handkerchief. Suddenly down dropped that handkerchief; and this was just the signal four active lads were waiting for. Up they sprang like monkeys behind the surgeon, who had hardly reached the lubber-hole. Alas! the good medico didn't reach it that day, for before you could have said "cutlass" he was seized, hand and foot, and lashed to the rigging, St. Andrew's-cross fashion.

The surgeon of the *Arrandoon* was spread-eagled, and Rory, the wicked boy! had his revenge.

"My conscience!" cried Sandy; "what next, I wonder?"

"It's a vera judeecious arrangement," sung Rory from the top.

But the men were not hard on the worthy doctor, and the promise of several ounces of nigger-head procured him his freedom, and he soon regained the deck, a sadder and a wiser man.

They were quickly among the ice—not bergs, mind you, only a stream of bits and pieces, of every shape and form, some like sheep and some like swans, and some like great white oxen. Here was a piece like a milking-pail; here was a lump like a hay-cock; yonder a gondola; yonder a boat; and yonder a couch on which the Naiades might recline and float, or Ino slumber.

It was Rory who made the last remark.

A SCHOOL OF WHALES. [*Page* 103.

"And by this and by that!" he exclaimed, "there is a Naiad on it now! or it's Ino herself, by all that's amusing!"

"Away, second whaler!"—this from McBain. " Get your rifle, boy Rory, and jump on board and fetch that seal!"

Down rattled the boat from the davits, Rory in the bows; the next moment she was off, and tearing through the glazed water as fast as sturdy arms could row. The seal took one look up to see what was coming. Rory's rifle rang out sharp and clear in the frosty air, and the poor seal never lifted head again.

The ship was by this time a goodly mile ahead, but there she stopped; then she went ahead again, rounded, and came back full speed to meet the boat, for they on board could see a danger that Rory couldn't—couldn't, did I say? Ah! but he soon did, and, with the roar of a maelstrom, down they came upon him—an enormous school of whales!

The men lay on their oars thunderstruck. The sea around them seemed alive with the mighty monsters. How they plunged and ploughed and snorted and blew! The sea became roughened, as if a fierce wind was blowing over it; pieces of ice as large as boats were caught on the backs or tails of these brutes and pitched aside as one might a football.

It occurred to Rory to fire at some of them.

"Stay, stay!" roared the coxswain; "if you love your life, sir, and care for ours, fire not. *You* may never have seen a whale angry—I have. Fire not, I beseech you!"

It was a strange danger to have encountered, and Rory and his boat-mates were not sorry when it passed, and they once more stood in safety on the deck of the *Arrandoon*.

But Rory soon regained his equanimity

" Five hundred whales!" he cried; "and they were all

mine, Ralph, 'cause I found them! Sure, they were worth a million of money!"

"So you've been a millionaire, Rory?" said McBain.

"Yes, worse luck!" said Rory, in a voice of comic sadness, "a millionaire for a minute!"

CHAPTER XII.

THE ISLE OF JAN MAYEN—RETROSPECTION—THE SEA OF ICE—THE DESERTED VILLAGE—CARRIED OFF BY A BEAR—DANCING FOR DEAR LIFE.

WHAT a tiny speck it looks in the map, that island of Jan Mayen, all by itself, right in the centre of the great Arctic Ocean. Of volcanic origin it undoubtedly is—every mountain, rock, and hill in it—and there is ample evidence that from yonder gigantic cone, that rises, like a mighty sugar-loaf or the Tower of Babel itself, to a height of 6,000 feet sheer into the blue and cloudless sky, at one time smoke and flames must oftentimes have burst, and showers of stones and ashes, and streams of molten lava.

I have gazed on it by night, and my imagination has carried me back, and back, and back, through the long-distant past, and I have tried to fancy the sublimity of the scene during an eruption.

The time is early spring. The long, dark winter has passed away; the cold-looking, rayless sun rises now, but skirts hurriedly across a small disc of southern sky, then speedily sinks to rest again, as though he shuddered to gaze upon scenery so bleak and desolate. The island of Jan Mayen, with its ridgy hills and its one mighty mountain, is clad in dazzling robes of virgin snow. Its rocky and precipitous shores rise not up, as yet, from the dark waters that in summer time wash round them, but from the sea of ice itself. As far as eye can reach, or north or south, or east or west, stretches this immeasurable ocean of ice. All flat and all snow-clad is it, like the wildest and loneliest of Highland moorlands in winter, and its very flatness gives it an air of greater lonesomeness, which the solitary hummocks here and there but tend to heighten. And through the short and dreary day one solitary cloud has rested like a pall on the summit of the mountain. But it is midnight now: in the deep blue of the sky big, bright stars are shining, that look like moons of molten silver, and seem far nearer than they do in southern climes. In the north the radiant bow of the Aurora is spread out, its transverse beams glancing and glistering, spears of light, that dance and glide and shimmer, changing their colours every moment from green to blue or red, from pale yellow to the brightest of crimson.

And the silence that reigns over all this field of ice is one that travellers have often experienced, often been impressed and awed by, but never yet found words to describe.

Silence did I say? Yes! but listen! Subterranean thunders suddenly break it—thunders coming evidently from the bosom of the great mountain yonder, thunders that shake and crack and rend the very ice on which you stand, causing the bergs to grind and shriek like monsters in agony. The great cloud pall has risen higher and spread itself out, and now hangs horizontally over half the island, black and threatening, its blackness lit up ever and anon with flashes of lightning, sheet and forked, while, peal after peal, the thunder now rolls almost without intermission.

And onward and onward rolls the cloud athwart the sky, blotting out the starlight—blotting out the beautiful Aurora—till the sea of ice for leagues around is canopied in darkness. But behold, over the mountain-top the cloud gets lighter in colour, for immense volumes of steam, solid sheets of water, and pieces of ice tons in weight, are being belched forth, or hurtled into the air with a continued noise that drowns the awful rhythm of the thunder itself. Then flames follow, shooting up into the sky many hundreds of feet, lighting up the scene with a lurid glare, while down the snow-clad sides of the great cone streams of fiery lava rush in fury, crimson, blue, or green. And gigantic rocks are precipitated into the air—rocks so large that, as they fall upon the ice miles distant from the burning crater, they smash the heaviest floes, and sink through into the sea. Great stones, too, are incessantly emited, like balls of fire, that burst in the air, and keep up a sound like that of the loudest artillery.

The sun will rise in due course, but his beams cannot penetrate the veil of saturnine darkness that envelops the sea of ice. And the fire will rage, the thunders will roll, and showers of stones and ashes fall for days, ay, mayhap for weeks or months, ere the mighty convulsion ceases, and silence once more reigns in and around this island of Jan Mayen.

Towards this lonely isle of the ocean the *Arrandoon* had been beating and pushing her way for days; and she now lay, with clewed sails and banked fires, among the flat but heavy bergs not five miles from it. There was no water in sight, for the iceless ocean had been left far, far astern, and the ship was now to all intents and purposes beset. Yet the ice was loose; it was not welded together by the fingers of King Frost, and if it remained so, the difficulty of getting out into the clear water again would be by no means insurmountable.

Our heroes, the doctor included, were all on deck, dressed to kill, in caps of fur with ear lapels, coats of frieze with pockets innumerable, with boots that reached over the knees, and each was armed with a rifle and seal-club, with revolver in belt and short sheaf-knife dangling from the left side.

"And so," said the doctor, "this is the mighty sea of ice that I've heard so much about! Man! boys! I'm no so vera muckle struck with it. It is not unlike my father's peat moss in the dreary depths of winter. Where are the lofty pinnacled bergs I expected to see, the rocks and towers of ice, the green glistening gables, and the tall spires, like a hundred cathedrals dang into one?"

"Ah!" said McBain, laughing, "just bide a wee, doctor lad, till we go farther north, and if you don't see ice that will outdo your every dream of romance, I'm neither Scot nor sailor.

"But what is this?" continued the captain. "Who in the name of all that is marvellous have we here?"

"I 'spects I'se Freezin' Powders, sah," was the reply of the little negro boy. "Leastways I hopes I is." Here the urchin touched his cap. "Freezin' Powders, at your service, sah—your under-steward and butler, sah!"

"Well, my under-steward and butler," said McBain; "but whoever could have expected to see you rigged out in this fashion—pilot suit, fur cap, boots, and all complete? Why, who dressed you, my little Freezin' Powders?"

"De minor ole gem'lam," replied the boy; "but don't dey fit, sah? Don't dey become dis chile? Look heah, sah!" and Freezing Powders went strutting up and down the quarter-deck, as proud as a pouter pigeon; and finished off by presenting arms with his seal-club in front of his good-natured captain.

"Well," said McBain, much amused, "you are a comical customer. By 'the minor ole gem'lam' I suppose you mean honest Magnus? But your English is peculiar, youngster."

"My English is puffuk, sah!" replied the boy; "but lo! sah! suppose I not have dis suit of close, I freeze, sah! I no longer be Freezin' Powders, 'cause I freeze all up into one lump, sah! Now, sah, I can go on shoh wid de oder officers."

"Ho! ho!" laughed McBain; "the *other* officers. It's come to that, has it? But," he added, turning to Allan and Rory, "you'll look after the lad, won't you?"

"That will we," said both in a breath.

Here are the names of those who went on shore in Jan Mayen on this memorable day—Allan, Ralph, Rory, Seth, and the doctor, with three club-armed retainers, and lastly, Freezing Powders himself.

They were a merry band. You could have heard them laughing and talking when they were miles away from the ship. They had to leap from one piece of ice to another; but as the bergs were from forty to fifty feet square—thus affording them a good run for their leaps—and as the pieces were pretty closely packed, jumping was no great hardship. When now and then they came to a bit of water that required a tolerable spring to get over, tall Ralph vaulted first, then brawny-chested Allan pitched Freezing Powders after him, whom Ralph caught as easily as if he had been a cricket-ball.

They landed on the island in a kind of bay, where the land sloped down to the snow-clad beach. Not far from the sea they were much surprised to find the ruins of huts that had been. No smoke issued therefrom now, but there was ample proof that roaring fires had once burned in each hut. They were partly underground, and though built of wood and sealskins they were thatched and fortified with snow. The largest cot of all was in the centre, and entering this they found a key to the seeming mystery, for here were evidences of civilisation. Pots and pans stood on the empty hearth; a chair or two, a truckle bed, a deal table and a book-cupboard, formed the furniture, and to cap all a written document was found, which informed them that this village had been the encampment for the summer months of a party of American walrus-hunters, the captain of which had aided science by making innumerable observations of a meteorological and scientific nature.

"I reckon," said Seth, "there ain't many parts o' the world where my enterprising countrymen hain't shown their noses."

"All honour to them for that same," said Rory; "and troth, there isn't a mightier nation on the face of the earth bar the kingdom of Ireland."

"Now, look here," said Allan, "this wee chap, Freezing Powders, will be far too tired if he goes with us; and here, by good luck, is a frozen ham in this enterprising Yankee's cupboard. I move we light a fire, hang it over it, and leave the little black butler as cook till we come back."

"Bravo!" said Ralph. "Allan, you're a brick. You won't be afraid, will you, Freezing Powders?"

"I stop and do de cookin', plenty quick," answered the boy, briskly. "Freezin' Powders never was afraid of nuffin in his life."

So the fire was lighted—there was fuel enough in the hut to keep it going for a month; then, leaving the boy to watch the ham, away went our explorers, upwards and onwards, through the ruggedest glens imaginable; winding round rocks and hills of ice and snow, they soon lost sight of the primitive village, the distant ship, and the sea of ice itself. They wandered on and on for miles, pausing often to allow Rory to make a sketch of some more than usually wild and fantastic group of ice-clad rocks or charming bit of scenery; but wherever they went, or whichever way they turned, there loomed the great mountain cone of Jan Mayen above them.

The scene was everywhere silent and desolate in the extreme, for not a breath of wind was blowing, not a cloud was in the sky, and no sign of life was there to greet them, not even a solitary gull or snowbird.

It wanted two good hours to sunset when they once more returned to the deserted village, eager to test the flavour of the Yankee's ham, for walking on the snow had given them the appetite of healthy hunters.

Their astonishment as well as horror may be imagined when, on entering the hut, they found a scene of utter confusion. The fire still burned, it is true, and yonder hung the ham; but the table and chairs were overturned, and the contents of even the rude bookcase scattered about the floor.

And Freezing Powders was gone!

He had been carried off by a bear. Of this there was plenty of testimony, if only in the huge footprints of the monster, which he had left in the snow. Not very distinct were they, however, for the surface of the snow was crisp and hard. But Seth was equal to the occasion, and at once—walking in a bee line, the trapper leading—they set out to track the bear, if possible, to his lair. The footprints led them southwards and west, through a region far more wild than that which they had already traversed.

For a whole hour they walked in silence, until they found themselves at the top of a ravine, the rocks of which joined to form a sort of triangle. Half-roofed over was this triangle with a balcony of frozen snow, from which descended immense icicles, on which the roof leant, forming a kind of verandah.

Seth paused, and pointed upwards. "The b'ar is yonder!" he whispered. "Stay here; the old trapper's feet are moccasined, he won't be heard. Gentlemen, Seth means to have that b'ar, or he won't come back alive!"

So leaving his companions, onwards, all alone, steals Seth. A bear itself could not have crept more silently, more cautiously along than the trapper does.

Those left behind waited in a fever of almost breathless suspense. The doctor stretched out his arm and took gentle hold of Rory's wrist. His pulse was over a hundred;

so was the doctor's own, and he could easily hear his heart beat.

How slowly old Seth seems to move. He is on hands and knees now, and many a listening pause he makes. Now he has reached the edge of the icy verandah, and peers carefully over. The bear is there, undoubtedly, for, see, he gives one anxious glance at his rifle—it is a double-barrelled bone-crusher.

Crang-r-r-r! goes the rifle, and every rock in the island seems to re-echo the sound. The reverberation has not ceased, however, when there mingles with it a roar—a blood-curdling roar—that seems to shake the very ground. "Wah-o-ah! waugh! waugh! wah-o!" and a great pale-yellow bear springs from the cave, then falls, quivering and bleeding, on his side in the snow.

Our heroes rush up now.

"Any more of them?" cries Rory.

"Wall, I guess not," said the old trapper. "Yonder lies the master; I've given him a sickener; and the missus ain't at home. But there is suthin' black in thar, though!"

"Why," cried Allan, "I declare it is Freezing Powders himself!" and out into the bright light stalked the poor nigger boy, staring wildly round about, and seemingly in a dream.

"Ah, gem'lams!" he said, slowly, "so you have come at last! What a drefful, *drefful* fright dis poor chile have got! 'Spect I'll nebber get ober it; nebber no more!"

"Come along," said Ralph. "Get on top of my shoulder. That's the style! You can tell us all about it when we reach the village."

"Now," cried Allan, "look alive, lads, and whip old Bruin out of his skin, and bring along his jacket and paws!"

When they did get back to the hut, and poor Freezing Powders had warmed himself and discussed a huge slice of broiled ham and a captain's biscuit, the boy got quite cheery again, and proceeded to relate his terrible adventure.

"You see, gem'lams," he said, "soon as ebber you leave me I begin for to watch de ham, and turn he round and round plenty much, and make de fire blaze like bobbery. Mebbe one whole hour pass away. De flames dey crack, and de ham he frizzle. Den all to once I hear somebody snuff-snuffing like, and I look round plenty quick, and dere was—oh! dat great big awful bear—bigger dan a gator [alligator]. Didn't I scream and run jus'! And de bear he knock down de chairs and de tables, and den he catchee me in his mouf, all de same I one small mouse and he one big cat. You see, gem'lam, he smell de ham. 'Dat bery nice,' he tink, 'but de nigga boy better.' So he take dis chile. He nebber have take one nigga boy before dis, p'r'aps. Den he run off wid me ober de mountains. He no put one tooth in me all de time. When he come to de cave he put me down and snuff me. Den he say to himself, 'I want some fun; I make play wid dis nigga boy befoh I gobbles 'im up.' So he make me run wid his big foot, and when I run away den he catchee me again, and he keep me run away plenty time, till I so tired I ready to drop.* All de same, I not want to be gobble up too soon, gem'lams, so I make all de fun I can. I stand on my head, and I run on my four feet. I jump and I kick, and I dance, and I sing to de tune ob—

"'Plenty quick, nigga boy,
Plenty fast you run,
De bear will nebber gobble you up
So long's you make de fun.'

Den de big, ugly yellow bear he berry much tickled, and he tink to hisself, 'Well,' he tink, ''pon my word and honah! I nebber see nuffin like dis before—not in all my

---

* Greenland bears have been known to play this cat-and-mouse game with seals before devouring them.

born days! I not eat dis nigga boy up till my mudder come home.' And all de time I make dance and sing—

"'Quicker, quicker, nigga boy,
  Faster, faste go,
Amoosin' ob ᴄe ole bear,
  Among de Ahtic snow.

"'Jing-a-ring, a-ring-a-ring,
  Sich somersaults I frow,
In all his life dis nigger chile
  Ne'er danced like dis befoh.'

But now, gem'lams, I notice dat de bear he begin to make winkee-winkee wid both his two eyes. Den I dance all de same, but I begin to sing more slow and plaintive, gem'lams—

"'Oh! I'm dreaming 'bout my mudder dear
  Dat I leave on Afric's shoh,
And de little hut among de woods
  Dat I ne'er shall see no moh.

"'Sierra-lee-le-ohney,
  Sierra-lee-leon,
Ah! who will feed de cockatoo
  When I is dead and gone?'

Dat song fix de yellow bear, gem'lams. He no winkee no more now; he sleep sound and fast, wid his big head on his big paws. Den I sing one oder verse, and I sleep, too, and I not hear nuffin more until de rifles make de bobbery and de yellow bear begin to cough."

"Bravo!" cried Ralph, when Freezing Powders had finished his story. "Now, Allan, lad, cut us all another slice of that glorious ham, and let us be moving."

"Yes," said Allan. "Here goes, then, for night is falling already, and the captain will be longing to hear of our adventures."

CHAPTER XIII.

MORE ABOUT FREEZING POWDERS—"PERSEVERANDO"—
DINING IN THE SKY—THE DESCENT OF THE CRATER.

A BLACK man in a barrel of treacle is said by some to be emblematical of happiness. So situated, a black man without doubt enjoys a deal of bliss, but I question very much if it equals the joy poor Freezing Powders felt when he found himself once more safe on board the *Arrandoon*, and cuddled down in a corner with his old cockatoo.* What a long story he had to tell the bird, to be sure!—what a "terrible tale," I might call it!

As usual, when greatly engrossed in listening, the bird was busily engaged helping himself to enormous mouthfuls of hemp-seed, spilling more than he swallowed, cocking his head, and gazing at his little black master, with many an interjectional and wondering "Oh!" and many a long-drawn "De-ah me!" just as if he understood every word the boy said, and fully appreciated the dangers he had come through.

"Well, duckie?" said the bird, fondly, when Freezing Powders had concluded.

"Oh! der ain't no moh to tell, cockie." said the boy; "but I 'ssure you, when I see dat big yellow bear wid his big red mouf, I tink I not hab much longer to lib in dis world, cockie—I 'ssure you I tink so."

* It may be as well to state here that neither the negro boy nor the cockatoo is a character drawn at random; both had their counterparst in real life.

Freezing Powders was the hero for one evening at all events. McBain made him recite his story and sing his daft, wild songs more than once, and the very innocence of the poor boy heightened the general effect. He was a favourite all over the ship from that day forth. Everybody in a manner petted him, and yet it was impossible to spoil him, for he took the petting as a matter of course, but always kept his place. His duties were multifarious, though light—he cleaned the silver and shined the boots, and helped to lay the cloth and wait at table. He went by different names in different parts of the ship. Ralph called him his cup-bearer, because he brought that young gentleman's matutinal coffee, without which our English hero would not have left his cabin for the world. Freezing Powders was message-boy betwixt steward and cook, and bore the viands triumphantly along the deck, so the steward called him "Mustard and Cress," and the cook "Young Shallots," while Ted Wilson dubbed him "Boss of the Soup Tureen;" but the boy was entirely indifferent as to what he was called.

"Make your games, gem'lams," he would say; "don't be afraid to 'ffend dis chile. He nebber get angry I'ssure you."

When Freezing Powders had nothing in his hand his method of progression forward was at times somewhat peculiar. He went cart-wheel fashion, rolling over and over so quickly that you could hardly see him, he seemed a mist of legs, or something like the figure you see on a Manx penny.

At other times "the doctor," as the cook was invariably called by the crew, would pop up his head out of the fore-hatch and bawl out,

"Pass young Shallots forward here."

"Ay, ay, doctor," the men would answer. "Shalots! Shalots! Shalots!"

Then Freezing Powder's curly head would beam up out of the saloon companion.

"Stand by, men!" the sailor who captured him would cry; and the men would form themselves into a line along the deck about three yards apart, and Freezing Powders would be pitched from one to the other as if he had been a ball of spun-yarn, until he finally fell into the friendly arms of the cook.

About a week after the bear adventure De Vere, the aëronaut, was breakfasting in the saloon, as he always did when there was anything "grand in the wind," as Rory styled the situation.

"Dat is von thing I admire very mooch," said the Frenchman, pointing to a beautifully-framed design that hung in a conspicuous part of the saloon bulkhead.

"Ah! said Allan, laughing, "that was an idea of dear foolish boy Rory. He brought it as a gift to me last Christmas. The coral comes from the Indian Ocean; Rory gathered it himself; the whole design is his."

"It's a vera judeecious arrangement," said Sandy McFlail, admiringly.

The arrangement, as the doctor called it, was simple enough. Three pieces of coral, in the shape of a rose, a thistle, and shamrock, encased—nay, I may say enshrined —in a beautiful casket of crystal and gilded ebony. There was the milk-white rose of England and the blood-red thistle of Scotland side by side, and fondly twining around them the shamrock of old Ireland—all in black.

Here was the motto underneath them—

"Perseberando."

"There is nothing like perseverance," said Allan. "The little coral insect thereby builds islands, ay, and founds continents, destined to be stages on which will be worked out or fought out the histories of nations yet unborn. 'Perseverando!' it is a grand and bold motto, and I love it."

The Frenchman had been standing before the casket;

he now turned quickly round to Allan and held out his hand.

"You are a bold man," he said; "you will come with me to-day in de balloon?"

"I will," said Allan.

"We vill soar far above yonder mountain," continued De Vere; "we vill descend into the crater. We vill do vat mortal man has neever done before. Perseverando! Do you fear?"

"Fear?" said Allan; "no! I fear nothing under the sun. Whate'er a man dares he can do."

"Bravely spoken," cried the Frenchman. "Perseverando! I have room for two more."

"Perseverando!" says Rory. "Perseverando for ever! Hoorah! I'm one of you, boys."

Ralph was lying on the sofa, reading a book. But he doubled down a leaf, got up, and stretched himself.

"Here," he said, quietly, "you fellows mustn't have all the fun; I'll go too, just to see fair play. But, I say," he added, after a moment's pause, "I don't suppose there will be any refreshment-stalls down there—eh?"

"No, that there won't," cried Allan. "Hi! Peter, pack a basket for four."

"Ay, ay, sir!" said Peter.

"And, I say, Peter—" This from Ralph.

"Yes, sir," said the steward, pausing in the doorway.

"Enough for twenty," said Ralph. "That's all, Peter."

"Thank'ee, sir," said Peter, laughing; "I'll see to that, sir."

It was some time before De Vere succeeded in gaining Captain McBain's consent to the embarkation of his boys on this wild and strange adventure, but he was talked over at last.

"It is all for the good of science, I suppose," he said, half doubtfully, as he shook hands with our heroes before they took their places in the car. "God keep you, boys. I'm not at all sure I'll ever see one of you again."

"HE ANXIOUSLY WATCHED IT TILL IT DISAPPEARED FROM SIGHT."
[*Page* 119.

The ropes were let go, and upwards into the clear air rose the mighty balloon.

"Here's a lark," said Allan.

"A skylark," said Rory. "Let us sing, boys—let us sing as we soar, 'Rule Britannia, Britannia rules the waves.'"

Standing on the quarter-deck, and gazing upwards, McBain heard the voices growing fainter and fainter, and saw the balloon lessening and lessening, till the song could no longer be heard, and the balloon itself was but a tiny speck in the heaven's blue. Then he went down below, and busied himself all day with calculations. He didn't want to think.

Meanwhile, how fared it with our boys? Here they were, all together, embarked upon as strange an expedition as it has ever probably been the lot of any youth or youths to try the chance of. Yet I do not think that anything approaching to fear found place in the hearts of one of them. The situation was novel in the extreme. With a slow and steady but imperceptible motion—for she was weightily ballasted—the "Perseverando," as they had named the balloon, was mounting skywards. There was not the slightest air or wind, nor the tiniest of clouds to be seen anywhere, and down beneath and around them was spread out a panorama, which but to gaze upon held them spellbound.

There was the island itself, with its rugged hills looking now so strangely flattened and so grotesquely contorted; to the west and to the north lay the white and boundless sea of ice, but far to the eastward and south was the ocean itself, looking dark as night in contrast with the solid ice.

But see, yonder; where the ice joins the water, and just a little way from its edge, lie stately ships—two, three, five in all can be counted, and their sails are all clewed; and those innumerable black ticks on the snow; what can they be but seals, and men sealing?

"Don't you long to join them?" said Allan, addressing his companions.

"I don't," replied Rory; "in spite of the cold I feel a strange, dreamy kind of happiness all over heart and brain. Troth! I feel as if I had breakfasted on lotus-leaves."

"And I," said Ralph, "feel as I hadn't breakfasted on anything in particular. Let us see what Peter has done up for us."

And he stretched out his hand as he spoke towards a basket.

"Ah!" cried the Frenchman, "not dat basket; dat is my Bagdads—my pigeons, my letter-carriers! You see, gentlemen, I have come prepared to combat eevery deeficulty."

"So I see," said Ralph, coolly undoing the other basket; "what an appetite the fresh air gives a fellow, to be sure!"

"Indeed," says Rory, archly, "it is never very far from home you've got to go for that same, big brother Ralph. But it's hardly fair, after all, to try to eat the Bagdads."

"Remember one thing, though," replied Ralph; "if it should occur to me suddenly that you want your ears pulled you cannot run away to save yourself."

"Indeed," said Rory, "I don't think that the frost has left any ears at all on me worth pulling, or worth speaking about either."

"Ha!" cried Allan, "that reminds me; I've got those face mufflers. There! I'll show you how to put one on. The fur side goes inside—thus; now I have a hole to breathe through, and a couple of holes for vision."

"And a pretty guy you look!"

"Oh! bother the looks," responded Ralph, let us all be guys. Give us a mask, old man."

They did feel more comfortable now that they had the masks on, and could gaze about them without the risk of being frozen.

The cold was intense; it was bitter.

"I'd beat my feet to keep them warm," said Rory, "if I didn't think I'd beat the bottom of the car out. Then we'd all go fluttering down like so many kittywakes, and it's Captain McBain himself that would be astounded to see us back so soon."

"Gentlemen," said the Frenchman, "we are right over the mouth of the crater. I shall now make descent, with your permission. Then it vill not be so cold."

"And is it inside the volcano," cries Rory, "you'd be taking us to warm us? Down into the crater, to toast our toes at Vulcan's own fireside? Sure, Captain De Vere, it is splicing the main-brace you're after, for you want to give us all a drop of the craytur."

"Oh!—oh!" this from Ralph. "Oh! Rory—oh! how can you make so vile a pun? In such a situation, too!"

The gentlest of breezes was carrying the balloon almost imperceptibly towards the north and west; meanwhile De Vere was permitting a gradual escape of gas, and the *Perseverando* sunk gradually towards the mountain-top, the mouth of which seemed to yawn to swallow them up. There was a terrible earnestness about this daring aëronaut's face that awed even Rory into silence.

"Stand by," he whispered; for in the dread silence even a whisper could be heard,—"stand by, Allan, to throw that bag of ballast over the moment I say the word."

Viewing it from the sea of ice, no one could calculate how large is the extent of the crater on the top of that mighty mountain cone. It is perfectly circular, and five hundred yards at least in circumference, but it is deeper, far and away, than any volcanic crater into which it has ever been my fortune to peer. Even when the great balloon began to alight in its centre the gulf below seemed bottomless. The *Perseverando* appeared to be sinking down—down—down into the blackness of darkness. To the perceptions of our heroes, who peered fearfully over the car and gazed below, the gulf was rising towards them and swallowing them up.

I do not think I am detracting in the slightest from their character for bravery, when I say that the hearts of Ralph, Rory, and Allan, at all events, felt as if standing still, so terrible was the feeling of dread of some unknown danger that crept over them. As for De Vere, he was a fatalist of the newest French school, and a man that carried his life in his hand. He never attempted, it is true, any feat which he deemed all but impossible to perform; but, having embarked on an enterprise, he would go through with it, or he cared not to live.

Strange though it may appear, it is just men like this that fortune favours. Probably because the wish to continue to exist is not uppermost in their minds, the wish and the hope to achieve success is the paramount feeling.

Still slowly, very slowly, sunk the balloon, as if unwilling to leave her aërial home. And now a faint shade of light begins to mingle with the darkness beneath them; they are near the bottom of the crater at last.

"Stand by once again," whispers De Vere, "to throw that anchor over as soon as I tell you."

A moment of awful suspense.

"Now! now!" hisses De Vere.

Two anchors quit the car at the same time—one thrown by the aëronaut himself, one by Allan, and the ropes are speedily made fast. The balloon gives an upward plunge, the cables tighten, then all is still!

"Ha! ha! she is fast!" cried De Vere, now for the first time showing a little excitement. "Oh, she is a beauty! she has behave most lofely! Look up, gentlemen!—look up!—behold the mighty walls of blue ice that surround us!—behold the circle of blue sky dat over-canopies us!—look, the stars are shining!"

"Can it be night so soon?" exclaimed Allan, in alarm.

"Nay, nay, gentlemen," said the enthusiastic Frenchman, "be easy of your minds. It is not night in the vorld outside, but here it is alvays night; up yonder the stars shine alvays, alvays, when de clouds are absent. And shine dey vill until de crack of doom. Now gaze around you. See, the darkness already begins to vanish, and you can see the vast and mighty cavern into which I have brought you. If my judgment serves me, it extends for miles around beneath de mountain. There!—you begin to perceive the gigantic stalactites that seem to support the oof!"

"Ralph," cried Rory, seizing his friend by the hand, "do you remember, years and years ago, while we all sat round the fire in the tartan parlour of Arrandoon Castle, wishing we might be able to do something that no one, man or boy, had ever done before?"

"I do—I do," answered Ralph.

"Descend with me here, then," continued Rory, "and let us explore the cavern. Only a little, *little* way, captain," he pleaded, seeing that De Vere shook his head in strong dissent.

"You know not vat you do ask," said De Vere, solemnly. "Here are caves within caves, one cavern but hides a thousand more; besides, there are, maybe, and doubtless are, crevasses in de floor of dis awful crater, into which you may tumble, neever, neever to be seen again. Pray do not think of risking a danger so vast."

* * * *

The day wore slowly to a close; many and many an anxious look did McBain take skywards, in hopes of seeing the returning balloon. But the sun set, tipping the distant hills with brightest crimson, twilight died away in the west, and one by one shone out the stars, till night and darkness and silence reigned over all the sea of ice.

He went below at last. His feelings may be better imagined then described. He tried to make himself believe that nothing had occurred, and that the balloon had safely descended in some snow-clad valley, and that morning would bring good tidings. But for all this he could not for the life of him banish a dread, cold feeling that something terrible had occurred, the very novelty of which made it all the more appalling to think of. Presently the mate entered the saloon.

"What cheer, Stevenson! Any tidings?"

"A pigeon, sir," replied the mate, handing the bird into the captain's grasp.

McBain's hands shook as he had never remembered them shake before, as he undid the tiny missive from the pigeon's leg.

It ran briefly thus:—

"We are detained here in the crater all night. Do not be alarmed. To-morrow will, please Providence, see us safely home."

CHAPTER XIV.

ANXIOUS HOURS—EXPLORATION OF THE MOUNTAIN CAVERN—THE CAVE OF THE KING OF ICE, AND GHOULS OF A THOUSAND WINTERS—TRANSFORMATION SCENES—SNOWBLIND—LOST.

IT would be difficult to say which was most to be pitied, McBain on board the *Arrandoon*, passing long hours of inconceivable anxiety, or our other heroes, left to spend the drear, cold night in the awful depths of that Arctic crater.

It was with light hearts that Ralph and Rory descended from the car of the *Perseverando* and commenced their perilous exploration of the vast and dimly-lighted cavern; but heavy hearts were left behind them, and hardly had they disappeared in the gloom ere the Frenchman exclaimed to Allan, "I greatly fear dat I have done wrong. Your two friends are big wid impulse; if anydings happen to them dere vill be for me no more peace in dis world."

Allan was silent.

But when hours passed away and there were no signs of their returning, when gloaming itself began to fall around them, and the stars at the crater's mouth assumed a brighter hue, Allan's anxiety knew no bounds, and he proposed to De Vere to go in search of his friends.

"Ah! if dat vere indeed possible!" was the reply.

"And why not?" said Allan.

"For many reasons: de balloon vill even now hardly bear de strain on her anchors; de loss of even your veight vould require such delicate manipulation on my part, dat I fear I could not successfully vork in such small space. Alas! ve must vait. But there yet is hope."

Meanwhile it behoves us to follow Ralph and Rory. They had faithfully promised De Vere they would go but a short distance from the car, and that promise they had meant to redeem. They found that the ground sloped downwards from the mouth of the crater, but there was no want of light, as yet at least, and thus not the slightest danger of being unable to find their way back, for were there not their footsteps in the snow to guide them? So onward they strolled, cheerfully enough, arm-in-arm, like brothers, and that was precisely how they felt towards each other.

The road—if I may say "road" where there was no road—was rough enough in all conscience, and at times it was difficult for them to prevent stumbling over a boulder.

"I wonder," said Rory, "how long these boulders have lain here, and I wonder what is beneath us principally, and what those vast stalactite pillars are formed of."

"'Bide a wee,' as the doctor says," replied Ralph; "don't hurry me with too many questions, and don't forget that though I am ever so much bigger and stronger than you, I don't think I am half so wise. But the boulders may have lain here for ages: those ghostly-looking pillars are doubtless ice-clad rocks, partly formed through the agency of fire, partly by water. I think we stand principally on rocks and on ice, with, far, far down beneath us, fire."

"Dear, dear!" said Rory, talking very seriously, and with the perfect English he always used when speaking earnestly; "what a strange, mysterious place we are in! Do you know, Ralph, I am half afraid to go much farther."

"Silly boy!" said his companion, "how thoroughly Irish you are at heart—joy, tears, sunshine and fun, but, deep under all, a smouldering superstition."

"Just like the fires," added Rory, "that roll so far beneath us. But you know, Ray,"—in their most affectionate and friendly moods Ralph had come to be "Ray" to Rory, and Rory "Row" to Ralph—"you know, Ray, that the silence and gloom of this eerie place are enough to make any one superstitious—any one, that is, whose soul isn't solid matter-of-fact."

"Well, it *is* silent. But I say, Row———"

"Well, Ray?"

"Suppose we try to break it with a song? I daresay they have never heard much singing down here."

"Who?" cried Rory, staring fearfully into the darkness.

"Oh!" said Ralph, carelessly, "I didn't mean any one in particular. Come, what shall we sing—'The wearing o' the green'?"

"No, Ray, no; that were far too melancholic, though I grant it is a lovely melody."

"Well, something Scotch, and stirring. The echoes of this cavern must be wonderful."

They were, indeed; and when Rory started off into that world-known but ever-popular song, "Auld lang syne," and Ralph chimed with deep and sonorous bass, the effect was really grand and beautiful, for a thousand voices seemed to fill the cavern. They heard the song even in the car of the balloon, and it caused Allan to remark, smilingly, for they had not yet been long gone, "Ralph and boy Rory seem to be enjoying themselves; but I trust they won't be long away."

Rory was quite lively again ere he reached the words—

"And we'll tak' a richt good-willy waught
   For auld lang syne."

He burst out laughing. "Indeed, indeed! there is no wonder I laugh," he said; "fancy the notion of taking a 'good-willy waught' in a place like this! And now," he added, "for a bit of a sketch."

"Don't be long in rubbing it in, then."

Rory was seated on a boulder now, tracing on his page the outlines of those strange, weird pillars that hands of man had never raised nor human eyes gazed upon before. So the silence once more became irksome, and the time seemed long to Ralph, but Rory had finished at last.

Then the two companions, after journeying on somewhat farther, began to awaken the echoes by various shouts; and voices, some coming from a long distance, repeated clearly the last words.

"Let us frighten those ghouls down there by rolling down boulders," said Rory.

"Come on, then," said Ralph; "I've often played at that game."

They had ten minutes of this work. It was evident this hill within a hill, this crater's point, was of depth illimitable from the distant hissing noises which the broken boulders finally emitted.

"It's a regular whispering gallery," said Rory.

"It is, Row. But do let us get back. See, there is already barely light enough to reveal our footsteps."

"Ah! but, my boy," said Rory, "the nearer the car we walk the more light we'll have. And I have just one more surprise for you. You see this little bag?"

"Yes. What is in it—sandwiches?"

"Nay, my Saxon friend! but Bengal fires. Now witness the effects of the grand illumination of the Cave of the King of Ice by us, his two ghouls of a thousand winters!"

The scene, under weird blue lights, pale green or crimson, was really magical. All the transformation scenes ever they had witnessed dwindled into insignificance compared to it.

"I shall remember this to my dying day!" Rory exclaimed.

"And I too!" cried Ralph, entranced.

"Now the finale!" said the artist; "it'll beat all the

others! This white light of mine will eclipse the glory of the rest as the morning sun does that of moonlight! It will burn quite a long time, too; I made it last night on purpose."

It was a Bengal fire of dazzling splendour that now was lit, and our heroes themselves were astonished.

"It beats the 'Arabian Nights'!" cried Rory. "Look, look!" he continued, waving it gently to and fro, "the stalactites seem to dance and move towards us from out the gloom arrayed in robes of transplendent white. Yonder comes the King of Ice himself to bid us welcome."

"Put it out! put it out!" murmured Ralph, with his hand on his brow.

It presently burned out, but lo! the change!—total darkness!

Rory and Ralph were snowblind!

"Oh, boy Rory!" said Ralph, "that brilliant of yours has sealed our fate. It will be hours ere our eyes can be restored, and long before then the darkness of night will have enshrouded us. We are lost!"

"Let us not lose each other, at all events," said Rory, feeling for his friend's arm, and linking it in his own.

"You think we are lost; dear Ralph, I have more hopes. Something within me tells me that we were never meant to end our days in the awful darkness of this terrible cavern. Pass the night here it is certain we must, but to-morrow will bring daylight, and daylight safety, for be assured Allan and De Vere will not leave us, unless——"

Here the hope-giver paused.

"Unless," added Ralph—"for I know what you would say—an accident should be imminent—unless they *must* leave. A balloon needs strange management."

"Even then they will return to seek us by morning light. Do you know what, Ray?" he continued, "our adventures have been too foolhardy. Providence has punished us, but He will not utterly desert us."

"Hope springs eternal in the human breast."

The lamp of hope was flickering—had, indeed, burned out—in Ralph's heart, but his friend's words rekindled it. Perhaps Rory's true character never shone more clearly out than it did now, for, while trying to cheer his more than friend, he fully appreciated the desperateness of the situation, and had but little hope left in him, except his extreme trust in the goodness of a higher Power.

"Could we not," said Ralph, "all snowblind as we are, try to grope our way upwards?"

"No, no, no!" cried Rory; "success in that way is all but impossible; and, remember, we have but the trail of our footprints to guide us even by day."

Something of the ludicrous invariably mixes itself up with the most tragic affairs of this world. I have seen the truth of this in the chamber of death itself, in storms at sea, and in scenes where men grappled each other in deadly strife. And it is well it should be so, else would the troubles of this world oftentimes swamp reason itself. The attempts of Rory to keep his companion in cheer, partook of the nature of the ludicrous, as did the attempts of both of them to keep warm.

So hours elapsed, and sometimes sitting, sometimes standing and beating feet and hands for circulation's sake, and doing much talking, but never daring to leave the spot, at last says Rory, "Hullo, Ray! joy of joys! I've found a lucifer!"

Almost at the same moment he lit it. They could see each other's faces—see a watch, and notice it was nearly midnight They had regained sight! Joy and hope were at once restored.

"Troth!" said Rory, resuming his brogue, "it's myself could be a baby for once and cry. Now what do ye say to try to sleep? We'll lie close together, you know, and it's warm we'll be in a jiffey!"

So down they lay, and, after ten long shivering minutes,

heat came back to their frozen bodies. They had not been talking all this time; it is but right to say they were better engaged.

With warmth came *le gaité*—to Rory, at least.

"Have you wound your watch, Ray?"

"No, Row? and I wouldn't move for the world!"

After a pause, "Ray," says Row.

"Yes, Row?" says Ray.

"You always said you liked a big bed-room, Ray, and, troth, you've got one for once!"

"How I envy you your spirits," answers Ray.

"Don't talk about spirits," says Row, "and frighten a poor boy. I've covered up my head, and I wouldn't look up for the world. I'm going to repeat myself to sleep. Good night."

"Good night," asks Ray, "but how do you do it?"

"Psalms, Ray," Row replies. "I know them all. I'll be out of here in a moment.

"'He makes me down to lie by pastures green,
He leadeth me the quiet waters by.'

Isn't that pretty, Ray?"

"Very, Row, but 'pastures green' and 'quiet waters' aren't much in my way. Repeat *me* to sleep, Rory boy, and I promise you I won't pull your ears again for a month."

"Well, I'll try," says Row. "Are your eyes shut?"

"To be sure. A likely thing I'd have them open, isn't it?"

"Then we're both going to a ball in old England."

"Glorious," says Ray. "I'm there already."

Then in slow, monotonous, but pleasing tones, Row goes on. He describes the brilliant festive scene, the warmth, the light, the beauty and the music, and the dances, and last but not least the supper table. It is at this point that our Saxon hero gives sundry nasal indications that this strange species of mesmerism had taken due effect, so Row leaves him at the supper table, and goes back to his "pastures green" and "quiet waters," and soon they both are sound enough. Let us leave them there; no need to watch them. Remember what Lover says in his beautiful song,—

> "O! watch ye well by daylight,
> For angels watch at night."

*   *   *   *   *

Poor McBain! Worn out with watching, he had sunk at last to sleep in his chair.

And day broke slowly on the sea of ice. The snow-clad crater's peak was the first to welcome glorious aurora with a rosy blush, which stole gradually downwards till it settled on the jagged mountain tips. Then bears began to yawn and stretch themselves, the sly Arctic foxes crept forth from snow-banks, and birds in their thousands—brightest of all the snowbird—came wheeling around the *Arrandoon* to snatch an early breakfast ere they wended their way westward to fields of blood and phocal carnage.

And their screaming awoke McBain.

He was speedily on deck.

Yonder was the *Perseverando* slowly descending.

During all the long cruise of the *Arrandoon* nobody referred to the adventure at the crater of Jan Mayen without a feeling akin to sadness and contrition, for all felt that something had been done which ought not to have been done—there had been, as McBain called it, "a tempting of Providence."

*   *   *   *   *

"Well, well, well," cried the skipper of the *Canny Scotia* —and he seemed to be in anything but a sweet temper. Just, like my luck. I do declare, mate, if I'd been born a hatter everybody else would have been born without heads. Here have I been struggling away for years against fortune, always trying to get a good voyage to support a small wife and a big family, and now that luck seems to have all turned in our favour, two glorious patches of seals on the ice yonder, a hard frost, and the ice beautifully red with blood, and no ship near us, then you, mate, come down from the crow's-nest with that confoundedly long face of yours, for which you ought to have been smothered at birth——"

"I can't help my face, sir," cried the mate, bristling up like a bantam cock.

"Silence!" roared the burly skipper. "Silence! when you talk to your captain. You, I say, *you* come and report a big steamer in sight to help us at the banquet."

The mate scratched his head, taking his hat off for the purpose.

"Did I make the ship?" he asked with naive innocence.

"Pooh!" the skipper cried; and next moment he was scrambling up the rigging with all the elegance, grace, and speed of a mud turtle.

He was in a better humour when he returned.

"I say, matie," he said, "yonder chap ain't a sealer; too dandy, and not boats enough. No, she is one of they spectioneering kind o' chaps as goes a prowling around lookin' for the North Pole. Ha! ha! ha! Come below, matie, and we'll have a glass together. She ain't the kind o' lady to interfere with our blubber-hunting."

The mate was mollified. His face was soaped, and he shone.

CHAPTER XV.

THE "ARRANDOON" ANCHORS TO THE "FLOE"—THE VISIT TO THE "CANNY SCOTIA"—SILAS GRIG—A SAD SCENE —RORY RELIEVES HIS FEELINGS—STRANGERS COMING FROM THE FAR WEST.

SEEING the skipper of the *Canny Scotia* and his mate come below together smiling, the steward readily guessed what they wanted, so he was not dilatory in producing the rum-bottle and two tumblers. Then the skipper pushed the former towards the mate, and said,

"Help yourself, matie."

And the mate dutifully and respectfully pushed it back again, saying,

"After you, sir."

This palaver finished, they both half-filled their tumblers with the ruby intoxicant, added thereto a modicum of boiling coffee from the urn that simmered on top of the stove, then, with a preliminary nod towards each other, emptied their glasses at a gulp. After this, gasping for breath, they beamed on each other with a newly-found friendliness.

"Have another," said the skipper.

They had another, then went on deck.

After ten minutes of attentive gazing at the *Arrandoon*, "Well," said the skipper, "I do call that a bit o' pretty steering; if it ain't, my name isn't Silas Grig."

"But there's a deal o' palaver about it, don't you think so, sir? remarked the mate.

"Granted, granted," assented Silas ; "granted, matie."

The cause of their admiration was the way in which the *Arrandoon* was brought alongside the great ice-floe. She didn't come stem on—as if she meant to flatten her bows —and then swing round. Not she. She approached the ice with a beautiful sweep, describing nearly half a circle, then, broadside on to the ice, she neared it and neared it. Next over went the fenders; the steam roared from the pipe upwards into the blue air, like driven snow, then dissolved itself like the ghost of the white lady; the ship was stopped, away went the ice anchors, the vessel was fast.

And no noise about it either. There may not be much seamanship now-a-days, but I tell you, boys, it takes a clever man to manage a big steamer prettily and well.

The *Arrandoon* was not two hundred yards from the *Canny Scotia*. Now round go the davits on the port quarter, outward swings the boat, men and officers spring nimbly into her, blocks rattle, and down goes the first whaler, reaching the water with a flop, but not a plash, and with keel as even and straight as a ruled line.

"I say, matie," said Silas Grig, in some surprise, "if that boat ain't coming straight away here, I hope I may never chew cheese again."

So far as that was concerned, if Silas chose, he would at least have the chance of chewing cheese again, for the *Arrandoon's* boat came rippling along towards them with a steady clŭck-ĕl-tēe clŭck-ĕl-tēe, which spoke well for the men at the oars.

"Well," continued Silas, who, rough nut though he was, always meant well enough, "let us do the civil, matie ; tell the steward to fill the rum-bottle, and pitch 'em a rope."

The rope came in very handy; but there was no need for the rum ; even in Greenland men can live without it— the officers of the *Arrandoon* had found that out.

McBain, with Allan and Rory,—the latter, by the way,

seemed to have registered a vow to go everywhere and see everything,—stood on the quarter-deck of the *Canny Scotia*, the skipper of which craft was in front of him, a comical look of admiration on his round brick-coloured countenance, and his two hands deep in the pockets of his powerful pilot coat.

"Ay, sir! ay!" he was saying; "well, I must say ye do surprise *me*."

He put such an emphasis on the "me" that one would have thought that to surprise Silas Grig was something to be quite boastful of ever after.

"All the way to the North Pole? Well, well; but d'ye think you'll find it?"

"We mean to," said Rory, boldly.

"*Perseverando!*" said Allan.

"The *Perseverance*!" cried the skipper. "I know the ship, a Peterheader. Last time I saw her she had got in the nips, and was lying keel up on the ice, yards and rigging all awry of course; and, bother her, I hope she'll lie there till Silas Grig gets a voyage [a cargo], then when the *Scotia* is full ship, the *Perseverance* can get down off the shelf, and cabbage all the rest. Them's my sentiments. But come below, gentlemen, come below; there is room enough in the cabin of the old *Scotia* for every man Jack o' ye. Come below."

Silas was right. There was room, but not much to spare, and, squeezed in between Allan and McBain, poor Rory was hardly visible, and could only reach the table with one hand.

The cabin of this Greenlandman can be described with a stroke of the pen, so to speak. It was square and not very lofty—a tall man required to duck when under a beam; the beams were painted white, the bulkheads and cabin doors—four in number—were grey picked out with green. One-half at least of the available space was occupied by the table; close around it were cushioned lockers; the only other furniture was the captain's big chair and a few camp-stools, a big square stove with a roaring fire, and a big square urn fixed on top thereof, which contained coffee, had never been empty all the voyage, and would not be till the end thereof. I suppose a bucket of water could hardly be called furniture, but there it stood close to the side of the stove, and the concentric rings of ice inside it showed the difficulty everybody must experience who chose to quench his thirst in the most natural way possible.

Above, in the hollow of the skylight, hung a big compass, and several enormously long sealer's telescopes.

"No rum, gentlemen?" said Silas; "well, you do astonish *me*; but you'll taste my wife's green-ginger wine, and drink her health?"

"That we will," replied McBain, "and maybe finish a bottle."

"And welcome to ten," said Silas; "and the bun, steward, bring the bun. That's the style! My wife isn't much to look at, gentlemen, but, for a bun or o' drop o' green ginger, I'll back her against the whole world."

After our heroes had done justice to the bun, and pledged the skipper's good lady in the green ginger, that gentleman must needs eye them again and again, with as much curiosity as if they had been some new and wonderful zoological specimens, that he had by chance captured.

"All the way to the North Pole!" he muttered. "Well, well, but that *does* get over Silas."

Rory could not help laughing.

"Funny old stick," said Silas, joining in his merriment, "ain't I?"

He did look all that and more, with his two elbows on the table, and his knuckles supporting his chin, for his face was as round as a full moon orient, and just the colour of a new flower-pot; then he laughed more with one side of his face than the other, his eyes were nowhere in the folds of his face, and his nose hardly worth mentioning.

After the laugh, beginning with Rory, had spread fairly round the table, everybody felt relieved.

"I'm only a plain, honest blubber-hunter,* gentlemen," said Silas Grig, apologetically, "with a large family and—and a small wife—but—but you do surprise *me*. There!"

But when McBain informed him that the *Arrandoon* would lay alongside him for a week or more, and help him to secure a voyage, and wouldn't ship a single skin herself, Silas was more surprised than ever. Indeed, until this day I could not tell you what would have happened to Silas, had the mate not been providentially beside him to vent his feelings upon. On that unfortunate officer's back he brought down his great shoulder-of-mutton fist with a force that made him jump, and his breath to come and go as if he had just been popped under a shower-bath.

"Luck's come," he cried. "Hey? hey?"

And every "hey?" represented a dig in the mate's ribs with the skipper's thumb of iron.

"Told ye it would, hey? Didn't I? hey?"

"What'll the old woman say, hey? Hey, boys? Hey, matie? Hey? Hey?"

"You gentlemen," said Silas, after his feelings had calmed down a trifle, "are all for sport, and Silas has to make a voyage. But you'll have sport, gentlemen, that ye will. My men are sealing now. They're among the young seals. It has been nothing but flay, flay, flay, for the last two rounds of the sun, and there isn't such a very long night now, is there? And you saw the blood?"

Saw the blood, reader! Indeed, our heroes had. Where was it that that blood was not? All the beautiful

* It is but fair to say that, as a rule, captains of Greenlandmen are far more refined in manner than poor Silas.

snow was encrimsoned with it on the distant field of ice, where the men were carrying on their ghastly work. It was as if a great battle had been fought there, and the dead crangs lay in dozens and hundreds. A crang means a carcass. Is the adjective "dead," then, not unnecessary? What else can a carcass or crang be but "dead"? Nay, but listen: let me whisper a truth in your ear, and I know your brave young blood will boil when I tell you: I've known our men, Englishmen and Scotchmen, flense the lambs while still alive.

From the field of slaughter the skins were being dragged to the ship by men with ropes, so there were streaks of red all the way to the ship, and all the vessel's starboard side was smeared with blood. Indeed, I do not wish to harrow the feelings of my readers, and I shall but describe a few of the cruelties of sealing—no, on second thoughts, I will not even do that, because I know well you will believe me when I tell you these cruelties are very great, and believing this, if ever you have an opportunity of voting for a bill or signing a petition to get poor Greenland seals fair play, I know you will.

Silas Grig and our heroes took a walk to the field of unequal strife, and Rory and Allan, to whom all they saw was very new, were not a little horrified as well as disgusted.

"This," said McBain, "is the young sealing. We are not going to assist you in this; we are sportsmen, not butchers, Captain Grig."

Silas grasped McBain's hand. "Your feelings do you credit, sir," he said—"they do. But I have feelings, too. Yes, a weather-beaten old stick like me has feelings! But I'm sent out here to make a voyage, and what can I do? I've a small wife and a large family; and my owners, too, would sack me if I didn't bring the skins. I say," he added, after a pause, "you know my mate?"

"Yes," said McBain.

"Well," said Silas, "you wouldn't imagine that a fellow with such an ugly chunk o' a figure-head as that had feelings, eh? But he has, though; and during all this young sealing business we both of us just drowns our feelings in the rum-bottle. Fact, sir! and old Silas scorns a lie. But, gentlemen, when all this wicked work is over, when we are away north from here, among the old seals, and when we can look at that sun again without seeing blood, then my matie and I banishes Black Jack* and sticks to coffee and arrowroot; that we do!"

They had turned their backs on the by no means inviting scene, and were walking towards the *Canny Scotia* as Silas spoke.

"But," said the Greenland mariner, "come and dine with the old man to-morrow. The last of the young seals will be on board by then, and we'll have had a wash down; we'll be clean and tidy like. Then hurrah for the old seals! That's sport, if you like!—that's fair play."

"Ah!" said McBain, "your heart is in the right place, I can see that. I wish there were more like you. Do *you* seal on Sunday? Many do."

Silas looked solemn. "I knows they do," he said, "but Silas hasn't done so yet, and he prays he never may be tempted to."

"Captain Grig, we'll come and dine with you, and we expect you to pay us the same compliment another day."

"I daresay you fellows are glad to get home?" said Ralph, rising from the sofa and throwing down the volume he had been dreaming over.

"Not a bit of it!" said Rory and Allan, both in one breath; and Rory added, "You don't know what a funny ship a real Greenlandman is! I declare you've lost a treat!"

* The gallon measure from which rum is served is so called.

"Does it smell badly?" asked Ralph, with a slight curl of his upper lip.

"Never a taste!" says Rory; "she's as sweet as cowslips or clover, or newly-made hay; and the bun was beautiful!"

"The what?" said Ralph.

"Don't tell him!" cried Allan; "don't tell him!"

"And the green ginger!" said Rory, smacking his lips.

"Ah, yes! the green ginger," said Allan; "I never tasted anything like that in all my born days!"

"Hi, you, Freezing Powders!" cried Rory, "take my coat and out-o'-doors gear. D'ye hear? Look sharp!"

"I'm coming, sah; and coming plenty quick!"

"De-ah me!" from Cockie.

"Now bring my fiddle, you young rascal, into my cabin;" for Rory, reader, had that young-sealing scene on his brain, and he would not be happy till he had played it away. And a wild, weird lilt it was, too, that he did bring forth. Extempore, did you ask? Certainly, for he played as he thought and felt; all his soul seemed to enter the cremona, and to well forth again from the beautiful instrument, now in tones of plaintive sorrow, now in notes of wrath; and then it stopped all at once abruptly. That was Rory's way; he had pitched fiddle and bow on the bed, and presently he returned to the saloon.

"Are you better?" inquired Allan.

Rory only gave a little laugh, and sat down to read.

It had taken McBain nearly a fortnight to get clear away from the Isle of Jan Mayen, for the frost had set in sharp and hard, and the great ice-saws had to be worked, and the aid of dynamite called in to blast the pieces. They were now some ten miles to the north and east of the island, but, so far as he knew on the day of his visit to the *Scotia*, he had bidden it farewell for ever.

It had not been for the mere sake of sport or adventure

he had called in there, he had another reason. Old Magnus, before the sailing—ay, or even the building—of the *Arrandoon*, had heard that the island was inhabited by a party of wandering Eskimos. Wherever Eskimos were McBain had thought there must be dogs, and that was just what was wanting to complete the expedition—a kennel of sleigh dogs. But, as we have seen, the Eskimo encampment was deserted, so McBain had to leave it disappointed. But, as it turned out, it was only temporarily deserted after all, and on the very day on which they had arranged to dine with Skipper Grig, two daring men, chiefs of a tribe of Eskimos, drawn in a rude sledge, were making their way towards the island. Their team consisted of over a dozen half-wild dogs, harnessed with ropes of skin and untanned leather. They seemed to fly across the sea of ice. Hardly could you see the dogs for the powdery snow that rose in clouds around them. Well might they hurry, for clouds were banking up in the west, a low wind came moaning over the dreary plain, and a storm was brewing, and if it burst upon them ere they reached the still distant island, then——

CHAPTER XVI.

SILAS GRIG'S DINNER-PARTY—A NEW MEMBER OF THE MALACOPTERYGII—THE STORM ON THE SEA OF ICE—BREAK-UP OF THE MAIN PACK—ROUGHING IT AT SEA.

WHILE those two chiefs of the Eskimo Indians were hurrying their team of dogs across the sea of ice eastwards, ever eastwards, with the clouds rising behind them, with the wind whispering and moaning around them, and sometimes raising the powdery snow in little angry eddies, that almost hid the plunging dogs from their view, honest Silas Grig, though somewhat uneasy in his mind as to what kind of weather was brewing, busied himself nevertheless in preparing what he considered a splendid dinner for his coming guests.

"But," he said to his mate, "it will just be like my luck, you know, if it comes on to blow big guns, and we've got to leave good cheer and put out to sea."

"Ah! sir," said the mate, "don't forget luck has turned, you know."

"Ha! ha! ha!" laughed Silas, "really, matie, I *had* a'most forgotten."

And away forward he hurried, to see how the men were getting on scrubbing decks and cleaning brass-work, and how the cook was getting on with that mighty sirloin of beef. He took many a run forward as the day advanced, often pausing, though, to give an uneasy glance windward, and at the sun, not yet hidden by the rising clouds. And often as he did so he shook his head and made some remark to his mate.

"I tell ye, matie," he said once, "I don't quite like the looks o' 't. Those clouds ain't natural this time o' the year, and don't you see the spots in the sun?* Why, he is holed through and through like an old Dutch cheese. Something's brewin'. But, talking of brewin', I wonder how the soup is getting on?"

Silas's face was more the colour of a new flower-pot than ever, when McBain and our three heroes came alongside in their dashing gig, with its beautiful paint and varnish, snow-white oars, flag trailing astern, and rudder-ribbons, all complete.

Rory was steering, and he brought her alongside with a regular admiral's sweep.

"Why, she's going away past us!" cried Silas; "no, she ain't. It is the bow-and-bow business the young 'un's after."

"In bow!" cried Rory. "Way enough—oars!"

These were the only three orders Rory needed to give to his men. There was no shouting of "Easy sta'board!" or "Easy port!" as when a lubber is coxswain.

Next moment they were all on deck, shaking hands with the skipper and his mate. The latter remained on deck; he didn't care for the company of "quality;" besides, he had to loosen sails, and have all ready to get in anchors at a minute's notice and put out to sea.

The skipper of the *Canny Scotia* had contrived another seat at table, so there was no such thing as crowding, and the dinner passed off entirely to his satisfaction. The pea-soup was excellent, neither too thick nor too thin, and the sippets done to a turn. Then came what Silas called the whitebait.

"Which is only my fun, gentlemen," he observed, "seeing that they are bigger than sprats. Where do I get

---

* In Greenland these are quite easily seen by the naked eye.

them? Hey? Why, turn up a piece of pancake ice, and there they be sticking in the clear in hundreds, like bees in a honeycomb, and nothing out but their bits of tails."

"It is curious," said Rory. "How do they bore the holes, I wonder?"

"That, young gentleman," replied Silas, "I can't say, never having seen them at work. Maybe they melt the ice with their noses; they can't make the holes with their teeth, their bows are too blunt and humble like. Perhaps, after all, they find the holes ready-made, and just go in for warmth. Queer, ain't it?"

"I believe," said Rory, "they belong to the natural order *Malacopterygii*."

"The what?" cried Ralph; "but, pray, Row, don't repeat the word. Think of the small bones; and McFlail isn't here, you know."

"Of which," continued Rory, "the *Clupeidæ*" [Ralph groaned] "form one of the families, belonging to which are the herring, the sardine, the whitebait, and sprat."

"They may be sprats, or they may be young sperm-whales, for anything I care," said Ralph; "but I do know they are jolly good eating. Captain Grig, may I trouble you again?"

With the pudding came the green ginger, that Ralph was so anxious to taste.

"The peculiarity of that pudding, gentlemen, is this," said Silas—"eaten hot it *is* a pudding, eaten cold it is a bun. The peculiarity of the green——"

What more he meant to have said will never be known, for at that moment the *Canny Scotia* gave an angry cant to leeward, and away—extemporised seat and all—went the skipper down upon the sta'board bulkheads; the coal-scuttle, the water-bucket, and the big armchair followed suit, and there was consequently some little confusion, and a speedy break-up of the dinner-party.

McBain's boat was called away, for the ship had slipped

her ice-anchors, and was drifting seaward, with the wind roaring wildly through rigging and cordage. The gale had come upon them as sudden as a thunderclap. Good-byes were hastily said, and away pulled the gig. She was in the lee of the ice and partly sheltered, otherwise they never would have regained the *Arrandoon*. As it was, the men were almost exhausted when they got alongside.

Her anchors were well fast, and her cables were strong; there was little fear of dragging for some time, so the order was given to at once get up steam, and that, too, with all speed, for the force of the wind seemed to increase almost momentarily. On the *Arrandoon's* decks you could scarcely have seen anything, for the snow blew blindingly from off the ice; there was little to be heard either, for the shrill, harsh whistling of the wind. Men flitted hither and thither like uneasy ghosts, making things snug, and battening down the principal hatches; on the bridge, dimly descried, was McBain, speaking-trumpet under arm, and beside him Stevenson.

Down below, from fore to aft, everybody was engaged. In the stoke-hole they were busy, and making goodly use of the American hams; in the engine-room the engineers were looking well to their gear, with bits of greasy "pob" in their hands, humming songs as they gave a rub here and a rub there, though to what end or purpose I couldn't tell you, but evidently on the best of terms with themselves and their beautiful engine. The doctor was busy stowing his bottles away, and the steward was making the pantry ship-shape, and our heroes themselves were stowing away all loose gear in their cabins. Presently they entered the saloon again, where was Freezing Powders making the cockatoo's cage fast with a morsel of lanyard.

"Here's a pretty to-do!" the bird was saying, half choking on a billful of hemp. "Call the steward!—call the steward!—call the steward!"

"You jus' console yourse'f," said the boy, "and don't

take sich big mou'fuls o' hemp. Mind, you'll be sea sick p'esently."

" De-ah me ! "

" Yes, ye will—dreffully sea-sick. Den you wants to call de steward plenty quick."

One ice-anchor came on board ; the other—the bow—was cut adrift as the ship's stern swung round seaward. Almost at the same moment an explosion was heard close alongside, as if one of the boilers had burst. The great berg to which they had been anchored had parted company with the floe, and was evidently bent on going to sea along with the *Arrandoon*.

Once they were a little way clear of the ice they could look about them, the snow no longer blowing over the vessel. The scene was peculiar, and such as can only be viewed in Greenland under like circumstances.

The whole field of ice, as far as it was visible, was a smother of whirling drift ; the lofty cone of Jan Mayen, which though miles to the south'ard and west, had been so well-defined an object against the blue of the sky, was now blurred and indistinct, and the grey, driving clouds every now and again quite hid the top of it from view. All along the edge of the pack the snow was being blown seaward like smoke, or like the white spray on the rocks where billows break. The eastern horizon was a chaos of dark, shifting billows, as tall as houses, and foam-tipped ; but near by the ice, although the wind blew already with the force of a gale, and the surface of the water was churned into froth, there was not a wave bigger than you would see on a farmer's mill-pond.

What a pity it seemed to leave this comparatively smooth water and steam away out into the centre of yonder mighty conflict 'twixt wind and wave. But well every one on board knew that to remain where they were was but to court destruction, for the noise that proceeded from the ice-fields told them the pack was breaking up. Ay, and bergs were already forging ahead of them, and surrounding them. Ere they were a mile from the floes they found this out, and the danger from the floating masses of ice was very real indeed. Every minute the pieces were hurtled with all the force of the waves against the sturdy vessel's weather-side, threatening to stave her; nor could McBain, who never left the bridge until the vessel was well out to sea, avoid at times stemming the bergs that appeared ahead of him. For often two would present themselves at one time, and one must be stemmed—the smaller of the twain; for to have come in collision bow on, would have meant foundering.

But at length the danger was past as far as the ice was concerned, though now the seas were mountains high, and of Titanic force; so after an hour or two the *Arrandoon* lay to, and having seen the lights all properly placed, and extra hands put on the look-out—having, in fact, done everything a sailor could do for the safety of his ship, McBain came down below.

In shining oil-skins and dripping sou'-wester, he looked like some queer sea-monster that had just been caught and hauled on board.

He looked a trifle more human, however, when the steward had marched off with his outer garments.

"Is she snug?" asked Allan.

"Ay, lads, as snug as she is likely to be to-night," replied McBain; "but she doesn't like it, I can tell you, and the gale seems increasing to hurricane force. How is the glass, Rory?"

"Not so very low," said Rory; "not under twenty-nine degrees."

"But concave at the top?"

"Yes, sir."

"Well, well," said McBain, "content yourselves, boys, for I think we'll have days of it. I for one don't want to see much more of the ice while this blow lasts. But what a splendid fire you have! Steward, mind you put on the guard last thing to-night."

"Why the guard?" asked Rory.

"Because," explained McBain, "I feel certain that many a good ship has been burned at sea by the fire falling out of the grate; a wave or a piece of ice hits her on the bows, the fire flies out of the stove, no one is below, and so, and so——"

"Yes," said Ralph, "that is very likely, and pray don't let us speak of anything very dreadful to-night. List! how the wind roars, to be sure! But to change the subject—Peter."

"Ay, ay, sir."

"Is supper ready?"

"Very nearly, sir."

"Well, tell Seth to come, and Magnus."

"Ho! ho!" said McBain, "that's it, is it?"

"What a comfort on a night like this," Allan remarked, "it is to be shipmates with two such fellows as Ray and Row, the epicure and the poet—the one to cater for the corporeal, the other for the mental man."

The ship was pitching angrily, dipping her bows deep down under the solid seas and raising them quickly again, but not neglecting to ship tons of water every time, which found its way aft, so that down in the saloon they could hear it washing about overhead and pouring past the ports into the sea.

"Steady, sir, steady," cried Magnus, entering the saloon. He was speaking to Seth, who had preceded him. He didn't walk in, he came in head first, and was now lying all his length on the saloon floor.

But Rory and Allan lifted him tenderly up again and seated him on the couch, amid such remarks as, "No bones broken, I do hope," "Gently does it, Seth, old man," "Have you really left your sea-legs forward?" "Call the steward," the last remark being the cockatoo's.

"I reckon," said the old trapper, rubbing his elbows and knees, "there ain't any bones given way this time, but that same is more chance than good management."

After supper—which was of Ralph's own choosing, I need not say more—a general adjournment was made to the after-cabin, or snuggery, and here every one adopted attitudes of comfort around the blazing stove, in easy-chairs, on sofas, or on rugs and skins on the deck; there they sat, or lounged, or lay. The elders had their pipes, the youngsters coffee. But with the pitching and rolling of the ship it was not very easy either to sit, or lounge, or lie, nor was it advisable to leave the coffee in the cup for any length of time; nevertheless everybody was happy, for wondrous little care had they on their minds. Oh! how wild and tempestuous the night was, and how madly the seas leapt and tossed around them! But they had a ship they could trust, and, better by far, a Power above them which they had learned to put confidence in.

Seth, to-night, was in what Ralph called fine form. His stories of adventure, told in his dry, droll, inimitable way, were irresistible. De Vere's face never once lacked a smile on it; he loved to listen though he could not talk.

Old Magnus also had some queer tales to tell, his relation of them affording Seth breathing space. Several times during the evening Rory played, and the doctor tooted, as he called it.

Thus merrily and pleasantly sped the time—every one doing his best to amuse his neighbours—until eight bells rang out, then all retired.

It is on such a night as this that the soundest sleep visits the pillow of your thorough sailor—the roar of the wind overhead, the rocking of the ship, and the sound of the waves close by the ear, all conduce to sweetest slumber.

There was little if any improvement in the weather next day, nor for several days; but cold and stormy though it was, to be on the bridge, holding on—figuratively speaking

—by the eyelids, was a glorious treat for our sailor heroes. The masts bent like fishing-rods beneath the force of the gale. At times the good ship heeled until her yard-ends ploughed the waves, and if a sea struck her then, the spray leapt higher than the main truck, and the green water made a clean breach over her. On the second day the clouds were all blown away, but the wind retained its force, and the waves their power and magnitude. Every wave threatened to come in board, and about one out of ten did. Those that didn't went singing astern, or got in under the *Arrandoon*, and tossed her all they could. The frost was intense, and in some way or other, I think, accounted for the strange singing noise emitted by those waves that went past without breaking. But it was when one great sea followed swiftly on the heels of another that the good ship suffered most, because she would probably be down by the head when she received salute number two. It was thus she had her bulwarks smashed, and one good boat rent into match-wood and cast away.

It was no easy task to reach the bridge, nor to rush therefrom and regain the saloon companion. You had to watch the seas, and were generally pretty safe if you made use of arms and legs just after one or two big waves had done their worst; but Allan once, and Rory three times, were washed into the scuppers, and more bruised than they cared to own. Ralph seldom came on deck, and the doctor just once got his head above the companion; for this piece of daring he received a sea in the teeth, which he declared nearly cut his head off. He went down below to change his clothes, and never came up again.

On the third day, in the dog watch, the wind fell, and the sea went down considerably. Had the gale blown from the east, the sea would have been in no such hurry to go down, but it had continued all the time to blow steadily from off the ice. What a strange sight the *Arrandoon* now presented! She was a ship of glass and snow. Funnel, masts, and rigging were, or seemed to be, composed of frosted crystal. The funnel, Rory declared, looked like a stalactite from "the cave of a thousand winters." Her bows were lumbered with ice feet thick, and from stem to stern there was no more liveliness in the good *Arrandoon* than there is in a Dutch collier.

As soon as the wind fell a man was sent up aloft, and the order was given,

"All hands clear ship of ice."

But hark! there is a shout from the crow's-nest.

"Large ship down to leeward, sir, apparently in distress."

CHAPTER XVII.

THE STORM—THE "CANNY SCOTIA" IN DISTRESS—RUM, MUTINY, ANARCHY, AND DEATH—SAVED—ADVENTURE WITH A SHE-BEAR—CAPTURE OF THE YOUNG.

HAS it not been said that the greatest pleasure on earth is felt on the sudden surcease of severe pain? I am inclined, though, to doubt the truth of this statement, and I think that nothing can equal the feeling of quiet, calm joy that is instilled into the heart on the instant one is plucked from the jaws of impending death. When the King of Terrors comes speedily, while the blood is up and the heart beating high, as he does to those who fall in the field of battle, his approach does not seem anything like so terrible as when he lags in his march towards his victim. One needs to have a hope that leads his thoughts beyond this world, to be brave and calm at such a moment.

When the *Canny Scotia* slipped her ice anchors and was driven out to sea, to encounter all the fury of the gale that had so suddenly sprung up, she had not the advantages of the *Arrandoon*. She had no steam power, nor was she so well manned. She could therefore only scud under bare poles, or lie to with about as much canvas spread as would make a mason's apron.

Silas didn't mean to be caught napping, however, and, as quickly as he could, he got the tarpaulins down over the hatches, took in all spare canvas, and did all he could for the best. Alas! the best was bad. The *Scotia* made fearful weather, and twenty-four hours after it had come on to blow, she had not a topmast standing, two of her best boats had been carried away, her bulwarks looked like a badly-built farmer's paling, and, worse than all, she was stove amidships on the weather side and under the water-line. When this last disaster was reported to Silas Grig, he called all hands to "make good repairs," and stem the flow of the water, which was rushing inboard like a mill-stream through the ugly hole in the vessel's side. Had it been calm weather, this might have been done effectually enough, but, under the circumstances, it was simply an impossibility. Everything was done, however, that could be done, but still the seas poured in at every lurch to windward.

Then it was "All hands to the pumps." The men worked in relays, and cheerily, too, and for a time the water was sent overboard faster than it came in, albeit there were times when the green seas poured over the ship like mountain cataracts. But after some hours, either through the men flagging, or from the hole in the ship's side getting larger, the water in the hold began to gain rapidly on them.

"Bring up black-jack!" cried the skipper to the steward, "and we'll splice the main-brace."

"Now hurrah! lads!" he exclaimed, addressing the men after a liberal allowance of rum had been handed round. "Hurrah! heave round again. The storm has about spent itself and the sea is going down. We can keep her afloat if we try. Hurrah then, hurrah!"

"Hurrah!" echoed the men in response, and, flushed with artificial strength, they once more set themselves with redoubled energy to keep the water under. There was no danger now from ice. The piece that had wrought them so much mischief was about the last they had seen. So for a time all went well, and if the water did not decrease it certainly did not rise. An hour went by, then a deputation came aft to beg for more rum, and the fate of this vessel, like that of many another lost at sea, seemed sealed by the awful drink curse.

"It's hardly judicious," said Silas to his mate, "but I suppose they must have it."

Ah! Silas Grig, it was not judicious to serve them with the first allowance. When hard work is over and finished, and men are worn out and tired, then is the time, if ever, to splice the main-brace; but when work has to be done that needs clear heads, and when danger is all around a ship, the farther away the rum is the better.

They had it, though, and presently they were singing as they pumped—singing, but not working half so hard as before. Then even the singing itself ceased; they were getting tired and drowsy, and yet another allowance of rum was asked and granted.

The water rose higher in the hold.

When the men heard this report they would work no more. With one accord they desisted from their labours, and a deputation of the boldest found their way aft.

"It is no use Captain Silas Grig," they said, addressing their skipper; "the ship is going down, and we mean to die jolly. Bring up the rum."

"This is mutiny," cried the captain, pulling out a revolver. "I'll shoot the first man dead that dares go down that cabin staircase."

"Captain," said one of the men, stepping forward, "will you let me speak to you? I've nothing but friendly feelings towards you.'

"Well," replied the skipper, "what have you to say?"

"This," said the man; "let us have no murder. Put up your shooting-irons. It is all in vain. The men *will* have rum. Hark! d'ye hear that?"

"I heard a knocking below," said the skipper. "What does it mean?"

Before the man could reply there was a wild shout from the half-deck.

"It means," replied the man, "that the men have broken through the cabin bulkheads and supplied themselves."

"Then Heaven help us!" said poor bewildered Silas.

He staggered to the seat beside the skylight and sat down, holding on by the brass glass-guards.

A moment after the mate joined him.

"You haven't been drinking, matie," said Silas, glancing gloomily upwards, " have you ?"

" No, sir, nor the second mate, nor the steward, nor the spectioneer," was the mate's reply. "Give us your hand, sir. We've had words together often; let us forgive each other now. God bless you, sir, and if die together we must, we won't die like pigs, at all events."

There was anarchy forward, anarchy and wild revelry, and cruel brawls and fighting, but the five men aft stuck together, and tried to comfort each other, though there was hardly a hope in their hearts that their vessel would be saved. A long evening wore away, a kind of semi-darkness settled over the sea, but this short night soon gave place once more to day. Then down forward all was quiet; the revellers were sleeping the stertorous sleep of the drunkard.

But the wind had fallen considerably, and the seas had gone down; the broken waves no longer sung in the frosty air, but the ship rolled like a half-dead thing in the trough of the sea. She was water-logged.

With infinite difficulty the mates, with the steward's assistance, stretched more canvas, while the captain took the helm. She heeled over to it, and looked as if she hardly cared to right again. But this brought the hole in her side into view. Then they got heavy blankets up, and, working as they had never worked before, they managed in an hour and a half to staunch the leak from the outside.

Hope began to rise in their hearts, and, at the bidding of the skipper, the steward went below and brought up a large tin of preserved soup.

"Ah! men," said poor Silas, "this is better than all the rum in the world."

And it was, for it gave them strength and heart. They went away down below next to the galley and half-deck, and tried to rouse some of the men. They found five of them stark and stiff, and from the others came nothing but groans and oaths.

So they went to the pumps themselves, and worked away for hours for dear life itself.

Oh! what a joyful sight it was for them when, in answer to their signal of distress, they saw the good ship *Arrandoon* coming steaming down towards them.

Then the grim raven Death, who had been hovering over the seemingly doomed ship, flapped his ragged wings and flew slowly away.

They were saved!

Oil was pumped upon the water between the *Arrandoon* and *Scotia*, to round off the curling, comb-like peaks of the waves, and a boat was lowered from the steamer and sent to the assistance of the distressed vessel.

The ship was pumped out, and next day, the weather becoming once more fine, she was towed towards the island of Jan Mayen, and made fast to a floe. She was next heeled over and the repairs completed. The *Arrandoon* spared them a few spars, and plenty of willing hands to hoist them, so that in a few days the Greenland sealer was as strong as ever.

Silas Grig was a very happy man now. The unfortunate wretches who had flown to meet their fate were sunk in the dark waters of the sea of ice, but this rough but kindly-hearted skipper never let one upbraiding word escape him towards his men, and the men knew they were forgiven, and liked their skipper none the less for his extreme forbearance.

"Do you know what I have done?" said Silas to McBain.

"You have forgiven your men, haven't you?" replied McBain.

"Ay, that I have," said Silas, "but I have staved every cask of rum on board, and black-jack is thrown overboard."

All along the west coast or shore of the island of Jan Mayen our heroes, on their re-arrival there, found that the water was comparatively clear, the bergs having been driven away out to sea on the wings of the wind, so that by breaking the light bay-ice the boats could approach quite close to the snow-clad cliffs.

Our three boys—for boys we must continue to call them for the sake of the days of "auld lang syne"—were glad to set foot on shore again, and with them went old Seth and the doctor. Freezing Powders was also invited, but his reply was, "No, sah! thank you all de same. But only dis chile not want anoder bad winter wid a yellow bear!"

"'Adventure' you mean, don't you?" said Rory.

"Dat is him, sah!" replied the boy. "I not want no more dancin' for de dear life.

"But the yellow bear was killed, Freezing Powders," persisted Allan.

"But him's moder not killed," said the lad, with round, open eyes. "You seem to hab 'tirely forgotten dat, sah; and p'raps de moder is much worse dan de son."

So they went without him. Well armed were they, and provisioned for a day at all events.

Somewhat to their surprise, they found smoke issuing from the once deserted huts, while a whole pack of dogs started up from where they had been lying and attempted to bar their progress. But the same two hardy chiefs of the Eskimos whom we last saw speeding along over the sea of ice, with the snow-wind roaring around them, came forth, quieted the dogs, and bade them kindly welcome.

In their broken English they told them the tale of their adventurous journey across the pack from the far-off western land of Greenland, and of the narrow escape they had had from the violence of the sudden storm.

Then they led the way, not into one of the small huts, but into the large central one.

"We are making him fit and warm and good," they explained, "for our big 'Melican masta. He come directly. To-day we see his boat not far off—a two-stick boat, with plenty mooch sail."

The "two-stick boat" which the chiefs referred to was a saucy little Yankee yacht, that on this very morning was cruising off the island.

Our heroes spent several hours in the hut, seated by the blazing logs, listening delightedly to a description of the strange country these chiefs called their home—a country that few white men have ever yet visited, and where certainly none have ever wintered.

But I cannot repeat all the strangers told them about the manners and customs of their countrymen, the dress of the men and women, their fishing and hunting exploits, their fierce though petty wars with other tribes, and the wonderful life they lead throughout the summer and during the long, drear, sunless season of winter.

"Ah!" said Rory, with a bit of a sigh, "I do like to hear these men talk about their wild land in the Far West. We must come again and make them tell us a deal more. I've half a mind to set out with them when they return, and live among them for some months. I say, Ray, wouldn't it be glorious to go surging over the ice-fields drawn by a hundred fleet-footed hounds?"

"Drawn by a hundred hounds!" cried Allan, laughing. "Draw it mild, Rory."

"Well," said Rory, "more or less, you know."

"Besides," Ralph put in, "these are not hounds, Rory; there is more of the wolf about them than the hound."

"Och, botheration!" replied Rory; "you're too particular. But if I went with these men, and dwelt among their tribes for a time, then I'd go to press when I came back to old England."

"A book of adventure?" said Allan.

"Ah, yes!" said Rory; "a book, if you please, but not dry-as-dust prose my boys! I'd write an epic poem."

Talking thus, away they went on an exploring expedition, Rory riding the high horse, building any number of castles in the air, and giving the reins to his wonderful imagination.

"I reckon, Mr. Rory," said Seth, "that you'd make the fortune of any publisher that liked to take you up. You try New York, I guess that'd suit you; and, if you like, you shall write the life of old trapper Seth."

"Glorious!" cried Rory; "'A Life in the Forests of the Far West.' Hurrah! I'll do it! You wait a bit. Look, look! What is that?"

"It's a white fox," said Seth, bowling the animal over before the others had time to draw a bead on it.

But that white fox, with a few loons, and five guillemots—which, by the way, when skinned, are excellent eating—were all they bagged that day.

McBain and Stevenson had better luck though, they had seen a gigantic bear prowling around among the rough ice beneath the cliffs, and had called away a boat and gone after it.

"O! sah!" cried Freezing Powders, running up to McBain as he was going over the side. "Don't go, sah! I can see de yellow bear's moder and two piccaninnies on de ice. She is one berry bad woman. She make you dance to please de piccaninnies, den she gobble your head off. Don't you go, sah! You not look nice widout a head. Dat am my impression, sah."

There was nothing of the sensational about McBain's adventure with the bear, but something of the sad. The captain of the *Arrandoon* was not the man to take the life of even a bear while in company of her young ones, but he well knew how terrible and how bloodthirsty such an animal is, and how cunning in her ferocity. He shuddered as he thought of Allan or Rory heedlessly passing the cave or crevasse in the rocks where she lay concealed, and being pounced upon and dragged in to be torn limb from limb. So he determined she must die.

Once landed, they almost immediately sighted her, and gave chase. Alone she might have escaped; but in dread terror the young ones leapt on her back and thus hampered her movements.* She then turned fiercely at bay, coming swiftly on to the attack, bent upon a fearful vengeance if she could only accomplish it.

"Stand by, Stevenson," cried McBain, dropping on one knee, "to fire if I don't kill at once."

The monster held her head low as she advanced, and a less experienced hunter would have made this the target. McBain knew better. He aimed at the lower part of the neck, and the bear fell pierced through the great artery of the heart. Yet so near had he allowed the animal to come before firing, that Stevenson, trembling for his safety, had brought his own rifle to the shoulder.

Then those two poor young bears stood up to fight for their dead dam, giving vent to growls of grief and rage.

"We can take them alive, sir," said Stevenson. "Come along, lads." This last sentence was addressed to the boat's crew. "Come along quick, and bring the ropes."

Had old Seth been there, these young Bruins would soon have been lassoed. But McBain's men were not over expert at such work. They did manage to rope one in a few minutes, but the other gave them a deal of trouble—sport one man erroneously called it. He invariably flew at the man who tried to throw the rope, and the man invariably made his feet his friends, thus giving another man a chance to try his skill. If he failed he had to run next.

---

* She-bears with young ones are easily got up to and killed on this account.

and so on until at long last one more adroit or more fortunate than his fellow succeeded in throwing the lasso over the young bear's neck, and brought it half strangled to the ice.

"A present for you, Captain Grig," cried McBain, pulling alongside the *Canny Scotia* with his double capture.

Silas was delighted when he saw the two live bears. "Heaven bless you, sir!" he exclaimed. "Why, sir, they'll fetch forty pounds each in the London Zoo. Forty pounds, sir! Think o' that. Eighty pounds for the two o' them. Keep my little wife and all the family for a month o' Sundays. Hurrah! matie, luck's turned."

CHAPTER XVIII.

A NEW ARRIVAL—THE DOGS—TRAPPER SETH BECOMES KENNEL-MAN—PREPARATIONS FOR A GREAT SEAL HUNT—THE GREENLAND BEAR.

ON the very day that McBain shot the great she-bear —for it was one of the largest that ever fell before a sportsman's gun—on that day, and on the afternoon of that day, just as our heroes were about to leave the island and re-embark on the *Arrandoon*, there landed from off that saucy "little two-stick yacht" one of the tallest Yankees that ever stepped in boots.

Seth squeezed the hand of this countryman of his till tears sprang into the stranger's eyes; and they were not tears of emotion, nor sentiment either, but of downright pain.

"I say, siree!" cried the new-comer, shaking his hand and looking at the tips of his fingers, "patriotism and brotherly love are both beautiful things in their way, but when it comes to squeezing the blood out from under a fellow's finger-nails, then I say, bother brotherly love."

"I'm proud to meet you, sir," exclaimed Seth, "let us shake hands once more."

"Never a shake, old man," said the stranger; "let us admire each other at a respectable distance. But come, gentlemen all," he continued, turning to the others, "you ain't going on board just yet. Come up with me to my house. I daresay you've been there already; but come back and break bread with Nathaniel Cobb, sometimes called the Little Wonder, because I ain't much more'n seven feet high."

Nat Cobb's boat's crew were Norwegians every one of them, short, somewhat squat, fair-haired fellows, but as active and bustling as a corresponding number of well-bred fox-terriers. A couple of them were moving on ahead now, with an immense basket between them.

"That's the dinner," said the Little Wonder; "and you'll find there's enough for all hands, too."

"Well, gentlemen," Nat said, when everybody had done justice to the good things placed before them, "let us drink each other's healths in a cup of fragrant mocha, for that's the wine for Greenland weather. Gentlemen, I look around me at your smiling faces, and I pledge you and bid you welcome to my island of Jan Mayen."

"Hallo!" thought Rory "*your* island"

"Yes, gentlemen," continued Nat, looking as if he really read Rory's thoughts, "*my* island. Six months and more ago I annexed it, and to-morrow once again the stars and stripes will proudly flutter from yonder flag-staff, and the bird o' freedom will soar over this wild mountain land."

Apart from his queer, half-boastful speech, Nat Cobb was a very agreeable companion.

He was very frank at all events.

After looking at Rory for the space of half a minute, he suddenly stretched out his hand.

"I like you," he said, "muchly, and I like you all. It from men like you that the mightiest republic in the world has been built. But why don't you speak more, Rory, as your messmates call you?"

"Ach! troth!" said Rory, "and sure I'm driving *tandem* with the thinking."

And you're wondering," said Nat, "where a piece of elongated mortality like myself stretches himself of a night on board the *Highflier?*"

"Seeing," replied Rory, laughing, "that you're about as long as the keel, and maybe a bit longer, I may well wonder that same; and unless you lean against a mast, I don't quite see how you can stretch yourself."

"Well, young sir, I'll tell you how I do it. I double up into four, and lie on my back! that is how it's done."

The Little Wonder went off with our party to the *Arrandoon;* and as Yankees are ever ready to trade, he had not been long on board when McBain had purchased from him a dozen of his best dogs. They were to be kept until the ship returned from a week's sport among the old seals, then taken on board just before the *Arrandoon* left for the extreme north. Old Seth was duly told off to superintend the erection of kennels, forward near the bows, and old Seth was in his glory in consequence.

"I'll feel myself o' some kind o' use now," he said. "Kennel-man in ordinary to the *Arrandoon*, a free house and victuals found, I guess it ain't half a bad sitivation."

About a week after this—the Greenland sealer having been made as good as new again—the Jan Mayen fleet sailed away from the island, and directed its course about north-and-by-east. First on the line went the noble *Arrandoon*, sailing, not steaming, for a nice beam wind was blowing; next came the *Canny Scotia* with her tall, tapering spars; and the saucy *Highflier*, with her fore-and-aft canvas, brought up the rear.

Nathaniel Cobb was Arctic meteorologist to a private company of American scientists, but his time was pretty much his own, and he didn't mind spending a week or a fortnight of it among the old seals. He wanted a skin or two anyhow, he said, to make a warm carpet for his "house," and some oil to burn for fuel, but promised that everything beyond what he really wanted which happened to fall to his gun should be given to Silas.

Silas Grig was never happier in his life than he was now.

Luck had indeed turned, fortune was about to favour him for once in a way. His would be a bumper ship, full to the hatches, with a bing of skins on deck that he wouldn't be able to find room for below. And when he returned to Peterhead, flags would fly and bands would play, and his little wife and he would live happy ever after.

McBain wanted to show his young companions a little genuine sport, and at the same time do a good turn to honest Silas, by helping him to a voyage; while the former, on the other hand, were all excitement and bustle, for the *Arrandoon* was about to be transformed into a sealer; and the idea being such a perfectly new one, was correspondingly appreciated.

The little fleet kept well together; it would not have suited them to part company, although, even on a wind, without the aid of her boilers, the *Arrandoon* could easily have shown her consorts a pair of clean heels. The doctor himself was led away with enthusiasm, and longed to draw a bead, as Seth called it, on a bear itself. He had chosen a rifle from the box, cleaned and polished it, and called it his own.

"I've never shot a wild beast," he explained to Rory, "but, man, if I get the chance, I'll have a try."

"Bravo!" cried Rory, "and you're sure to get the chance, you know."

The ice was loose, although the weather was clear and very frosty. There was a heaving motion in the main pack that prevented the bergs from getting frozen together, but for all that the fleet kept well clear of it, for fear of getting beset. Patches of old seals might, it is true, have been found far in among the ice, but the risk was too great to run, so McBain kept to the outside edge, and the others followed his example.

Silas Grig was invited on board the *Arrandoon*; and proud he was when the captain told him that he could choose five-and-twenty of his best men, and superintend their preparations for going after the seals. The third mate might be one of the number, but neither Stevenson nor Mitchell was to be allowed to go, although McBain did not object to these officers, or even the engineers, having a day's sport now and then.

It was a glorious morning—for Greenland—when Captain McBain called all hands, in order that Silas might choose the men who were to assist him in making his fortune. The sun was shining as brightly as ever it does in England, and there wasn't too much wind to blow the cold through and through one. Either of the officers might have passed for old men, if white hairs make men look old, for their hair, whiskers, and moustachios were coated with hoar-frost ice. Our heroes had just finished breakfast, all of them having had a cold sea-bath to give them a glow before they sat down, and were now walking briskly up and down the quarter-deck, talking merrily and laughing.

The *Scotia* had her foreyard aback, and the *Arrandoon* had also stopped her way, and yonder was Silas in his boat coming rapidly over the rippling water towards the steamer, the skipper himself standing like a gondolier and steering with an oar in true whaler fashion.

"Now, lads," cried Silas, when the men of the *Arrandoon* lay aft in obedience to orders. "Your're a fine lot, I must say; every man Jack o' ye is better than the other; but I just want the men that have been to the country before. The men among ye that know a seal-club from a toastin'-fork, or a lowrie-tow * from a bell-rope, just elevate a hand, will ye?"

No less than fifteen gloved hands were waved aloft. Silas was delighted, and did not take long to choose the remaining ten.

"You'll go on the ice by twos, you know, men," he con-

* Lowrie-tow = the rope with which the men drag the skins to the ship's side.

tinued, "and when one o' ye tumbles into the water, why, the other'll simply pull him out. Nothing easier."

All these hands were to be clubsmen and draggers, while "the guns," as they were called, comprized the following: Ralph, Rory, Allan, Sandy the surgeon, De Vere the aëronaut, Seth trapper, and the third mate, seven in all, and warranted to give a good account of the seals, and keep the men steadily on drag if the sport was anything like good.

Having made these preliminary arrangements, the men were dismissed, and Silas spent the rest of the day forward with old Ap the carpenter and the sail-maker. And very busy the whole four of them were, too, for three dozen daggers or seal-knives had to be fitted with sheaths of leather, and belts to go round the men's waists, and three dozen lowrie-tows, with the same number of seal-clubs, had to be got ready.

I saw the other day an engraving of a sealing scene in Greenland, evidently done by an artist who had never been in the Arctic regions in his life, and who had therefore trusted to his imagination, which had led him far from the truth. In this picture there is a ship under canvas: error No. 1, for sealers always clue or brail up before the men go over the side. The ice is tall and pinnacled: error No. 2, for the ice the old seals lie on is either flat or hummocky. The men on the ice are leaping madly from berg to berg and clubbing *old* seals: error No. 3, for unless old seals get positively frozen out of the water by the pieces becoming fast together, they will not wait to be clubbed. You may catch a weasel asleep, but never an old seal. Lastly, in this picture, the men are wielding clubs that have evidently been borrowed from some gymnasium: this constitutes error No. 4, for seal-clubs are nothing like these. They are more like an ancient battle-axe; the shaft is about four or five feet long and made of strong, tough wood, while through the top of this terrible weapon is run the part that does the execution—a square piece of iron or steel sharpened at one end, hammer-like at the other, and nearly a foot long. With this instrument a strong man has been known to lay a Greenland bear dead with one blow. No one of course would dare to attack a bear armed with a club alone, but instances have occurred where the bear has been the aggressor, and where the man had to defend himself as best he could.

One word parenthetically about the great Polar or ice bear. Until I had first seen the carcass of one lying flensed on the ice, I could not have believed that any wild beast could attain such gigantic proportions. The footprints of this monster were as large as an ordinary pair of kitchen bellows. The pastern, or ankle, seemed as wide as the paw, and as near as I could guess about thirty inches round; the forearms and hind-legs were of tremendous strength; so too were the shoulders and loin. An animal like this with one stroke can slay the largest seal in Greenland, and could serve the biggest lion that ever roared in an African jungle precisely the same. As to the voice, it is hardly so fearful as the lion's, but heard, as I heard it one night on the pack, within two yards of me, it is sufficiently appalling, to say the least of it. It is a sort of half-cough, half roar. As trapper Seth described it after his adventure at the cave in Jan Mayen, when little Freezing Powders so nearly lost the number of his mess:

"The roar of a healthy Greenland bear, when the owner of it is so close ye could kick him, is a kind o' confusin'; it shakes your innards considerable, and makes ye think the critter has swallowed the thick end of a thunder-storm and is tryin' to work it up again."

An elephant—a tusker—is no joke when he loses his temper and comes after you, nor is a lion or tiger when he thinks he can do you a mischief, but I would rather face either of them twice over than I would an ice bear with his back up, if I myself were unarmed. I was very young, by the way, when I found myself confronted with my first Greenland bear, but I well remember both what my thoughts were at the time, and what were my feelings. The truth is, I had made the captain promise he would give me a chance to go and fight one of these terrible giants of the ice. He did so in good time, and I confess that as the boat neared the pack—I being in the bows—I suddenly discovered that I was not half so brave as I had previously imagined. The bear did not run away, as I fear I had almost wished that he would. He simply waited, looking at us somewhat inquiringly; and when I landed, all alone, mind you, he came along to meet me, and inquire what I wanted, and I hated him while I envied him for his coolness. He seemed to say, "Why, you're only a boy; just wait till I get alongside you, and I'll show you how I treat boys. I'll turn you inside out." I had to wait. Wild horses couldn't have torn me from the spot, where I had dropped on one knee. Oh! I can assure you, I would have liked, well enough, to run away, but with all the ship's crew looking at me—? No; death rather than live a coward. On came Bruin, much to my disgust; I would have felt as brave as a lion had he only shown me his heels. Then these questions chased each other through my brain: "How near will I let the beggar come before I fire? Shall I hit him on the head, or shoot him in the chest? and, What shall I do if the rifle misses fire?"

Bruin still advanced at a shambling trot. Then I brought my rifle to the shoulder and took aim, glancing along the glimmering barrel till I could only see the *visé* at the end, and immediately beyond that Bruin's yellow breast. Bang, bang! I dare say it really was myself who pulled those two triggers of my double barrelled rifle, but at the time I felt as if I had nothing at all to do with it. Then there was a shout from the boat, and a shout from the ship. Bruin was dead, and I was the hero; but somehow I did not feel that I deserved the praise which I received.

Yet, after all, I daresay I only felt in this encounter as most boys would have felt. Doing anything dangerous is always nasty at first, but when one gains confidence in himself, then is the time one knows

> "That strange joy that warriors feel
> In foemen worthy of their steel."

CHAPTER XIX.

"SILAS GRIG, HIS YARN"—THE WHITE WHALE—AFLOAT ON AN ICEBERG—A DREARY JOURNEY—BEAR ADVENTURES—"THE SEALS! THE SEALS!!"

THERE was only one subject in the whole world that Silas Grig was thoroughly conversant with, and that was the manners and customs of his friends the seals. Had you started talking upon either politics or science, or the state of Europe or Ireland, Silas would have become silent at once. He would have retired within himself; his soul, so to speak, would have gone indoors, and not come out again until you had done. Such was Silas; and he confessed frankly that he had never sung a song nor made a speech in his lifetime. He was a perfect enthusiast while talking about the natural family *Phocidæ*. No naturalist in the world knew half so much about them as Silas. On the evening of the day in which he had chosen his men from the crew of the *Arrandoon*, he was pronounced by both Ralph and Rory to be in fine form. He was full of anecdote, and even tales of adventure, so our heroes allowed him to talk, and indeed encouraged him to do so.

"What!" he cried, his honest, fear-nothing face lighting up with smiles as he eyed Rory across the table after dinner. "Spin you a yarn, d'ye say? ah! boy, and you'll excuse me calling ye a boy. Silas never could tell a story, and I don't suppose he ever had an adventure as signified much to you in his life."

"Never mind," insisted Rory, "you tell us something, and I'll play you that old tune you so dearly love."

"Ah! but," said Silas, " if my matie were only here; now you wouldn't think, gentlemen"—here he glanced round the table as seriously as if contradiction were most unlikely—"you wouldn't think that a fellow like that, with such an ugly chunk of a head, had any sentiment; but he has, though, and he owns the prettiest wife and the smartest family in all Peterhead."

"Look here," cried Rory, "be quiet about your matie. Sure this is what we're waiting for."

He exhibited the doctor's slate as he spoke, and on the back thereof, behold! in large letters, the words,

"SILAS GRIG, HIS YARN."

Silas laughed till his sides ached, his eyes watered, the chair creaked, and the rafters rang. It was a pleasant sight to see. After this he lit up a huge meerchaum pipe, "hoping there was no offence," cleared his throat, turning his face upwards at the pendent compass, as if seeking help there. Then he began,—

"Of the earlier days of Silas Grig little need be said. I daresay he was no better and no worse than other boys. He nearly plagued the life out of his grandmother, and drove three maiden aunts to the verge of distraction, and made any amount of work for the tailor and the shoemaker; and when they couldn't stand him any longer at home they sent him to school, reminding the teacher ere they left him there, that to spare the rod was to spoil the child. The teacher didn't forget that; he whipped me three times a day, drilled me through the English grammar and Grey's arithmetic, then flogged me into Cæsar; and when I translated the passage, 'Cæsar triduas vias fecit' * into 'Cæsar made three roads,' the dominie gave me such a dressing that I followed Cæsar's example—I made three

* "Cæsar made three days' journey."

days' journey due north, and never returned to my maiden aunts, nor the dominie either.

"I found myself now in the heart of what I then took to be a big town, for I wasn't very big myself, you know. It was only Peterhead, after all. I marched boldly down to the docks, and on board a great raking-masted Greenlandman.

"'What use would you be?' inquired the skipper when I told him what I wanted. 'Bless me!' he added, 'you ain't any size at all; the bears would eat you up.'

"'I'll have him,' said the doctor, 'if you'll let me, captain. He can be my lob-lolly-boy and body-guard.'

"And so, gentlemen, from that day to this I've been a sailor o' the northern seas; and there isn't much to be seen in these regions that old Silas hasn't come across, from Baffin's Bay to Kamschatka, from lonely Spitzbergen in the north to Iceland in the south."

"And so you've been in Spitzbergen, have you?" said McBain.

"Why, bless you, yes," replied Silas. "It was there I was in at the death of the great white whale, and a sad day it was for us, I can tell you. He was white with age.* I should think he couldn't have been much under a hundred years old, and just as sly and wary as a hundred and forty foxes all rolled in to one. Many and many a boat had tried to catch him, but he had a way of diving and doubling to avoid the harpoons that some believed was rather more than natural; then when you thought he was miles and miles away, pop! up he would come among the very midst of the boats, and a funny thing it would be if he didn't knock one o' them to smithereens with that tail o' his. We killed him though. Our skipper himself speared him, but it was hours after that before

* Very old whales are sometimes found in the far northern seas covered with a kind of parasite, which gives them a white or light-grey appearance.

he died. And before he died terrible was the revenge he took on his destroyers. Gentlemen, Silas Grig has no language in his vocabulary to describe the vicious wrath of that sea-demon. I think I see him now as he rose to the surface, blowing blood and spray, snorting with fury, with fire seeming to flash out of his little evil eyes. We in the boats thought our last hour had come, as he ploughed down through us. But our hearts stood still with fear and dread when he dashed past us and made for the ship itself. Onward with lightning speed went the brute, leaving a wake astern such as a man-o'-war might have left.

"Our craft—a small brig—was lying with her foreyard aback. She looked as if sleeping on the gently rippling water. No one spoke in the boats, every eye was fixed on our ship—our home, and on the fearful monster advancing to attack her. We could see that the people left on the brig knew the whole extent of their danger, for they seemed all on deck. There were wild shouts, and guns were fired, but nothing availed to avert the catastrophe. Then, oh! the sad, despairing cry that rose to heaven from that doomed ship! It seems to ring in my ears whenever I think of it. The whale struck her right amidships, and she went over and down at once. No soul was saved; and when we rode up to the spot, there was nothing to be seen, and nothing to be heard, save the body of the great white whale, dead, on his side, with the waves lap-lapping against it as it slowly rose and fell.

"For six long, cold, weary days we lived in the open boats, feeding on the flesh of the seals we happened to kill, and quenching our thirst with the snow we gathered from the ice. When we had almost despaired of being saved, for we were far to the nor'ard and east of the usual fishing-grounds, a Norwegian walrus-hunter picked us up, and landed us at last, in mid-winter, on a dreary shore in Lapland. But, gentlemen, that is nothing to what we, the survivors of the ill-fated *Jonathan Grey*, suffered some years afterwards. The ship got 'in the nips' coming out o' the pack. We were crushed just as you might crush an egg-shell between your fingers. Thirty of us embarked upon the very iceberg that had caused our ruin, with two casks of biscuit, and hardly clothes enough to cover us. Then it came on to blow, and, huddled together in the centre of the berg, we were blown out to sea, trying in vain to keep each other warm, and defend ourselves from the cruel cold seas that dashed over us, heavier than lead, more remorseless than the grave. Fifteen days were we on the berg, and every day some one dropped off, ay, and the living seemed to envy the quiet, calm sleep of the dead. A sail in sight at last; and how many of us, think you, were alive to see it? Three! only three! It was a year after this before I was fit to brave the Arctic seas again, and meanwhile I had met my Peggy—my little wife that is. Some difference, you will allow, gentlemen, between Silas Grig afloat on a solitary iceberg in a troubled northern sea, and Silas strolling on the top of a breezy cliff in the bright moonlight of midsummer, with Peggy on his arm, and just as happy as the sea-birds.

"Were these the only times that I was cast away? No—for I lost my ship by fire once in the northern ice of Western Greenland, and it was two whole years before either myself or my messmates placed foot again on British soil. There wasn't a ship anywhere near us, and the nearest settlement was a colony of transported Danes, that lived about three hundred miles south of us. We saved all we could from the burning barque, and that was little enough; then we constructed rough sledges, and tied our food and chattels thereon, and set out upon our long, dreary march. It took us well-nigh two months to accomplish our journey, for the way was a rough one, and the region was wild and desolate in the extreme. It was late in autumn, and the sun shone by day, but his beams were sadly shorn by the falling snow. Five suns in all we could count at times, though four, you know, were merely mirages. We did not all reach the colony; indeed, many succumbed to the fatigue of the march, to frost-bites, and to scurvy; and we laid them to rest in hastily-dug graves, and the snow was their only winding-sheet. It was more than a year before we found a passage back to our own country, and kind though the poor people all were to us, the governor included, we had to rough it, I can tell you. But you see, sailors who choose the Arctic Seas as their cruising-grounds must expect to suffer at times.

"Bears, did you say? Thousands! I've counted as many as fifty at one time on the ice, and I've had a few encounters with them too, myself, though I've known those that have had more. I've known men fight them single-handed, and come off scot free, leaving Bruin dead on the ice. Dickie McInlay fought a bear with a seal-club. You may be sure the duel wasn't of his own proposing; but coming across the ice one day all alone, he rounded the corner of a hummock, and lo! and behold! there was a monstrous bear washing the blood off his chops after eating a seal.

"'Ho! ho!' roared the bear. 'I have dined, but you'll come in handy for dessert. Oho! Waugh, O! oh!'

"Dick was a little bit of a fellow, but his biceps was as big, round, and just as hard as a hawser.

"'If you come an inch nearer me,' cried Dickie, quite undaunted, 'it'll be a dear day's work for ye, Mr. Bruin.'

"The bear crouched for a spring. He never did spring, though; but Dickie did; and he will tell you to this day that he never could understand how he managed to clear the space betwixt himself and the bear so speedily. Then there was a dull thud; Bruin never lifted head again, for the iron of Dickie's club was planted deep into his brain.

"The doctor here," continued Silas, "can tell you what a terribly sharp and deadly weapon of offence a large amputating knife would prove, in the hands of a powerful man, against any animal that ever lived. But the doctor I don't think would care to attack a bear with one."

"Indeed, no," said Sandy; "I would rather be excused."

"But the surgeon of the *North Star* did," said Silas. "I was witness myself to the awful encounter. But the poor surgeon was mad at the time; he had given way to the rum-fever—rum-fiend it should be called. With his knife in his hand he wandered off and away all by himself over the pack. I saw the fight between the bear and him commence, and sent men at once to assist him. When they reached the scene of action they found the huge bear lying dead, stabbed in fifty places at least. The snow for yards around had been trampled down in the awful struggle, and was yellow and red with blood. The doctor lay beside the bear, apparently asleep. I need not tell you that he slept the sleep that knows no waking. The poor fellow's body was crushed to pulp.

"Charles Manning, a spectioneer of the *Good Resolve*, was lying on his back on the sunny side of a hummock, snatching a five-minutes' rest, for it was sealing time, when a bear crept up behind him, more stealthily than any cat could have done. He drew his paw upwards along the poor fellow's body. Only once, mind you, but he left him a mere empty shell.*

"Ah! but, gentlemen, you should have seen a two-mile run I had not five years ago from a bear. Silas himself wouldn't have believed that Silas could have done the distance in double the time. He was coming home all by

---

* The author is relating facts; names only are concealed.

himself, when he burst his rifle firing at a seal, and just at that moment up popped a bear.

"'All alone, are you, Silas?' Bruin seemed to say.

"'Yes,' replied Silas, moving off; 'and I don't want your company either. I know my way, thank you.'

"'Oh, I daresay you do!' says the bear. 'But it will only be friendly like if I see you home. Wait a bit.'

"'Never a wait!' said Silas; and so the race began.

"Of course they saw it from the ship, and sent men to meet me and settle Bruin. Puffed? I should think I was! I lay on my face for five minutes, with no more breath in my old bellows than there is in a dead badger!"

"You've seen the sea-lion, I suppose, Captain Grig?" said Allan.

"I have that!" replied Silas, "and the sea-bear, too, and I don't know which of the two I'd rather meet on the top of a berg, for they are vicious brutes both."

"I've read some very interesting accounts of them," said Allan, "in the encyclopædias."

"So have I," laughed old Silas, "written by men who had never seen them out of the Brighton Aquarium. Pardon me, but you cannot study nature from books.

"Do you know the *Stemmatopus cristatus?*" inquired Rory.

"What ship, my boy?" said Silas, with one hand behind his ear; "I didn't catch the name o' the craft."

"It isn't a ship," said Rory, smiling; "it is a great black seal, with a thing like a kettle-pot over his head."

"Oho!" cried Silas; "now I know. You mean the bladder-nose. Ay, lad! and a dangerous monster he is. A Greenland sailor would almost as soon face a bear as fight one of those brutes single-handed."

"But the books tell us," said Rory, "that, when surprised by the hunter, they weep copiously."

"Bother such books!" said Silas. "What? a bladder-nose weep! Crocodile's tears, then, lad! Why, gentlemen, this monstrous seal is more fierce than any other I know. When once he gets his back up and erects that kettle-pot o' his, and turns round to see who is coming, stand clear, that's what Silas says, for he means mischief, and he's as willing to take his death as any terrier dog that ever barked. I would like to see some o' those cyclopædia-building chaps face to face with a healthy bladder-nose on a bit o' bay ice. I think I know which o' them would do the weeping part of the business."

"Down south here," said McBain—"if we can call it south—the seals have their young on the ice, don't they?"

"You're right, sir," said Silas.

"And where do they go after that?"

"Away back to the far, far north," said Silas. "We follow them up as far as we can. They live at the Pole."

"Ah!" said McBain; "and that, Captain Grig, is in itself a proof that there must be open water around the Pole."

"I haven't a doubt about it!" cried Silas; "and if you succeed in getting there you'll see land and water too, mountains and streams, and maybe a milder climate. Seals were never made to live down in the dark water; they have eyes and lungs, even if they are amphibious. But look! look! look, men, look!"

Silas started up from the table as he spoke, excitement expressed in every lineament of his face. He pointed to the port from which at present the *Canny Scotia* was plainly visible, about half a mile off, on the weather quarter. The men could be seen crowding up the rattlings, and even manning the yards, and wildly waving their caps and arms in the air.

Silas threw the port open wide. "Listen!" he cried.

Our heroes held their breath, while over the water from the distant barque came the sound of many voices cheering. Then the *Arrandoon's* rigging is manned, and glad shout after glad shout is sent them back.

Next moment Stevenson rushed into the cabin. "The seals! the seals!" was all he could say, or rather gasp.

"Are there many?" inquired several voices at once.

"Millions on millions!" cried the mate; "the whole pack is black with them as far as ever we can see from the mainmast head."

CHAPTER XX.

SEAL-STALKING—A GLORIOUS DAY'S SPORT—PIPER PETER AND THE BEAR—A STRANGE DUET—THE SEAL-STALKERS' RETURN.

IT was about midnight on the 24th of April when the seals were sighted. Midnight, and the sun was low down on the horizon, but, for three long months, never more would it set or sink behind the sea of ice. The weather was bright, bracing, beautiful. Not a cloud in the sky, and hardly wind enough to let the ships get well in through the pack, towards the place where the seals lay as thick as bees, and all unconscious of their approaching fate. But the *Arrandoon* got steam up, and commenced forcing her way through the closely packed yet loosely floating bergs, leaving behind her a wake of clear water, which made it easy work for the *Scotia* and the saucy little "two-stick yacht" to follow her example.

My young reader must dismiss from his mind the idea of tall, mountainous, pinnacled icebergs, like those he sees in common engravings. The ice was in heavy pieces, it is true, from forty to sixty or seventy feet square, and probably six feet out of water, with hummocks here and there, and piles of bay ice that looked like packs of gigantic cards, but so flat and low upon the whole, that from the masthead a stretch of snow-clad ice could be seen, spreading westwards and north for many and many a mile.

When even the power of steam failed to force the *Arrandoon* farther into the pack, the ships were stopped, fires were banked and sails were clewed, and all hands prepared for instant action. The men girt their knives and steels around them, and threw their "lowrie-tows" across their broad shoulders, and the officers, dressed in their sealing costume, seized their rifles and shot-belts.

Next moment the bo's'n's shrill pipe sounded out in the still air, and the order was shouted,

"All hands over the side."

In five minutes more the ships were apparently deserted. You wouldn't have heard a sound on board, for few were left but stewards and cooks; while little boy Freezing Powders and his wonderful cockatoo had it all to themselves down in the saloon of the great steamship. The boy was bending down beside his favourite in the corner.

"What's the row? What's the row? What's the row?" the bird was saying.

"I don't know nuffin' more nor you do, Cockie," was the boy's reply; "but it strikes dis chile dat dey have all taken leave of der senses, ebery moder's son of dem. And de captain he have gone up into de crow's-nest, which looks for all de world like a big barrel of treacle, Cockie, and he have shut hisself in der, and nuffin' does he do but wave a long stick wid a black ball at de end of it.* Dat is all de knows; but oh! Cockie, don't you take such drefful big mouf-fuls o' hemp. Supposin' anyting happen to you, Cockie, den I hab nobody to talk to dat fully understand dis chile."

The *Canny Scotia* was moored to the ice so close to the *Arrandoon* that the captains of the respective ships could maintain a conversation without stressing their lungs to any very great extent. Talking thus, each in his own crow's-nest, they looked for all the world like a couple of chimney-sweeps conversing together from rival chimneys. The cooks were not idle in the galleys, they were busy

* The fan with which Greenland captains guide their men in the direction of the seals.

boiling hams and huge joints of beef, and these, when cooked, were taken on deck; for sealing is hungry work, and every time a man brings a drag to the vessel's side he helps himself to a lordly slice and a biscuit.

By-and-by the draggers began to drop in fast enough, each one hauling an immense skin with the fat or blubber attached; and these skins were all hoisted on board the *Scotia*, for all hands were working for Silas. But our heroes had the sport, and, taking it all in all, I do not think there is any sport in the world to compare to that of seal-stalking. Without any of the cowardliness of battue shooting, in which the poor surrounded animals are helpless, and cruelly and mercilessly slain, you have far more excitement, and the sport is not unattended with danger. To be a good seal-stalker you need the limbs of an athlete, the eye of an excellent marksman, and all the stealth and cunning of a tabby cat or a Coromanche Indian. If your nerves are not well strung, or your muscles not like iron, you may fail to leap across the lane of dark water that separates piece from piece; if you do fail and are not speedily helped out, the current may drag you beneath the bergs, or those dreadful sharks, that seldom are absent where blood is being spilled on the sea of ice, may seize and pull you down to a fearful death; if you are not a good shot, your seals will get away, for your bullet *must* pierce either neck or head; and, lastly, if you are not cunning, if you do not stalk with stealth, your seals will escape with the speed of lightning.

On warm, sunny days the seals lie close and sleep soundly, but they always have their sentries set. Kill the sentry, and many others are at your mercy; miss him, or merely wound him, and he gives the alarm *instanter*, and all the rest jump helter-skelter into the sea, according you a beautiful view of their tail-ends, which you don't find very advantageous in the way of making a bag.

A good sealer, like a good skirmisher, takes advantage

of every bit of cover, and many a death-blow is dealt from the shelter of a lump of loose ice.

The gunners to-day, as they usually do, went on after the seals in skirmishing order, in one long line, each taking a breadth of about seventy or one hundred yards.

It was an hour past midnight before they left the ships. When it was nine in the morning there was a kind of general assembly of the riflemen to breakfast, behind a large square hummock of packed bay ice,* and only the very oldest among them could believe that it was so late. Why, to our own particular heroes it seemed scarcely an hour since they had left their ship, so great is the excitement of seal-stalking. But Ralph and Rory and Allan had done so well, and had managed to lay so many splendid seals dead on every piece of ice, that they earned high encomiums from the mate of the *Canny Scotia;* and even the doctor hadn't shot amiss, and proud was he to be told so.

"But, my dear sirs," said Sandy, "I'd like to know why a good surgeon shouldn't be a good sportsman. Don't you know that the great Liston himself was sometimes summoned to an operation at the hospital, just as he was mounting his horse to ride off to the hunt, arrayed in scarlet and cords?"

"And what did he do?" asked Rory.

"Pass the pie," said Ralph.

"Why," continued the doctor, enthusiastically, "doffed his scarlet coat and donned an old gown, whipped off a leg in one minute ten and a half seconds, and was in the saddle again five minutes after that."

"Brayvo!" cried Captain Cobb, "doctor, you're a brick,

---

* These strange hummocks, which resemble, as already stated, huge packs of cards, are formed of pieces of bay ice about a foot thick, which has been broken up between two bergs, and finally thrown up out of the water altogether. They form quite a characteristic feature of a North Greenland icescape.

and if ever you come out to New Jersey, come and see Cobb, and I guess he'll give you a good time of it."

"Ray," said Rory.

"Well, Row," said Ray.

"Your face and hands are begrimed with powder, and there is a kind of wolfish look about you that is worth studying. You look like a frozen-out blacksmith who hasn't a penny to buy a bit of peas-pudding or a morsel of soap."

"I'm hungry, anyhow," said Ray. "How good of McBain to send such a jolly breakfast! But I say, Row, d'ye remember the proverb about Claudius? Well, don't you call my face and hands black till you've washed your own. You look like a chimney-sweep who has been out of work for a week, and got no food since the day before yesterday."

"Well, well," says Row, "but 'deed in troth, my dear big boy, nobody can wonder at your being successful as a seal-stalker, for what with the colour of your face, and the urgency, so to speak, of the two eyes of you, and that big fur cap, why the seals take you for one o' themselves, a big bladder-nose."

"Pass the ham," said Ray; "Allan, some more coffee, I begin to feel like a giant refreshed."

"I do declare upon mine honour," said De Vere, "dat dis is de most glorious pignig [picnic] I ever have de pleasure to attend. But just you look at mine friend Seth, how funnily he do dress."

"It may be a funny way," said Allan, "but it is a most effectual one; dear old trapper Seth has killed more seals this morning than any two of us."

Seth was dressed from top to toe in young seals' skins, the hair outwards, with the exception of the cap, which was of darker fur, and a black patch on his back. They were not loose garments, they were almost as tight as a harlequin's; but when Seth drew his fur cap over his face and threw himself on the ice, and began wriggling along, his resemblance to a saddle-seal was so preposterous that everybody burst into a hearty laugh.

"That's the way I gets so near them," said Seth, standing once more erect.

"Look, look!" cried Rory, and every eye was turned in the direction in which he pointed; and there, in a pool of dark water not twenty yards away, a dozen beautiful heads, with round, wondering eyes, had popped up to gaze at them.

It was a lovely sight, and never a rifle was lifted to shoot. Presently they disappeared, but on the mate of the *Scotia* giving vent to a loud whistle, up came the heads again, and there they remained as long as the mate whistled, for of all wild creatures in the world that I have ever come across, the Greenland seal is the most inquisitive; and no doubt the experience of some of my old-boy readers who have been to the country is the same as my own.

Onwards, steadily onwards, all that day went our sportsmen; they did not even assemble again for another meal, and at five of the clock they found themselves fully four miles from the place where the ships lay. The field of seals which they had attacked was some ten miles square, and although they had worked their way into it for miles, nevertheless when the flags were hoisted to recall them, at two bells in the first dog-watch, the field of seals still remained about ten miles square. This may seem strange, but is thus accounted for. Out of say twenty seals on each berg, fifteen at least would escape, and these swam away under the pack, and again took the ice on the far-off edge of the field of seals.

It being somewhat too far to drag the skins to the ship, bings had been made on the ice during the latter part of the day, so that no dead seals should be left unflensed upon the ice. When they wended their way homewards at the end of this glorious day's shooting a broom was stuck.

besom-side up, on each bing, with the name of the ship on the handles. This is done with the view of preventing other ships from appropriating the skins. This is the custom of the country—one of the unwritten laws of the sea of ice.

While the gunners and their merry men were yet a long way off from the ships, there came a hail from the crow's-nest of the *Arrandoon*, which, by the way, McBain had hardly left all the time. Peter had brought him up coffee and food, and he had danced in the interval to keep himself warm.

"On deck there!"

"Ay, ay, sir," roared Peter, looking up.

"Is dinner all laid?"

"Ay, sir, and the cook is waiting."

"Well, on with the kilt, Peter, if you're not afraid of getting your hocks frozen, get the bagpipes, and go and meet the hunters."

Down below dived Peter, and he was up again in what sailors call "a brace of shakes," arrayed in full Highland costume, with the bagpipes over his arm. No wonder the cockatoo cried,

"De-ah me!" when he saw Peter, and added, "Such a to-do! such a to-do! such a to-do."

Now the bears had been rather numerous on the pack that day, just as the sharks were in the water. Doubtless the sharks found many a poor wounded seal to close their vengeful jaws upon, for they are either too cowardly or not swift enough to catch a healthy phoca; but the bears had behaved themselves unusually well. They had had plenty to eat, at all events, and seemed to know that the men at work on the ice were laying up a store of provisions for them that would last them all the summer, so they had made no attempt to attack them. But on their way back to the ship the doctor, who was striding on a little way in advance of the rest, startled a huge monster who was sunning himself behind a hummock. It would be difficult to say whether the bear or the doctor was the more startled; at all events the latter fired and missed, and the former made off, running in the direction of the ships. But he hadn't gone above half a mile when who should Bruin meet but Peter, coming swinging along with his bagpipes under his arm. Never a gun had Peter, and never a club—only the pipes. As soon as they saw each other they both stopped short.

"I do declare," Bruin seemed to say to himself, "here is a man or something all alone. But what a strange dress! I never saw anybody dressed like that before. Never mind, he looks sweet and nice; I'll have a bit."

"I do declare," said Peter to himself, "if that isn't a big lump of a bear coming along, and I haven't even a stone to throw at him. Whatever shall I do at all, at all? Och! and och! this is the end of me now, at last. Sure enough it is marching to my own funeral I've been all the time, instead of going to meet the sportsmen. Oh! Peter, Peter! you'll never see your old mother in this world again, nor Scotland either. Yonder big bear is licking his chops to devour you. Yonder is the big hairy sarcophagus that'll soon contain your mangled remains. Who would have thought that Peter of Arrandoon would have lived to play his own coronach?"*

Hardly knowing what he did, poor Peter shouldered his pipes, and began to play a dreary, droning, yelling, squealing lament.

At the same moment Bruin commenced to perform some of the queerest antics ever a bear tried before. He stretched first one leg, then another, and he stretched his neck and described circles in the air with his nose, keeping time with the music. Then he sat up entirely on one end.

"Oh!" he seemed to say, "flesh and blood couldn't stand that; I must, yes, I must give vent to a Ho—o—o—o—o—

* Coronach—a funeral hymn or wail for the departed.

"And likewise to a

"Hoo—oo—oo—oo—oo!!"

Reader, the voice of an asthmatical steam-engine, heard at midnight as it enters a tunnel, is a melancholy sound, so is the Welsh hooter, and the fog-horn of a Newcastle coal brig; but all combined, and sounding together, would be but a feeble imitation of the agonising notes of that great white bear as he sat on his haunches listening to Peter's pipes. Peter himself saw the effect his music had produced, and, like the "towsy tike" in *Tam o' Shanter*,

"He hotched and blew wi' might and main."

And, as if Peter had been a great magician, Bruin felt impelled to try to follow the notes, though I am bound to say he did not always keep even in the key-note. Surely such a duet was never heard before in this world. There was a small open space of water not far from the hummock on which the piper of the *Arrandoon* had stationed himself; it was soon alive with the heads of hundreds of seals who had come up to listen; so, upon the whole, Peter had a most appreciative audience. But see yonder, is that a seal on the ice that is creeping closer and closer up behind the bear? Nay, for seals don't carry rifles; and now the new-comer levels his gun just for a moment, there is a puff of blue-white smoke, the bear springs high in the air, then falls prostrate on the snow. His ululations are over for ever and aye; the piper plays a merrier air, and advances with speed to meet old Seth and the rest of the sportsmen, who, glad as they are to see him alive, greet him with uproarious cheers and laughter. Then a procession is formed, and with Peter and his pipes striding on in front, thus do the seal-stalkers return to the *Arrandoon*.

CHAPTER XXI.

THE COMING FROST—SILAS WARNS THE "ARRANDOON" OF DANGER—FORGING THROUGH THE ICE—BESET—A STRANGE AND ALARMING ACCIDENT.

SO willingly and merrily worked all hands on the ice, that in less than three days the *Canny Scotia* was almost a full, though by no means a bumper ship, and poor Silas began to see visions of future happiness in his mind's eye, when he should return to his native land and complete the joy of his family. Unfortunately, however, his good fortune did not last for the present. How seldom, indeed, good luck does last in this world of ours! One day, towards midnight, the sky apparently assumed a brighter blue. This seemed to concern Silas considerably. The good man was walking the deck at the time with his inseparable companion the first mate, neither of whom ever appeared now to court sleep or rest.

"Matie," said Silas, pointing skywards, "do you see any difference in the colour yonder?"

"That do I!" replied the mate.

"And hasn't it got much colder?"

"Well, both of us have been walking," the chief officer returned, "at the rate of several knots, just to keep the dear life in us, and I never saw you, sir, with your hands so deep in your pockets before."

Down rushed the captain to consult his glass; he was speedily up again, however. "It is just as I thought," he said. "Now come up into the nest with me; there's room for both of us. Look!" he added, as soon as they had reached their barrel of observation, "the rascals know what is coming. They are taking the water, and before ten minutes there won't be a seal with his nose on that bit of pack. Heigho, matie! heigho! that is just like my luck. If I'd been born a tailor, every man would have been born a Highlander, and made his own kilts. But hi! up, matie, Silas doesn't mean to let his heart down yet for a bit. A black frost is on the wing. There is no help for that, but the *Arrandoon's* people don't seem to know it. I must off over and tell them;" and even as he spoke Silas began descending the Jacob's ladder. "Call all hands!" he cried, as he disappeared over the side; "we must work her round as long as the pieces are anything loose-like."

It was not a long journey to the big sister ship, and the sturdy legs of this ancient mariner would soon get him there. But he would not wait till alongside; he needs must hail her while still many yards from her dark and stately sides.

"What ho, there!" he bawled. "*Arrandoon* ahoy!"

That voice of his was a wonderful one. It might have awakened the dead; it was like a ten-horse power speaking-trumpet lined with the roughest emery-paper. Seals heard it far down beneath the ice, and came to the surface to listen and to marvel. A great bear was sitting not twenty yards from Silas. He thought he should like to eat Silas, but he could not swallow that voice, so he went across the ice instead. Then the voice rolled in over the vessel's bulwarks, startled the officer on duty, and went ringing down below through the state-rooms, causing our sleeping heroes to tumble out of their bunks with double-quick speed, even the usually late and lazy Ralph evincing more celerity than ever he had done in his life before.

They met, rubbing their eyes and looking cold and

foolish, all in a knot in the saloon. Cold and foolish, and a little bit frightened as well, for the words of Silas sounded terribly like "the *Arrandoon* on fire!"

Not a bit of it, for there came the hail again, and distinct enough this time.

"*Arrandoon* ahoy! Is everybody dead on board?"

"What *is* the matter?" cried McBain, as soon as he got on deck, dressed as he was in the garments of night.

"Black frost, Captain McBain," answered Silas, springing up the side, "and you'll soon find that matter enough, or my name ain't Grig, nor my luck like a bad wind, always veering in the wrong direction. The seals are gone, sir—every mother's son o' them! My advice is—but, dear me, gentlemen! go below and rig out. Why, here's four more of you! That ain't the raiment for a black frost! You look like five candidates for a choking good influenza!"

This first bit of advice being taken in good part,

"Now," continued Silas, " your next best holt, Captain McBain, will be to get up steam, and get her head pointed away for the blue water, else there is no saying we may not leave our bones here."

"Ah!" exclaimed McBain, "we've no wish to do that. And here comes our worthy engineer. The old question, chief—How soon can you get us under way?"

"With the American hams, sir," was the quiet reply, "in about twenty minutes; with a morsel of nice blubber that I laid in especially for the purpose of emergencies, in far less time than that."

"Thanks!" said McBain, smiling; "use anything, but don't lose time."

The ships lay far from the open sea. They had been "rove" a long way in through the pack, to get close to the seals, but, independently of that, floating streams of ice, one after another, had joined the outer edge of this immense field of bergs, placing them at a greater distance from the welcome water.

Steam was speedily roaring, and ready for its work. Then, not without considerable difficulty, the vessel was put about, and the voyage seaward was commenced. Slow and tedious this voyage was bound to be, for there was so little wind it was useless to shake the sails loose, so the duty of towing her consorts devolved upon the *Arrandoon*. Instead of remaining on his own ship, Silas Grig came on board the steamer, where his services as iceman were fully appreciated.

As yet the frost had made no appreciable difference to the solidity of the pack; a very gentle swell was moving the pieces—a swell that rolled in from seaward, causing the whole scene around to look like a tract of snow-clad land, acted on by the giant force of an earthquake. Forging ahead through such ice, even by the aid of steam, is hard, slow work; and, assisted as the *Arrandoon* was by men walking in front of her and pushing on the bergs with long poles, hardly could she make a headway of half a mile an hour, and there were twenty good miles to traverse! It was a weary task, but the men bent their backs cheerfully to it, as British sailors ever do to a duty that has to be performed.

[Light lie the earth on the breast of the gallant Captain Brownrigg, R.N., and green be the grass on his grave. My young readers know the story; it is such stories as his they ought to read; such men as he ought to be enshrined in their memory. Betrayed by treacherous Arabs, with a mere handful of men he fought their powerful dhow and guns; and even when hope itself had fled he made no attempt to escape, but fought on and fought on, till he fell pierced with twenty wounds. He was a heroic sailor, and *he was doing his duty.*]

Even had it been possible to keep up the men's strength, forty hours must have elapsed ere the *Arrandoon* would be rising and falling on blue water. But many hours had not gone by ere the men got a rest they little cared for—for down went the swell, the motion among the bergs was stilled, and frost began its work of welding them together.

"Just like my luck, now, isn't it?" said Silas, when he found the ship could not be budged another inch, and was quite surrounded by heavy ice.

"I don't believe in luck," said Captain McBain; "and, after all, things might have turned out even worse than they have."

"Oh!" said Silas, "I'm not the man to grumble or growl. We are comfortable and jolly, and we have plenty to eat."

"We won't have much sport, though," said Rory, with a sigh, "if we have to remain here long, for the bears will follow the seals, won't they?"

"That they will," replied Silas, "and small blame to them; it is exactly what I should like to do myself."

"Well, you can, you know," said McBain, laughing. "We have a splendid balloon. De Vere will take you for a fly I'm sure, if you'll ask him."

"What! trust myself up in the clouds!" cried Silas; "thank you very much for the offer, but if ill-luck has kept following my footsteps all my life, ill-luck would be sure to follow me if I attempted any aërial flights, and I'd come down by the run."

"Well, we're fairly beset, anyhow," said Rory, "and I daresay we'll have to try to make the best of it."

So guns were placed disconsolately in the racks, as soon as the terrible black frost had quite set in, or if they were taken out when a walk was determined on, it was only for fashion's sake, and for the fear that an occasional bear might be met with. But it was good fun breaking bottles with rifle bullets, and good practice as well. As the days went on, and there were no signs of the pack breaking up, a number of books were taken down to be perused, much time was spent in playing piano or violin, or both together, while after dinner the hours were devoted to talking.

Many a racy yarn was told by Cobb, many an adventure by Seth, and many a queer experience by Silas Grig, and duly appreciated, too. So the evenings did not seem long, whatever the days did.

Said Silas one morning to McBain, as they stood together leaning on the bulwarks,

"I don't quite like the look of that ice, captain; it is precious big, and if it came on to press a bit, why, it would go clean through the ribs of us, strong though our good ships are. And that cockle-shell of Cobb's would be the very first to go down to the bottom."

"Or up to the top," suggested McBain.

"What?" laughed Silas; "would you clap your balloon top of her, and lift her out like?"

"No, not that; but we could hoist her high and dry on top of the ice easily enough."

"Well, I declare," cried Silas, clapping one brawny hand on his knee, "that is a glorious idea. And an old iceman like me to never think of it!"

Then Silas's face fell, as he said,

"Ah! but you couldn't hoist me up too. The *Canny Scotia* would go down; that would be more of my luck."

"Well, but I've thought of a plan. I have torpedoes on board. I'll have a go at this ice, anyhow."

"Make a kind of harbour, you mean?" inquired Silas.

"That's it," was the reply.

"But," said Silas, still somewhat dubious, "you know the currents run like mill-streams in under the ice. Well, suppose your torpedos were to be floated in under my ship, and went bursting off there?"

"Well, your ship would be hoisted," replied McBain; "that would be all."

"Ay!" said Silas, "that would be all; that would end all the luck, good or bad."

"But there is no fear of any such accident. And now let us just have a try at it."

Blowing up icebergs with torpedoes is by no means difficult, when you know how to do it, but sometimes the current will shift the guiding-pole or rope, and were it to get under the stern of the ship itself, it would make it awkward for the Arctic explorers. In the present instance everything went well, and berg after berg succumbed to the force of the gun-cotton, until the last, when, by some mismanagement, one torpedo was shifted right under a piece of ice on which stood, tools in hand, about ten men, besides Silas, Rory, and Captain McBain himself. Of course it was not likely that boy Rory was going to be far away when any fun was going on, so that is why he happened to be on top of this identical berg when the blowing-up took place. And here is precisely what was seen by disinterested bystanders—a smother of snow and water and ice, mixed, rising in shape of a rounded column over ten feet high, and, dimly visible in the misty midst thereof, a minglement of hands and heads and arms and legs. The sound accompanying the columnar rising was something between a puff and a thud; I cannot better describe it. Then there was a sudden collapse, and next moment the arms and the legs and the hands and the heads were all seen sprawling and struggling in the frothy, seething water below. It simply and purely looked as if they were all being boiled alive in a huge cauldron. But the strangest part of the story is to come. With the exception of a few trifling bruises, not one of those who were thus surprised by so sudden a rise in the world was a bit the worse. The ducking in the cold sea was certainly far from pleasant, but dry clothes and hot coffee soon put that to rights, and they came up smiling again.

Freezing Powders, who was on deck at the time of the accident, was dreadfully frightened, and ran down below instantly to report matters to his favourite.

"What's the row? What's the row? What's the row?" cried the bird as the boy entered the saloon.

"Don't talk so fast, Cockie, and I'll tell you," said Freezing Powders, sinking down on the deck with one arm on the cage. "I tink I'se all right at present, though my breaf is all frightened out of my body, and I must look 'bout as pale as you, Cockie."

"De-ah me!" said Cockie.

"But don't hang by de legs, Cockie. When you wants a mouf-ful of hemp just hop down for it, else de blood all run to your poor head, den you die in a fit!"

"Poor de-ah Cockie! Pretty old Cockie!" said the bird, in mournful tones.

"And now I got my breaf again, I try to 'splain to you what am de row. De dreful world round de ship is all white, Cockie, and to-day dey has commenced blowing it up, and jus' now, Cockie, dey has commenced to blow derselves up!"

"De-ah me!" from Cockie.

"Dat am quite true, Cockie, and de heads and de legs am flying about in all directions! It is too dreful to behold!"

"Now then, young Roley Poley!" cried Peter, entering at that moment, "toddle away forward for some boiling-hot coffee, and run quicker than ever you ran in your life."

"I'se off like a bird!" said Freezing Powders, darting out of the cabin as if there had been a boot after him.

CHAPTER XXII.

CAPTAIN COBB RETIRES—MORE TORPEDOING—THE GREAT ICE-HOLE—STRANGE SPORT—THE TERRIBLE ZUGÆNA—THE DEATH STRUGGLE.

BOTH Captain McBain and Silas Grig felt more easy in their minds when they had got fairly rid of the green-rooted monsters of icebergs that had lain so placidly yet so threateningly alongside their respective ships. And oh! by the way, how very calm, harmless, and gentle bergs like these *can* look, when there is no disturbing element beneath them, their snow-clad tops asleep and glistening in the sunlight; but I have seen them angry, grinding and crashing together, each upheaval representing a height of from fifteen to thirty feet; each upheaval representing a strength hydraulic equal in force to the might of the great ocean itself.

Our heroes had taken time by the forelock. They had "guncottoned the bergs," as Captain Cobb termed it, and lay for the time being in square ice-locked harbours, and could bid defiance to almost any ordinary occurrence, whether gale of wind in the pack or swell from the distant sea.

As the days went by the black frost seemed only to increase in severity.

"How long d'ye think," said Captain Cobb, one morning, while at breakfast in the *Arrandoon*—"how long d'ye think this state of affairs'll last? 'cause, mind ye, I begin to feel a kind o' riled already."

McBain looked inquiringly at Silas.

"If it's asking me you are," said the latter, "I makes answer and says, it may be for months, but it can't be for ever."

"But the frost isn't likely to go for a week, is it now?"

"That it won't, worse luck," was the reply.

"Well, then, gentlemen," said Cobb, "this child is going off, straight away out o' here back to Jan Mayen."

"Back to Jan Mayen!"

"Back to Jan Mayen!" everybody said, or seemed to say, in one breath.

"I reckon ye heard aright," said the imperturbable Yankee.

"It's just like this, ye see," he continued. "I'm paid by my employers to make observations on the old island down yonder; stopping here ain't taking sights, but it's taking the company's dollars for nothing, so if you'll—either o' ye—lend me a hand or two, and promise to hoist up Cobb's cockle-shell in the event of a squeeze, Cobb himself is off home, 'tain't mor'n fifty miles."

The journey was a dangerous one, nobody knew that better than the bold American himself, and it was a true sense of duty to his employers that caused him to undertake it. But having once made up his mind to a thing, Cobb was not the man to be deterred from accomplishing it.

So, with many a good wish for his safety, accompanied by only three men, he set out on his long journey over the snow. Rory, from the deck of the *Arrandoon*, and McBain from the nest, watched them as long as they were in sight. Indeed, I am not at all sure that Rory did not feel a little sorry he had not asked leave to accompany them, so fond was he of adventure in every shape and form.

It was a relief for him—and not for him alone—when McBain, in order to break the monotony of existence, and by way of doing something, proposed trying the effects of his torpedoes again at some distance from the ship, and forming a great ice-hole.

"Things will come up to breathe, and look about them, you know," he explained, "and then we may get some sport, and Silas may bag a seal or two."

Our heroes were overjoyed when the working party was called away. At last there was a prospect of doing something, and seeing an animal of some kind, for not only the bears, but the very birds had deserted them. Sometimes, indeed, a solitary snow-bird would come flying around the ships. It would hover for awhile in the air, giving vent to many a peevish, mournful chirp, then fly away again.

"No, no, no!" it seemed to say, "there is nothing good to eat down there—no raw flesh, no blood—and so I'm off again to the distant sealing-ground, where the yellow bear prowls, and the snow is red with blood.

A few hours' work with torpedoes, picks, and ice-saws was enough to form an opening big enough for the purpose required. The broken pieces were either "landed high and dry," or sunk beneath the pack, and so the work was completed.

"It'll entail a deal of trouble, gentlemen," said Dr. McFlail, "to keep that hole clear with the temperature which we are at present enjoying—or rather enduring."

"There is that in the sea, doctor," said Silas, with a knowing nod, "which will save us the trouble."

He wasn't wrong. Not an hour elapsed ere a few black heads, with great wondering eyes, appeared above the surface and peered around them, and blinked at the sun, and seemed to enjoy mightily a sniff of the fresh air and a blink of the daylight.

"This is nice, now," they said, "and ever so much better than being down there in the dark—quite an oasis in the desert."

Bang! bang!

Two of them slowly sunk to rise no more.

"This won't do," said Allan; "it is only murder to shoot poor seals that we cannot land and make some good out off. What is to be done?"

"Be quiet with ye!" said Rory. "Sure yonder is Seth himself, coming straight from the ship, in his suit of skins, and if he isn't up to some manœuvre then my name isn't Roderick, that is all."

Seth *was* up to something; he had a coil of rope with him, and the nattiest little harpoon that ever was handled.

"Fire away, gentlemen!" he said, lying down on the sunny side of a small hummock pretty close to the water's edge, "only don't hit the old trapper; he'd rather die in his bed if it be all the same to you."

Undeterred by the fate that had befallen their companions, it was not long before other seals popped up to breathe. Our heroes were ready for them, and two again were killed, one being missed. Seth was ready for them, too. He sprang to his feet, and ere the smoke had melted in the thin air, one of the seals was neatly harpooned and dragged to the edge. Here it was gaffed, and lifted or pulled bodily on to the ice by help of Ralph's powerful arm. The harpoon was released, and before the other seal had time to sink it was served in precisely the same manner.

The sport was exceedingly novel, and combined, as Rory said, "all the pleasures of shooting and fishing in one glorious whole."

No work on natural history, so far as my reading goes, remarks upon the exceedingly great speed exhibited by the Greenland seal in his flight—it is in reality a flight—through and beneath the water. I have often been astonished at the rapidity of their movements; so swiftly do they dart along that the eye can barely follow them for the moment or two they are visible. This power of swimming enables them to pursue their finny prey for many miles under an ice-pack; it doubtless also enables them to escape the fangs of their natural enemy, the great Greenland shark (*Scymnus borealis*), and on the present occasion it accounted for their appearance at the great breathing-hole made for them by the torpedoes and ice-saws of the *Arrandoon*. The water under the pack would be everywhere else as black and dark as midnight, but through this opening the sunshine would stream in straight and powerful rays, and not seals alone, but fishes and monsters of the deep of many kinds, would naturally come towards the light, as the salmon does to the glimmer from the torch of the Highland poacher.

The sport obtained at the opening was not of a very exciting character on the first day, but next morn, to their joy, they found that a bear had been around, and had left the marks of his broad soles in the snow. Many more seals, too, came up to breathe, and more harpoons had to be requisitioned. Silas was once more in his glory at the prospect of adding a few more skins, and a few more tons of oil, to the cargo he had already shipped.

Towards afternoon the fun grew fast and furious, and when Peter came in person to announce dinner, he could hardly get his officers to pay any heed to the summons. Even Cockie down in the saloon heard the noise, and must needs inquire, as he stretched his neck and fastened one bead of an eye on his little black master,

"What's all the to-do about? What's all the to-do about?"

"I don't know," was the reply of Freezing Powders. "I don't know no more nor you do, Cockie. I tinks dey has gone to blow derselves all to pieces again."

Dinner was partaken of in a merrier mood that day than it had been for weeks. Silas was there, of course; in fact, he had become an honorary member of the *Arrandoon* mess.

"You see, Captain Grig," McBain had observed, "we

must have you as much with us now as we can, for we soon go different roads, don't we?"

"Ah! yes," replied Silas, with a bit of a sigh; "you go north; God send you safe back; and I go back to my little wife and large family."

"Happy reunion, won't it be?" said Allan.

The eyes of Silas sparkled, but his heart was too full of happy thoughts to say more than simply,

"Yes."

"Won't the green ginger fly?" said Rory.

"I say, boys," Ralph put in, "this sort of thing positively gives a man a kind of an appetite."

Rory looked at him with such a mischievous twinkle in his eyes that Ralph longed to pinch him.

"Just as if ever you lost yours," said Rory.

At this moment the sound of a rifle was heard, apparently close to the ship.

"It's the trapper," cried Rory; "it's friend Seth. Sure enough I know the charming music of his long gun. Now, Ray, I'll wager my fiddle he has bagged a bear."

Rory was right for once, and here is how it fell out. Several bears had that day scented the battle from afar, or were attracted by the noise of the malleys and gulls that were now wheeling around the ships in thousands. They stood aloof while shooting was going on, sitting on their haunches licking their chops, greedy, hungry, expectant; but as soon as the sportsmen went off to dine,

"Now is our time," said one, "to get a bit of fresh meat."

"Come on, then," cried another; "there are a hundred seals lying on the ice. Hurrah!"

So down they came, to the feast. They had not had such a treat for a whole day, and that is a long time for a bear to fast, and they made good use of their time, you may be sure, and so earnest were they, that they did not perceive a long, hairy creature that came creeping stealthily towards them. When at last one of them did observe this strange animal " with the tail of his eye," he said to himself,

" Oh ! it is only a tiny bit of a young seal, hunting for a lost mother, perhaps. Well, I'll have it presently by way of dessert."

And almost immediately after, the sound that had startled our friends at *their* dessert rang out in the clear, frosty air, and Bruin's head dropped never more to rise. His brother bears suddenly discovered they had eaten enough; anyhow, they remembered that it was always best to rise up from the table feeling that you could eat a little more, so they shambled away across the pack as fast as four legs could carry them.

"Bravo, Seth, old boy," cried Rory and Allan, coming on the scene.

Ralph only waited to finish some pastry, then he too joined them.

"Why," said the latter, " it is the biggest bear we have seen yet."

In true trapper fashion, Seth was already on his knees beside the enormous carcass, engaged with knife and fist and elbow, " working the rascal out of his jacket," as he called it, when Rory, who was not far from the edge of the water, started, or rather sprang back in horror.

"Oh! Allan, Allan ! Ray, Ray ! look !" he cried.

Well might he cry " look," for a more terrible or revolting apparition never raises head over the black waters of the Greenland ocean than the zugæna, or hammer-headed shark. The skull is in shape precisely what the name indicates, that of a gigantic hammer, with a great eye at each end, and the mouth beneath. This shark is not unfrequently met with in the northern seas, and he is just as fierce as he is fearful to behold.

Allan and Ralph both saw the brute, and neither could repress a shudder. It appeared but for a few moments, then dived below again.

Silas and McBain, coming up at the time, were told of the occurrence.

"I know the vile beasts well," said Silas, "and they do say that they never appear in these seas without bringing a big slice o' ill-luck in their wake. That is unless you catches them, and sometimes that doesn't save the ship. When I was skipper o' the *Penelope*, and that is more than ten years ago, there wasn't a lazier chap in the crew than snuffy Sandy Foster. He wasn't a deal o' use down below, he did nothing on deck, and he never went aloft. He had two favourite positions: one was sitting before a joint of junk, with a knife in his hand; t'other was leaning against the bulwarks with a pipe in his mouth, and we never could make out which he liked best.

"'Did ever you do anything clever in your life, Sandy?' I asked one day.

"Sandy took his pipe out of his mouth and eyed the mainmast for fully half a minute. Then he brought his eyes round to my face, and said,

"'Not that I can remember o', sir.'

"'The first time, Sandy,' says I, 'that you do anything clever, I'll give you a pair of the best canvas trousers in the ship.'

"Sandy's eyes a kind of sparkled; I'd never seen them sparkle before.

"'I'll win them,' said Sandy, 'wait till ye see.'

"And, indeed, gentlemen, I hadn't long to wait. One day the brig was dead before the wind under a crowd o' cloth, for there wasn't much wind, but a nasty rumble-tumble sea; there was no doubt, gentlemen, from the looks o' that sea, that we had just come through a gale o' wind, and there was evidence enough to go to jury on that there was another not far away. Well, it was just in the dusk o' the evening—we were pretty far south—that the cry got up,

"'Man overboard.'

"It was our bo's'n's boy, a lad of fourteen, who had

gone by the run. Singing out to the mate to lay to, I ran forward, and if ever I forget the expression of the poor bo's'n's face as he wrung his hands and cried, 'Oh, save my laddie! Oh, save my laddie!' my name will change to something else than Silas.

"'I'll save him,' cried a voice behind me. Some one rushed past. There was a splash in the water next moment, and I had barely time to see it was Sandy. Before the boat reached the spot they were a quarter of a mile astern, but they were saved; they found the bo's'n's laddie riding 'cockerty-coosie' on Sandy's shoulder, and Sandy spitting out the mouthfuls of salt water, laughing and crying,

"'I've won the breeks! I've won the canvas breeks, boys!'

"He had won them, and that right nobly, too. Well, after he had worn them for over a month, it became painfully evident even to Sandy that they sorely needed washing; but, woe is me! Sandy was too lazy to put a hand to them. But he thought of a plan, nevertheless, to save trouble. He steeped them in a soda ley, attached a strong line to them, and pitched them overboard to tow.

"When, after two hours' towing, Sandy went to haul them up, great was his astonishment to find a great hammer-head spring half out of the water and seize them. Sandy had never seen so awful a monster before; he put it down as an evil spirit.

"'Let go,' he roared; 'let go my breeks, ye beast.'

"Now, maybe, with those hooked teeth of his, the shark could not let go; anyhow, he did not.

"'I dinna ken who ye are, or what ye are,' cried Sandy, 'but ye'll no get my breeks. Ah! bide a wee.'

"Luckily the dolphin-striker lay handy, Sandy made a grab at it, and next minute it was hard and fast in the hammer-head's neck. To see how that monster wriggled and fought, more like a fiend than a fish, when we got him on deck, would have—but look—look——"

Seth had not been idle while his companions were talking. He had cut off choice pieces of blubber and thrown them into the sea; he had coiled his rope on the ice close by; then, harpoon in hand, he knelt ready to strike. Nor had he long to wait. The bait took, the bait was taken, the harpoon had left the trapper's hand and gone deep into the monster's body.

I will not attempt to describe the scene that followed— it was a death-scene that no pen could do justice to—the wild struggle of the giant shark in the water, his mad and frantic motions ere clubbed to death on the ice, and his terrible appearance as he snapped his dreadful jaws at everything within reach; but here is a fact, strange and weird though it may read—fully half an hour after the creature seemed dead, and lying on its side, while our heroes stood silently round it, with the wild birds wheeling and screaming closely overhead, the zugæna suddenly threw itself on its stomach as if about to swim away. It was the last of its movements, and a mere spasmodic and painless one, though very distressing to witness.

CHAPTER XXIII.

RORY'S REVERIE—SILAS ON THE SCYMNUS BOREALIS—THE BATTLE WITH THE SHARKS—RORY GETS IN FOR IT AGAIN—THROWN AMONG THE SHARKS.

THE ships still lay hard and fast in the ice-pack, many miles to the nor'ard and eastward of the Isle of Jan Mayen. There was as yet no sign of the frost giving way. Day after day the bay ice between the bergs got thicker and thicker, and the thermometer still stood steadily well down below zero. But the wind never blew, and there never was a speck of cloud in the brilliant sapphire sky, nor even haze itself to shear the sun of his beams; so the cold was hardly felt, and after a brisk walk or scamper over the ice our heroes felt so warm that they were in the habit of throwing themselves down on the snow on the southern side of a hummock of ice. Book in hand, Rory would sometimes lie thus for fully half an hour on a stretch. Not always reading, though; the fact of Rory's having a book in his hand was no proof that he was reading, for just as often he was dreaming; and I'll tell you a little secret—there were a pair of beautiful eyes which were filled with tears when last he had seen them, there were two rosy lips that had quivered as they parted to breathe the word "good-bye." These, and a soft, small hand that had lain for a moment in his, haunted him by night and by day, and seemed ever present with him through all his wild adventures.

Ah! but they didn't make him unhappy, though; no, but quite the reverse.

He was reclining thus one day all by himself, about a quarter of a mile from his ship, when Ralph and McBain came gently up behind him, walking as silently as the crisp snow, that felt like powdered glass under their feet, would permit them.

"Hullo! Rory," cried McBain, in a voice of thunder.

Startled from his reverie, Rory sprang to his feet, and instinctively grasped his rifle.

His friends laughed at him.

"It is somewhat late to seize your rifle now, my boy," said McBain; "supposing now we'd been a bear, why, we would be eating you at this present moment."

"Or making a mouse of you," added Ralph, "as the yellow bear did of poor Freezing Powders; and at this very minute you'd be

>'Dancin' for de dear life
> Among de Greenland snow.'"

"I was reading," said Rory, smiling, "that beautiful poem of Wordsworth, *We are seven*."

"Wordsworth's *We are seven*?" cried Ralph, laughing. "Oh! Row, Row, you'll be the death of me some day. Since when did you learn to read with your book upside down?"

"Had I now?" said Rory, with an amused look of candour. "In troth I daresay you are right."

"But come on, Row, boy," continued Ralph, "luncheon is all ready, Peter is waiting, and after lunch Silas Grig is going to show us some fun."

"What more malley-shooting?" asked Rory.

"No, Row, boy," was the reply; "he is going to lead us forth to battle against the sharks."

"Against the sharks!" exclaimed Rory, incredulous.

"I'm not in fun, really," replied Ralph. "Silas tells us

they are in shoals of thousands at present under us; that the sea swarms with them, some fifteen feet long, others nearer twenty."

"Oh!" said Row; "this *is* interesting. Come on; I'm ready."

While the trio stroll leisurely shipwards over the snow, let me try to explain to my reader what Rory meant by malley-shooting, as taught them by Silas Grig. The term, or name, "malley," is that which is given by Greenlandmen to the Arctic gull. Although not so charming in plumage as the snowbird, it is nevertheless a very handsome bird, and has many queer ways of its own which are interesting to the naturalist, and which you do not find described in books. These gulls build their nests early in the season on the cliffs of Faroe and Shetland, and probably, though I have never found them, in sheltered caves of Jan Mayen and Western Greenland as well. Despite the extreme cold, they manage to bring forth and rear their young successfully, and are always ready to follow Greenland ships in immense flocks. Wherever work is going on, wherever the crack of the rifle is heard on the pack, wherever the snow is stained crimson and yellow with blood, the malleys will be there in daring thousands. The most curious part of the thing is this: they possess a power of either scent or sight, which enables them to discover their quarry, although scores of miles away from it. For example—the Arctic gulls, as a rule, do not follow a ship for sake of the bits of bread and fat that may be thrown overboard. Some of them do, I know, but I look upon these as merely the lazaroni, the beggars of their tribe; your healthy, youthful, aristocratic malley prefers something he considers better. Give him blubber to eat, or the flesh of a new slain seal, and he will follow you far enough. Now a ship may be lying becalmed off this pack, with no seals in sight, and doing nothing; if so she will be deserted by these birds. Not from the crow's-nest, though aided by the most powerful telescope, will you be able to descry a single gull ; but no sooner is a sealskin or two hauled on deck to be cleared of their fat, than notice seems to be flashed to the far-off gulls, and in a few minutes they are winging around you, making the welkin ring with their wild, delighted screams. They alight in the water around a morsel of meat in such bunches, that a table-cloth would cover two dozen of them.

Having had enough—and that "enough" means something enormous—they go off for a "fly," just as tumbling pigeons do. You may see them in hundreds high in air, sailing round and round, enjoying themselves apparently to the very utmost, and shrieking with joy. Now is the time for the skua to attack them. A bold, black, hawk-like rascal is this skua, a robber and a thief. He never comes within gunshot of a ship. He is as wild and untamable as the north wind itself; yet, no sooner have the malleys commenced their post-prandial gambols than he is in the midst of them. He does not want to kill them; only some one or more must disgorge their food. On this the skua lives. No wonder that Greenland sailors call him the unclean bird.

The malley-gull floats on the waves as lightly and gently as a child's toy air-ball would. His usual diet is fish, except in sealing times, and of the fish he catches the marauding skua never fails to get his share. It is for the sake of the feathers sailors shoot these birds on the ice, for they are nearly as well feathered as an eider duck.

Getting tired of shooting seals in the water, Rory and Allan one day, leaving the others on the banks of the great ice-hole, determined to make a bag of feathers. And here is how they bagged their game.

Armed with fowling-pieces, they retired to some distance from the water party and lay down behind a hummock of ice. Here they might have lain until this day without a bird looking twice in their direction had they not provided themselves with a lure. This lure was simply a pair of the wings of a gull, which one waved above his head, while the other prepared to fire right and left. And not a minute would these wings be waved aloft ere the gulls, with that strange curiosity inherent in all wild creatures, would begin to circle around, coming nearer and nearer, tack and half-tack, until they were within reach of the guns, when— down they came. But the untimely end of one brace nor twenty did not prevent their companions from trying to solve the mystery of the waving wings.

Luncheon was on the table, and our friends were seated around it, all looking happy and hungry. Rory would have liked to have asked Silas Grig right straight away about the expedition against the sharks but for one thing—he didn't like to appear too inquisitive; and, for another, he was not quite sure even now that it was not one of Ralph's pretty jokes. But when everybody had been served, when weather and future prospects, the state of the thermometer and height of the barometer, had been discussed, Rory found he could not contain himself any longer.

"What are you going to be doing after lunch?" he asked Silas, pointedly.

"Aha, boy Rory!" was the reply; "we'll have such sport as you never saw the likes o' before!"

Rory now began to see there really was no joke about the matter; and Ralph, who was sitting next to him, pinched him for his doubt and misbelief. The two young men could read each other's thoughts like books.

"Do you mean to say you are going to catch sharks in earnest, you know?" asked Rory.

"Well," said Silas, with a bit of a laugh, "I'm going to have as good a try at it as ever I had. And as for catching 'em in earnest, I'm thinking it won't be fun—for the sharks!"

"It is the *Scymnus borealis*, isn't it?" said Dr. Sandy McFlail, "belongin', if my memory serves me, to the natural family *Squalidæ*—a powerful brute, and a vera dangerous, too."

"You may call him the *Aurora borealis* if you like, doctor," said Silas; "and as for his family connections I know nought, but I daresay he comes from a jolly bad stock."

"Natural history books," said Allan, "don't speak of their being so very numerous."

"Natural history books!" reiterated Silas, with some warmth of disdain. "What do they know? what can they teach a man? Write a complete history of all the creatures that move about on God's fair earth, that fly in His air or swim in His sea, and you'd fill St. Paul's with books from top to bottom—from the mighty cellars beneath to the golden cross itself. No, take my advice, boy Rory; if you want to study nature, put little faith in books. The classification is handy, say you? Yes, doctor; and I've seen a stripling fresh from college look as proud as a two-year-old peacock because he could spin you off the Greek names of a few specimens in the British Museum, though he couldn't have told you the ways and habits of any one of them to save him from having his leave stopped. There is only one way, gentlemen, to study natural history; you must go to the great book of Nature itself—ay, and be content, and thankful, too, if, during even a long lifetime, you are able to learn the contents of even a single page of it."

Rory, and the doctor, too, looked at Silas with a kind of newborn admiration; there was more in this man, with his weather-beaten, flower-pot-coloured face, than they had had any idea of.

"If I had time, gentlemen," Silas added, "I could tell you some queer stories about sharks. 'I reckon,' as poor old Cobb used to say, that some o' them would raise your hair a bit, too!"

"And what kind of a monster is this Greenland shark?" asked Allan.

"No more a monster," said Silas, "than I am. God made us both, and we have each some end to fulfil in life. But if you want me to tell you something about him, I'll confess to you I love the animal about as much as I do an alligator. He comes prowling around the icebergs when we are sealing to see what he can pick up in the shape of a dead or wounded seal, a chunk o' blubber, or a man's leg. He is neither dainty nor particular, he has the appetite of a healthy ostrich, and about as much conscience as a coal-carter's horse. He is as wary as a five-season fox, and when he pays your ship a visit when out at sea, he looks as humble and unsophisticated as a bull trout. He'll take whatever you like to throw him, though—anything, in fact, from a cow's-heel to the cabin boy—and he'll swallow a red-hot brick rather than go away with an empty stomach. But when he comes around the ice at old-sealing time he doesn't come alone, he brings his father and mother with him, and his uncles and aunts, and apparently all his natural family, as the doctor calls it. And fine fun they have, though they don't agree particularly well even *en famille*. I've seen five of them on to one seal crang, and there was little interchange of courtesies, I can tell you. He's not a brave fish, the Greenland shark, big and all as he is. If you fall into the water among a score of them your best plan is to keep cool and kick. Yes, gentlemen, by keeping cool and kicking plenty I've known more than one man escape without a bite. The getting out is the worst, though, for as long as you splash they keep at a distance and look on; they don't quite know what to make of you; but as soon as you get a hold of the end of the rope, and are being drawn out, look sharp, that's all, or it will be 'Snap!' and you will be minus one leg before you can wink, and thankful you may be it isn't two. A mighty tough skin has the Greenland shark," continued Silas; "I've played upon the back of one for over half an hour with a Colt's revolver, and it just seemed to tickle him—nothing more. I don't think sharks have much natural affection, and they are no respecters of persons. I do believe they would just as soon dine off little Freezing Powders here as they would off a leg of McBain."

"Oh, oh, Massa Silas!" cried Freezing Powders, "don't talk like dat; you makes my flesh all creep like nuffin' at all!"

"They are slow in their movements, aren't they?" said the doctor.

"Ay!" said Silas, "when they get everything their own way; but they are fierce, revengeful, and terrible in their wrath. An angry shark will bite a bit out of your boat, collar an oar, or do anything to spite you, though it generally ends in his having his own head split in the long run." *

"The men are all ready, sir," said Stevenson, entering the cabin at that moment, "to go over the side, sir."

"Thank you," said the captain; "send them on to the ice, then, for a general skylark till we come up."

When the officers did come up they found all the men on the ice, and a pretty row they were having. They were running, racing, jumping high leap and low leap, boxing, and fencing with single-sticks, quarter-staves, and foils; and last but not least, a party were dancing the wild and exciting reels of Scotland, with Peter playing to them just as loudly as he knew how to, although his eyes seemed starting from his head, and his face was as red as a dorking's comb in laying season.

Then it was "Hurrah for the ice-hole!" and "Hurrah for the sharks!"

Silas did not take very long to get his party—his fishing-party, as he called it—into working order. He evidently meant business, and expected it, too. He had seven or eight long lines, to each of which was attached a piece of

* Silas Grig's description of the Greenland shark is a pretty correct one, so far as my own experience goes.—G. S.

chain and an immense shark-hook. These were baited with pieces of blubber; the men were armed with long knives and clubs. So sure was Silas Grig of capturing a big haul of these sea-fiends, the Greenland sharks, that he had a large fire of wood lighted on the ice at some little distance, and over it, suspended by a kind of shears, hung an immense cauldron. In this it was intended to boil the livers of the sharks in order to extract the oil, which is the most valuable part of the animal.

Until tempted by huge pieces of seal-flesh hardly a shark showed fin; but when once their appetites were wetted then——!

I cannot, nor will I attempt to describe this battle with the sharks, although such a fight I have been eye witness to. Sometimes as many as two were hauled out at once; it required the united strength of fifteen or twenty men to land them. Then came the struggle on the ice, the clubbing, the axing, and the death, during which many a man bit the snow, though none were grievously wounded. Before the sun pointed to midnight, between thirty and forty immense sharks had been captured, and the oil from their livers weighed nearly a ton.

Poor Rory—to whom all the best of the fun and all the worst misfortunes seemed always to fall—had a terrible adventure during the battle. Carried away by his enthusiasm, with club in hand, he was engaging one of the largest sharks landed. The brute bent himself suddenly, then as suddenly straightened himself out, and away went boy Rory, like an arrow from a cross-bow, alighting in the very centre of the pool. For a moment every one was struck dumb with horror!

But Rory himself never lost his presence of mind. He remembered what Silas had said about splashing and kicking to keep the sharks at bay. Splash? I should think he did splash, and kick, too; indeed, kicking is hardly any name for his antics. He made a wheel of himself in the water. He seemed all arms and legs, and as for his head, it was just as often up as down, and *vice versâ*; and all the while he was issuing orders to those on the bank—a word or two at a time, whenever his head happened to be uppermost, so that in the midst of the splashing and spluttering his speech ran like this:

"Stand by"—(splutter, splutter)—"you fellows"—(splash, splash)—"up there"—(splutter) "to pull quick" —(splash)—"as soon as I"—(splutter, splutter)—"catch the rope."—(splash, splash)—"Now lads, now!"—(splutter splutter, splash, splash, splutter, splutter, splash).

"Hurrah!" he cried, when he found himself on the ice. "Hurrah! boys. Cheer, boys, cheer. Safe to bank! Hurrah! and both my legs as sound as a bell, and never a toe missing from any single one of the two o' them. Hurrah! Sure it's myself'll be Queen o' the May to-morrow. Hurrah!"

Yes, reader, the very next day was May-day, and on that day there are such doings on Greenland ships as you never see in England.

CHAPTER XXIV.

MAY-DAY IN THE ARCTIC REGIONS.

MAY-DAY! May-day in England! Surely, even to the minds of the youngest among us, these words bring some pleasant recollections.

"Ah! but," I think I hear you complain, "the May-days are not now what they were in the good old times; not the May-days we read of in books; not the May-days of merrie England. Where are the may-poles, with their circles of rosy-cheeked children dancing gleesomely around them? Where are the revels? Where are the games? Where is the little maiden persistent, who plagued her mother so lest she should forget to wake and call her early—

'Because I'm to be Queen o' the May, mother,
I'm to be Queen o' the May'?

And echo answers, 'Where?'"

These things, maiden included, have passed away; they have fled like the fairies before the shriek of engine and rattle of railway wheels.

But May-day in England! Why, there is some pleasure and some joy left in it even yet. Summer comes with it, or promises it will soon be on the wing. Already in the meadows the cattle wade knee-deep in dewy grass, and cull sweet cowslips and daisies. A balmier air breathes over the land; the rising sun is rosy with hope; the lark springs from his nest among the tender corn, and mounts higher to sing than he has ever done before; flowers are blooming on every brae; the mossy banks are redolent of wild thyme; roses begin to peep coyly out in the hedgerows, and butterflies spread their wings, as a sailor spreads a sail, and go fluttering away through the gladsome sunshine. And yonder—why, yonder *is* a little maiden, and a very pretty one, too, though she isn't going to be Queen o' the May. No, but she is tripping along towards the glade, where the pink-blossomed hawthorn grows, and the yellow scented furze. She is going to—

> Bathe her sweet face in May-morn dew,
> To make her look lovely all the year through.

She glances shyly around her, hoping that no one sees her. You and I, dear reader, are far too manly to stand and stare so.

Hey! presto! and the scene is changed.

May-day! May-day in Greenland! An illimitable ocean of ice, stretching away on all sides towards every point of the compass from where those ships are lying beset. It looks like some measureless wold covered with the snows of midwinter. It is early morning, though the sun shines brightly in a sky of cloudless blue, and, save for the foot-fall of the solitary watchman who paces the deck of the *Arrandoon*, there is not a sound to be heard, the stillness everywhere is as the stillness of death. An hour or two goes slowly by, then the watchman approaches the great bell that hangs amidships.

Dong-dong! dong-dong! dong-dong! dong-dong! Eight bells. The men spring up from hatch and companion-way, and soon the decks are crowded and the crew are busy enough. They have discussed their breakfast long ago, and have since been hard at work on the May-day garland, which they now proceed to hoist on high, 'twixt fore and main masts. That garland is quite a work of art, and a very gay one, too. Not a man in the ship that has not contributed a few ribbons to aid in decorating it.

Those ribbons had been kept for this special purpose, and were the last loving gifts of sisters, wives, or sweethearts ere the vessel set sail for the sea of ice. But there is more to be done than hoisting the garland. The ship has to be dressed, and when this is finished, with her flags all floating around her, she will look as beautiful as a bride on her marriage morning.

None the worse for the ducking and fright of the previous day, Rory was first up on this particular May-day, and tubbed and dressed long before either Allan or Ralph was awake.

"Get up, Ray!" cried Rory, entering his friend's cabin.

"Ray, *Ray*, RAY!"

The last "Ray" was shouted.

"Hullo! hullo!" cried Ray. "Oh! it's you, is it, Row? Is breakfast all ready, old man?"

"Ray, arise, you lazy dog!" continued Row, shaking him by the shoulder. "This is May-morning, Ray, and I'm to be Queen of the May, my boy, I'm to be Queen of the May!"

At half-past eight our heroes, Captain McBain included, went on deck in a body, and this was the time for the crew to cluster up the rigging, man the yards, and give voice to a ringing cheer; nay, not one cheer only, but three times three; and hardly had the sound died away ere it was taken up and re-echoed back by the crew of the *Canny Scotia*. It seemed that Captain Cobb's cockle-shell was not to be left out of the fun either, for the crew of even that tiny craft must man the rigging and cheer, though after the lusty roar that had gone up from the other ships, their voices sounded like that of a chicken learning to crow.

After this, while the men went to work to rig a great platform on the upper deck, Peter, arrayed in fullest Highland costume, played pibroch after pibroch, and wild march after wild march, as he went strutting up and down the quarterdeck.

The decks were cleared of everything that could be removed, and a great tent erected from mizen to foremast; when this was lined with flags there was but little light, but lamps in clusters were hung here and there, and a stove was brought up to give heat, so that the whole place was as gay as could be, and comfortable as well.

At one end of the tent a platform was erected. There the piano was placed all handy, and Rory's fiddle and the doctor's flute, as well as several armchairs and a kind of a throne, the use of which will soon be seen. On the stage at one side was an immense tub nearly filled with cold, icy water; two steps led up to it, and on the edge thereof was a revolving chair. Very comfortable it looked indeed, but, on touching a spring, backwards it went, and whoever might be sitting on it had the benefit of a beautiful bath. My readers already guess what this is for. Yes, for May-day in Greenland is not only a day of fun and frolic, but the self-same kind of performance takes place as on southern ships while crossing the line.

The day itself was dedicated to games on the ice, for not until towards evening would the real fun begin. The seals had a rest to-day, and so had the sharks; even the terrible zugæna wasn't once thought of, and Bruin himself might sit on one end licking his chops and looking on, so long as he kept at a respectful distance. The games were both Scotch and English, a happy medley in which all hands joined. The morning saw cricket and football matches in full swing, the afternoon golf—and golf played on hummocky ice *is* golf—and hockey. Peter was the band, and right well he played; but when, tired of march quadrille, or pibroch, he burst into a Highland reel, and the crews began to dance—well, the scene on the snow grew exciting indeed. It was grotesque enough, too, in all conscience, for everybody, without exception, was dressed in fancy costume.

No wonder, too, that Cockie, whom his master had

brought on deck to look down on them from the bulwarks, lost all control of himself, and shouted, "Go on—go on—keep it up—keep it up." Then when Cockie began to throw his head back and shriek with laughter, the men couldn't resist it any longer; they joined in that laugh, and laughed till sides ached and eyes ran water, and many had to roll in the snow to prevent catastrophes. But the louder the men laughed, all the louder laughed Cockie, till Freezing Powders was obliged to run below with him at last.

"Oh!" said his master, as he restored the cage to its corner, "I tell you all day, Cockie, you eat too much hemp. It's drefful, Cockie, to hear you laugh like all dat."

Suddenly from the bows of the *Arrandoon* a big gun is fired, and the revel stops. Then comes a hail from the crow's-nest,

"Below there!"

"Ay, ay!" roared McBain.

"A procession coming along over the snow, sir, towards the ship."

A consultation was at once held, and it was resolved to march forth to meet them.

"It is Neptune, I know," said McBain, "for a snow-bird this morning brought me a note to say he'd dine with us."

It wasn't long before our friends came in sight of the royal party. It was Neptune, sure enough, trident and all, both his trident and he looking as large as life. He was drawn along in a sledge by a party of naiads, and Amazon jades they looked. On one side of him walked his wife, on the other the Cock o' the North, while behind him came the barber carrying an immense razor and a bucket of lather. Silas Grig, I may as well mention, played Neptune, and Seth his wife—and a taller, skinnier, bristlier old lady you couldn't have imagined; and her attempts to act the lady of fashion, and her airs and graces, were really funny. The Cock o' the North was Ted Wilson. He was dressed in feathers from top to toe, with an immense bill, comb, and wattles, and acted his part well. He was introduced by Neptune as—

> "One who ne'er has been to school,
> But keeps us fat—in fact, our fool;
> A fool, forsooth, yet full of wit
> As he can stand, or lie, or sit."

After the usual introduction, salaams, and courtesies, Neptune made his speech in doggerel verse, with many an interruption both from his wife and his fool, telling how "his name was Neptune"—"though it might be Norval," added the Cock o' the North. How—

> "From east to west, from pole to pole,
> Where'er waves break or waters roll,
> *My* empire is——"
>
> *His Wife*—"And *you* belong to *me*."
> *Cock o' the North.*—"All hail, great monarch of the sea!"
> *Neptune*—"The clouds pay tribute, and streams and rills
> Come singing from the distant hills."
> *His Wife.*—"*Do* stop, my dear; you're *not* a poet,
> And never were——"
> *Neptune.*— "Good sooth, I know it.
> But now lead on, our blood feels cold,
> For truth to tell, we're getting old.
> We and our wife have seen much service,
> Besides—the dear old thing is nervous,
> So to the ship lead on, I say,
> We'd see some fun on this auspicious day.
> My younger sons I fain would bless 'em."
> *His Barber.*—"And I can shave."
> *His Wife* (*rapturously*).—"And I can kiss 'em."

The six poor lads who were to be operated on, and whose only fault was that they had never before crossed the line, trembled in their prison as they heard the big guns thunder forth, announcing the arrival of King Neptune.

They trembled more when, dressed in white, they were led forth, a pair at a time, and seated blindfolded on the chair of the terrible tub, and duly shaved and blessed and kissed; but they trembled most when the bolt was drawn, and they tumbled head foremost into the icy water; but when, about twenty minutes thereafter, they were seen seated in a row in dry, warm clothing, you would not have known them for the same boys. Their faces were beaming with smiles, and each one busied himself discussing a huge basin of savoury sea-pie. They were not trembling then at all.

At the dinner which followed, Neptune took the head of the table, with his wife on his right and McBain himself as vice-president. The dinner was good even for the *Arrandoon*, and that is saying a deal. In size, in odour, and beauty of rotundity, the plum-pudding that two stalwart men carried in and placed in front of Neptune, was something to remember for ever and a day. Size? Why, Neptune could have served it out with his trident. Ay! and everybody had two helps, and looked all the healthier and happier after them.

Our three chief heroes were in fine form, Rory in one of his funniest, happiest moods. And why not? Had not he dubbed himself Queen o' the May? Yes, and well he sustained the part.

I am not sure how Neptune managed to possess himself of so many bottles of Silas Grig's green ginger, but there they were, and they went all round the table, and even the men of the crew seemed to prefer it to rum. The toasts given by the men were not a few, and all did honour to the manliness of their hearts. The songs sung ere the table was cleared were all well worth listening to, though some were ballads of extreme length.

Neptune was full of anecdotes of his life and adventures, and his wife also had a good deal to say about hers, which caused many a peal of laughter to rattle round the table.

Some of the men recited pieces of their own composition. Here is one by the crew's pet, Ted Wilson to wit:

THE GHOST OF THE COCHIN-SHANGHAI.

Tis a tale of the Greenland ocean,
    A tale of the Northern seas,
Of a ship that sailed from her native land
    On the wings of a favouring breeze;
Her skipper as brave a seaman
    As ever set sail before,
Her crew all told as true and bold
    As ever yet left the shore.

And never a ship was better "found,"
    She couldn't be better, I know,
With beef in the rigging and porkers to kill,
    And tanks filled with water below;
And turkeys to fatten, and ducklings and geese,
    And the best Spanish pullets to lay;
But the pride of the ship, and the pet of the mess,
    Was a Brahma cock, Cochin-Shanghai.
And every day when the watches were called,
    This cock crew so cheery O!
With a shrill cock-a-lee, and a hoarse cock-a-lo,
    And a long cock-a-leerie O!
But still as the grave was the brave bird at night,
    For well did he know what was best;
Yes, well the cock knew that most of the crew
    Were weary and wanted their rest.
But one awful night he awoke in a fright,
    Then wasn't it dreary O!
To hear him crow, with a hoarse cock-a-lo,
    And a shrill cock-a-leerie O!
                    Oh!

Then out of bed scrambled the men in a mass,
    "We cannot get sleep," they all cried;
"May we never reach dock till we silence that cock,
    We'll never have peace till the villain is fried."
All dressed as they were in the garments of night,
    Though the decks were deep covered with snow,

They chased the cock round, with wild yell and bound,
    But they never got near him—no.
And wherever he flew, still the bold Cochin crew,
    With a shrill cock-a-lee, and a hoarse cock-a-lo,
    And a long cock-a-leerie O !

Now far up aloft defiant he stands,
    Like an eagle in eerie O !
Till a sea-boot at last, knocked him down from the mast,
    And he sunk in the ocean below.
But the saddest part of the story is this :
    He hadn't quite finished his crow,
He'd got just as far as the hoarse cock-a-lo
    But failed at the leerie O !
              Oh-h !

And that ship is still sailing, they say, on the sea,
    Though 'tis hundreds of years ago ;
Till they silence that cock they'll ne'er reach a dock,
    Nor lay down their burden of woe ;
For out on the boom, till the crack of doom,
    The ghost of the Cochin will crow,
With his shrill cock-a-lee, and his hoarse cock-a-lo,
    But *never* the leerie O !
              No !

They tell me at times that the ship may be seen
    Struggling on o'er the billows o' blue,
That the hardest of hearts would melt like the snow,
    To witness the grief of that crew,
As they eye the cold waves, and long for their graves,
    Looking *so weary O !*
Will he *never* have done with that weird cock-a-lo,
    As get to the leerie O ?
              Oh-h !

Dinner discussed, the fun commenced. In the first place, there were sailors' dances, and the floor was kept pretty well filled one way or another. But certainly *the* dances of the evening were the barber's "break-down," Rory's "Irish jig," and the doctor's "Hielan fling." They were *solos*, of course, and the barber was the first to take the floor; and oh! the shuffling and the double-shuffling, and the tripleing and double-tripleing of that wonderful hornpipe! No wonder he was cheered, and encored, and cheered again. Then came Rory, dressed in natty knickerbockers and carrying a shillelah! nobody could say at times which end of him was uppermost, or whether he did not just as often strike his seemingly adamantine head with his heels as with his shillelah. Lastly came Sandy McFlail in Highland costume, and being a countryman of my own, I must be modestly mum on the performance, only, towards the end of the "fling," you saw before you such a mist of waving arms and legs and plaid-ends, that you could not have been sure it was Sandy at all, and not an octopus.

But hark! there comes a shriek from the pack, so loud that it drowns the sounds of music and merriment. Men grow suddenly serious. Again they hear it, and there is a perceptible movement—a kind of thrill under their feet. It is the wail that never fails to give the first announcement of the breaking up of the sea of ice.

CHAPTER XXV.

BREAKING-UP OF THE GREAT ICE PACK—IN THE NIPS—THE "CANNY SCOTIA" ON HER BEAM-ENDS—STAVING OF THE "ARRANDOON."

IN the very midst of joy and pleasure in this so-called weary world, we are oftentimes very nigh to grief and pain.

See yonder Swiss village by the foot of the mountain, how peacefully it is sleeping in the moonlight; not a sound is to be heard save the occasional crowing of a wakeful cock, or the voice of watch-dog baying the moon. The inhabitants have gone to bed hours and hours ago, and their dreams, if they dream at all, are assuredly not dreams of danger. But hark to that terrible noise far overhead. Is it thunder? Yes, the thunder of a mighty avalanche. Nearer and nearer it rolls, till it reaches the devoted village, then all is desolation and woe.

See yet another village, far away in sunny Africa; its little huts nestle around the banyan-tree, the tall cocoa-palm, and the wide-spreading mango. They are a quiet, inoffensive race who inhabit that village. They live south of the line, far away from treacherous Somali Indians or wild Magulla men; they never even dreamt of war or bloodshed. They certainly do not dream of it now.

"The babe lies in its mother's arms,
The wife's head pillowed on the husband's breast."

Suddenly there is a shout, and when they awake—oh! horror! their huts are all in flames, the Arab slavers are on them, and—— I would not harrow your young feelings by describing the scenes that follow.

But a ship—and this is coming nearer home—may be sailing over a rippling sea, with the most pleasant of breezes filling her sails, no land in sight, and every one, fore and aft, as happy as the birds on an early morning in summer, when all at once she rasps, and strikes—strikes on a rock, the very existence of which was never even suspected before. In half an hour perhaps that vessel has gone down, and those that are saved are afloat in open boats, the breeze freshening every moment, the wavetops breaking into cold spray, night coming on, and dark, threatening clouds banking up on the windward horizon.

When the first wail arose from the pack that announced the breaking-up of the sea of ice, a silence of nearly a minute fell on the sailors assembled at the entertainment. Music stopped, dancing ceased, and every one listened. The sound was repeated, and multiplied, and the ship quivered and half reeled.

McBain knew the advantage of remaining calm and retaining his presence of mind in danger. Because he was a true sailor. He was not like the sailor captains you read of in penny dreadfuls—half coal-heaver, half Herzegovinian bandit.

"Odd, isn't it?" he muttered, as he stroked his beard and smiled; then in a louder voice he gave his orders.

"Men," he said, "we'll have some work to do before morning—get ready. The ice is breaking up. Pipe down, bo'swain. Mr. Stephenson, see to the clearing away of all this hamper."

Then, followed by Rory and the doctor, he got away out into the daylight.

The ships were all safe enough as yet, and there was only perceptible the gentlest heaving motion in the pack. Sufficient was it, however, to break up the bay ice between the bergs, and this with a series of loud reports, which could be heard in every direction. McBain looked overboard somewhat anxiously; the broken pieces of bay ice were getting ploughed up against the ship's side with a noise that is indescribable, not so much from its extreme loudness as from its peculiarity; it was a strange mixture of a hundred different noises, a wailing, complaining, shrieking, grinding noise, mingled with a series of sharp, irregular reports.

"It is like nothing earthly," said Rory, "that ever I heard before; and when I close my eyes for a brace of seconds, I could imagine that down on the pack there two hundred tom-cats had lain down to die, that twenty Highland bag-pipers—twenty Peters—were playing pibrochs of lament, and that just forenenst them a squad of militia-men was firing a *feu-de-joie*, and that neither the militia-men nor the pipers either were as self-contained as they should be on so solemn an occasion."

The doctor was musing; he was thinking how happy he had been half an hour ago, and now—heigho; it was just possible he would never get back to Iceland again, never see his blue-eyed Danish maiden more.

"Pleasures," he cried, "pleasures, Captain McBain——"

"Yes," said McBain, "pleasures——"

"Pleasures," continued the doctor,

'are like poppies shed,
You seize the flower, the bloom is fled.'

I'll gang doon below. Bed is the best place."

"Perhaps," said McBain, smiling, "but not the safest. Mind, the ship is in the nips, and a berg might go through her at any moment. There is the merest possibility of your being killed in your bed. That's all; but that won't keep *you* on deck."

Mischievous Rory was doing ridiculous attitudes close behind the worthy surgeon.

"What!" cried Sandy, in his broadest accent. "*That* not keep me on deck! Man, the merest possibility of such a cawtawstrophy would keep me on deck for a month."

"A vera judeecious arrangement," hissed Rory in his ear, for which he was chased round the deck, and had his own ears well pulled next minute. The doctor had him by the ear when Allan and Ralph appeared on the scene.

"Hullo!" they laughed, "Rory got in for it again."

"Whustle," cried Sandy.

"I only said 'a vera——'" began Rory.

"Whustle, will ye?" cried the doctor.

"I can't 'whustle,'" laughed Rory. But he had to "whustle," and then he was free.

"It's going to be a tough squeeze," said Silas to McBain.

"Yes; and, worse luck, the swell has set in from the east," answered the captain.

"I'm off to the *Canny Scotia*; good morning."

"One minute, Captain Grig; we promised to hoist up Cobb's cockle-shell. Lend us a hand with your fellows, will you?"

"Ay, wi' right good will," said Silas.

There were plenty of spars on board the *Arrandoon* big enough to rig shears, and these were sent overboard without delay, with ropes and everything else required.

The men of the *Arrandoon*, assisted by those of the *Canny Scotia*, worked with a readiness and will worthy even of our gallant Royal Engineers. A shears was soon rigged, and a winch got up. On a spar fastened along the cockle-shell's deck the purchase was made, and, under the superintendence of brave little Ap, the work began.

For a long time the "shell" refused to budge, so heavily did the ice press around her; the spar on her deck started though, several times. "Worse luck," thought little Ap. He had the spar re-fastened. Tried again. The same result followed. Then little Ap considered, taking "mighty" big pinches of snuff the while.

"We won't do like that," he said to himself, "because, look you see, the purchase is too much on the perpendicular. Yes, yes."

Then he had the spar elevated a couple of yards, and fastened between the masts, which he had strengthened by lashing extra spars to them. The result of this was soon apparent. The hawsers tightened, the little yacht moved, even the pressure of the ice under her helped to lift her as soon as she began to heel over, and, in half an hour afterwards, the cockle-shell lay in a very ignominious position indeed—beam-ends on the ice.

"Bravo!" cried Silas, when the men had finished their cheering. "Bravo! what *would* long Cobb say now? what would he say? Ha! ha! ha!"

Silas Grig laughed and chuckled till his face grew redder than ever, but he would not have been quite so gay, I think, had he known what was so soon to happen to his own ship.

Stevenson touched McBain on the shoulder.

"The ice presses heavy on the rudder, sir."

"Then unship it," said McBain.

"And I'll unship mine," said Silas.

Unshipping rudders is a kind of drill that few save Greenland sailors ever learn, but it is very useful at times, nevertheless.

In another hour the rudders of the two ships were hoisted and laid on the bergs. So that was one danger past.

But others were soon to follow, for the swell under the ice increased, the bergs all around them rolled higher and higher. The noise from the pack was terrific, as the pieces met and clashed and ground their slippery sides together. In an hour or two the bay ice had been either ground to slush, or piled in packs on top of the bergs, so that the bergs had freedom to fight, as it were. Alas! for the two ships that happened to be between the combatants. Their position was, indeed, far from an enviable one. Hardly had an hour elapsed ere the ice-harbours McBain and Silas had prided themselves in, were wrecked and disintegrated. They were then, in some measure, at the mercy of the enemy, that pressed them closely on every quarter. The *Canny Scotia* was the worst off—she lay between two of the biggest bergs in the pack. McBain came to his assistance with torpedoes. He might as well have tried to blow them to pieces with a child's pop-gun. Better, in fact, for he would have had the same sport with less trouble and expense, and the result would have been equally gratifying.

For once poor Silas lost his equanimity. He actually wrung his hands in grief when he saw the terrible position of his vessel.

"My poor shippie," he said. "Heaven help us! I was building castles in the air. But she is doomed! My bonnie ship is doomed."

At the same time he wisely determined not to be idle, so provisions and valuables were got on shore, and all the men's clothes and belongings.

As nothing more could be done, Silas grew more contented. "It was just his luck," he said, "just his luck."

Long hours of anxiety to every one went slowly past, and still the swell kept up, and the bergs lifted and fell and swung on the unseen billows, and ground viciously against the great sides of the *Arrandoon*. Now the *Canny Scotia* was somewhat Dutchified in her build— not as to bows but as to bottom. She was not a clipper by any manner of means, and her build saved her. The ice actually ground her up out of the water till she lay with her beam ends on the ice, and her keel completely exposed.*

* As did the *P——e*, of Peterhead, once for weeks. The men lived on the ice alongside, expecting the vessel to sink as soon as the ice

But the *Arrandoon* had no such build. The ice caught under her forefoot, and she was lifted twelve feet out of the water. No wonder McBain and our heroes were anxious. The former never went below during all the ten hours or more that the squeeze lasted. But the swells gradually lessened, and finally ceased. The *Arrandoon* regained her position, and lost her list, but there lay the *Canny Scotia*, a pitiable sight to see, like some giant overthrown, silent yet suffering.

When the pumps of the *Arrandoon* had been tried, and it was found that there was no extra water in her, McBain felt glad indeed, and thanked God from his inmost heart for their safe deliverance from this great peril. He could now turn his attention to consoling his friend Silas. After dinner that day, said McBain,

"Your cabin is all ready, Captain Grig, for of course you will sleep with us now."

But Silas arose silently and calmly.

"I needn't say," he replied, "how much I feel your manifold acts of kindness, but Silas Grig won't desert his ship. His bed is on the *Canny Scotia*."

"But, my dear fellow," insisted McBain, "the ice may open in an hour, and your good ship go down."

"Then," said Silas, "I go with her, and it will be for you to tell my owners and my little wife—heaven keep her!—that Skipper Grig stuck to his ship to the last."

What could McBain say, what argument adduce, to prevent this rough old tar from risking his life in what he considered a matter of duty? Nothing! and so he was dumb.

Then away went Silas home, as he called it, to his ship. He lowered himself down by a rope, clambered

---

opened. The captain, however, would not desert his ship, but slept on board, his mattress lying on the ship's side. The author's ship was beset some miles off at the same time.

over the doorway of the cabin, took one glance at the chaos around, then walked tenderly *over* the bulkhead, and so literally *down* to his bed. He found the mattress and bed-clothes had fallen against the side, and so there this good man, this true sailor, laid him down and slept the sleep of the just.

But the *Scotia* did not go to the bottom; she lay there for a whole week, defying all attempts to move her, Silas sleeping on board every night, the only soul in her, and his crew remaining on the *Arrandoon*. At the end of that time the ice opened more; then the prostrate giant seemed to begin to show signs of returning life. She swayed slightly, and looked as if she longed once more to feel the embrace of her native element; seeing which, scientific assistance was given her. Suddenly she sprang up as does a fallen horse, and hardly had the men time to seek safety on the neighbouring bergs, when she took the water—relaunched herself—with a violence that sent the spray flying in every direction with the force of a cataract. It would have been well had the wetting the crew received been the only harm done.

It was not, for the bergs moved asunder with tremendous force. One struck the *Arrandoon* in her weakest part—amidships, under the water-line. She was stove, the timbers bent inwards and cracked, and the bunks alongside the seat of accident were dashed into matchwood. Poor old Duncan Gibb, who was lying in one of these bunks with an almost united fracture of one of his limbs, had the leg broken over again.

"Never mind, Duncan," said the surgeon, consolingly, "I didn't make a vera pretty job of it last time. I'll make it as straight as a dart this turn!"

"Vera weel, sir; and so be it," was poor contented Duncan's reply, as he smiled in his agony.

"Dear me, now!" said Silas, some time afterwards; "I could simply cry—make a big baby of myself and cry. It would be crying for joy and grief, you know—joy that my old shippie should show so much pluck as to right herself like a race-horse, and grief to think she should go and stave the *Arrandoon*. The ungrateful old jade!"

"Never mind," said McBain, cheerfully, "Ap and the carpenters will soon put the *Arrandoon* all right. We will shift the ballast, throw her over to starboard, and repair her, and the place will be, like Duncan's leg, stronger than ever."

It did not take very long to right Captain Cobb's cockle-shell, and all the vessels being now in position again, and the ice opening, it might have been as well to have got steam up at once, and felt the way to the open water. McBain decided to make good repairs first; it was just as easy to list the ship among the ice as out of it, and probably less dangerous. Besides, the water kept pouring in, and the beautiful arrangement of blankets and hammock-cloths which Ap had devised, hardly sufficed to keep it out.

This decision of the captain nearly cost the life of two of our best-loved heroes, and poor old Seth as well. But their adventure demands a chapter, or part of one at least, to itself.

CHAPTER XXVI.

AN ADVENTURE ON THE PACK—SEPARATED FROM THE SHIP—DESPAIR—THE DREAM OF HOME—UNDER WAY ONCE MORE.

NOTHING in the shape of adventure came amiss to Rory. He was always ready for any kind of "fun," as he called every kind of excitement. Such a thing as fear I do not believe Rory ever felt, and, as for failing in anything he undertook, he never even dreamt of such a thing. He had often proposed escapades and wild adventures to his companions at which they hung fire. Rory's line of argument was very simple and unsophisticated. It may be summed up in three sentences—first, "Sure we've only to try and we're bound to do it." If that did not convince Allan or Ralph, he brought up his first-class reserve, "Let us try, *anyhow;*" and if that failed, his second reserve, "It's *bound* to come right in the end." Had Rory been seized by a lion or tiger, and borne away to the bush, those very words would have risen to his lips to bring him solace, "It's bound to come right in the end."

The few days' delay that succeeded the accident to the *Arrandoon*, while she had to be listed over, and things were made as uncomfortable as they always are when a ship is lying on an uneven keel, threw Rory back upon his books for enjoyment. That and writing verses, and, fiddle in hand composing music to his own words, enabled him to pass the day with some degree of comfort; but when Mr.

Stevenson one morning, on giving his usual report at breakfast-time, happened to say,

"Ice rather more open to-day, sir; a slight breeze from the west, and about a foot of rise and fall among the bergs; two or three bears about a mile to leeward, and a few seals," then Rory jumped up.

"Will you go, Allan," he cried, "and bag a bear? Ralph hasn't done breakfast."

"Bide a wee, young gentleman," said McBain, smiling. "I really imagined I was master of the ship."

"I beg your pardon, Captain McBain," said Rory, at once; and with all becoming gravity he saluted, and continued, "Please, sir, may I go on shore?"

"Certainly not," was the reply; and the captain added, "No, boy, no. We value even Rory, for all the trouble he gives us, more than many bears."

Rory got hold of his fiddle, and his feelings found vent in music. But no sooner had McBain retired to his cabin than Rory threw down his much beloved instrument and jumped up.

"Bide a wee; I'll manage," he cried.

"Doctor," he added, disarranging all the medico's hair with his hand—Sandy's legs were under the mahogany, so he could not speedily retaliate—"Sandy, mon, I'll manage. It'll be a vera judeecious arrangement."

Then he was off, and presently back, all smiles and rejoicing.

"Come on, Allan, dear boy," he cried. "We're going, both of us, and Seth and one man, and we're going to carry a plank to help us across the ice. Finish your breakfast, baby Ralph. I wouldn't disturb myself for the world if I were you."

"I don't mean to," said Ralph, helping himself to more toast and marmalade.

"What are you grinning at now?" asked Rory of the surgeon.

"To think," said Sandy, laughing outright, "that our poor little boy Rory couldn't be trusted on the ice without Seth and a plank. Ha, ha, ha! my conscience!"

"Doctor," said Rory.

"Well?" said the doctor.

"Whustle," cried Rory, making a face.

"I'll whustle ye," said Sandy, springing up. But Rory was off.

On the wiry shoulders of Seth the plank was borne as easily as if it had been only an oar; the man carried the rope and sealing clubs. The plank did them good service, for whenever the space between two bergs was too wide for a safe leap it was laid down, and over they went. They thus made good progress.

There was a little motion among the ice, but nothing to signify. The pieces approached each other gradually until within a certain distance. Then was the time to leap, and at once, too, without fear and hesitation. If you did hesitate, and made up your mind to leap a moment after, you might fail to reach the next berg, and this meant a ducking at the very least. But a ducking of this kind is no joke, as the writer of these lines knows from experience. You strip off your clothes to wring out the superabundance of water, and by the time you put them on again, your upper garments, at all events, are frozen harder than parchment. You have to construe the verb *salto* * from beginning to end before you feel on good terms with yourself again. But falling into the sea between two bergs may not end with a mere ducking. A man may be sucked by the current under the ice, or he may instantly fall a prey to that great greedy monster, the Greenland shark. Well the brute loves to devour a half-dead seal, but a man is caviare to his maw. Again, if you are not speedily rescued, the bergs may come slowly together and grind you to pulp.

* *Salto*—I leap, or jump.

But our heroes escaped scot-free. So did the bears which they had come to shoot.

"It is provoking!" said Rory. "Let us follow them a mile or so, at all events."

They did, and came in sight of one—an immensely great brute of a Bruin—who, after stopping about a minute to study them, set off again shambling over the bergs. Then he paused, and then started off once more; and this he did many times, but he never permitted them to get within shot.

All this time the signal of recall was floating at the masthead of the *Arrandoon*, but they never saw it. They began to notice at last, though, that the bergs were wider apart, so they wisely determined to give up the chase and return.

Return? Yes, it is only a little word—hardly a simpler one to be found in the whole English vocabulary, whether to speak or to spell; and yet it is a word that has baffled thousands. It is a word that we should never forget when entering upon any undertaking in which there is danger to either ourselves or others. It is a word great generals keep well in view; probably it was just that word "return" which prevented the great Napoleon from landing half a million of men on our shores with the view of conquering the country. The man of ambition was afraid he might find a difficulty in getting his Frenchmen back, and that Englishmen would not be over kind to them.

Rory and his party could see the flag of recall now, and they could see also the broad black fan being waved from the crow's-nest to expedite their movements. So they made all the haste in their power. There was no leaping now, the plank had to be laid across the chasms constantly. But at last they succeeded in getting just half-way to the ship, when, to their horror, they discovered that all further advance was a sheer impossibility! A lane of open water effectually barred their progress. It was already a hundred yards wide at least, and it was broadening every minute.

South and by west, as far as eye could reach, stretched this canal, and north-west as well. They were drifting away on a loose portion of the pack, leaving their ship behind them.

Their feelings were certainly not to be envied. They knew the whole extent of their danger, and dared not depreciate it. It was coming on to blow; already the face of that black lane of water was covered with angry little ripples. If the wind increased to a gale, the chances of regaining their vessel were small indeed; more likely they would be blown out to sea, as men have often been under similar circumstances, and so perish miserably on the berg on which they stood. To be sure, they were to leeward, and the *Arrandoon* was a steamer; there was some consolation in that, but it was damped, on the other hand, by the recollection that, though a steamer, she was a partially disabled one. It would take hours before she could re-adjust her ballast and temporarily make good her leak, and hours longer ere she could force and forge her way to the lane of water, through the mile of heavy bergs that intervened. Meanwhile, what might not happen?

Both Rory and Allan were by this time good ice-men, and had there been but a piece of ice big enough to bear their weight, and nothing more, they could have embarked thereon and ferried themselves across, using as paddles the butt-ends of their rifles. But there was nothing of the sort; the bay ice had all been ground up; there was nothing save the great green-sided, snow-topped bergs. And so they could only wait and hope for the best.

"It'll all come right in the end," said Rory.

He said this many times; but as the weary hours went by, and the lane widened and widened, till, from being a lane, it looked a lake, the little sentence that had always brought him comfort before seemed trite to even Rory himself.

The increasing motion of the berg on which they stood

did not serve to reassure them, and the cold they had, from their forced inactivity, to endure, would have damped the boldest spirits. For a time they managed to keep warm by walking or running about the berg, but afterwards movement itself became painful, so that they had but little heart to take exercise.

The whole hull of the *Arrandoon* was hidden from their view behind the hummocky ice, and thus they could not tell what was going on on deck, but they could see no smoke arising from the funnel, and this but served further to dishearten them.

Even gazing at those lanes of water that so often open up in the very midst of a field of ice, is apt to stir up strange thoughts in one's mind, especially if one be, like Rory, of a somewhat poetical and romantic disposition. The very blackness of the water impresses you; its depth causes a feeling akin to awe; you know, as if by instinct, that it is deep—terribly, eeriesomely deep. It lies smiling in the sunshine as to surface, but all is the blackness of darkness below. Up here it is all day; down there, all night. The surface of the water seems to divide two worlds—a seen and an unseen, a known and an unknown and mysterious—life and death!

Tired at last of roaming like caged bears up and down the berg, one by one they seated themselves on the sunny side of a small hummock. They huddled together for warmth, but they did not care to talk much. Their very souls seemed heavy, their bodies seemed numbed and frozen, but their heads were hot, and they felt very drowsy, yet bit their lips and tongues lest they might fall into that strange slumber from which it is said men wake no more.

They talked not at all. The last words were spoken by Seth. Rory remembered them.

"I'm old," he was muttering; "my time's a kind o' up; but it do seem hard on these younkers. Guess I'd give the best puma's skin ever I killed, just to see Rory safe. Guess I'd——"

Rory's eyes were closed, he heard no more. He was dreaming. Dreaming of what? you ask me. I answer, in the words of Lover,

> "Ask of the sailor youth, when far
>   His light barque bounds o'er ocean's foam
> What charms him most when evening star
>   Smiles o'er the wave? To dream of home."

Yes, Rory was dreaming of home. All the home he knew, poor lad! He was in the Castle of *Arrandoon*. Seeing, but all unseen, he stood in the cosy tartan parlour where he had spent so many happy hours. A bright fire was burning in the grate, the curtains were drawn, in her easy-chair sat Allan's mother with her work on her lap, the great deerhound lay on the hearthrug asleep, and Helen Edith was bending over her harp. How boy Rory longed to rush forward and take her by the hand! But even in his partial sleep he knew this was but a dream, and he feared to move lest he might break the sweet spell. But languor, pain, and cold, all were forgotten while the vision lasted.

But list! a horn seems to sound beyond the castle moat. Rory, in his dream, wonders that Helen hears it not; then the boy starts to his feet on the snow. The vision has fled, and the sound of the horn resolves itself into the shout,

"Ahoy—oy—hoy! Ahoy! hoy!"

Every one is on his feet at the same time, though both Allan and Rory stagger and fall again. But, behold! a boat comes dancing down the lane of water towards them, and a minute after they are all safe on board.

The labour of getting that boat over the ice had been tremendous. It had been a labour of love, however, and the men had worked cheerily and boldly, and never flinched

DREAMING OF HOME.   [Page 244.

a moment, until it was safely launched in the open water and our heroes were in it.

The *Arrandoon*, the men told them, had got up steam, and in a couple of hours at most she would reach the water. Meanwhile they, by the captain's orders, were to land on the other side, and make themselves as comfortable as possible until her arrival.

Rory and Allan were quite themselves again now, and so, too, was honest Seth,

"Though, blame me," said he, "if I didn't think this old trapper's time had come. Not that that'd matter a sight, but I did feel for you youngsters, blame me if I didn't;" and he dashed his coat-sleeve rapidly across his face as he spoke.

And now a fire was built and coffee made, and Stevenson then opened the Norwegian chest—a wonderful contrivance, in which a dinner may be kept hot for four-and-twenty hours, and even partially cooked. Up arose the savoury steam of a glorious Irish stew.

"How mindful of the captain!" said Allan.

"It was Ralph that sent the dinner," said Stevenson, "and he sent with it his compliments to Rory."

"Bless his old heart," cried Rory. "I don't think I'll ever chaff him again about the gourmandising propensities of the Saxon race."

"And the doctor," continued the mate, "sent you some blankets, Mr. Rory. There they are, sir; and he told me to give you this note, if I found you alive."

The note was in the Scottish dialect, and ran as follows:—

"*My conscience, Rory! some folks pay dear for their whustle. But keep up your heart, ma wee laddie. It's a vera judeecious arrangement.*"

* * * * *

In a few days more the *Arrandoon* had made good her repairs, and as the western wind had freshened, and was blowing what would have been a ten-knot breeze in the open sea, the steamer got up steam and the sailing-ship canvas, and together they took the loose ice, and made their way slowly to the eastward. The bergs, though some distance asunder, were still sufficiently near to considerably impede their way, and, for fear of accident, the *Arrandoon* took the cockle-shell, as she was always called now, in tow.

For many days the ships went steadily eastward, which proved to them how extensive the pack had been. Sometimes they came upon large tracts of open water, many miles in extent, and across this they sailed merrily and speedily enough, considering that neither of the vessels had as yet shipped her rudder. This they had determined not to do until they were well clear of the very heavy ice, or until the swell went down. So they were steered entirely by boats pulling ahead of them.

Open water at last, and the cockle-shell bids the big ships adieu, spreads her white sails to the breeze, and, swan-like, goes sailing away for the distant isle of Jan Mayen. Ay, and the big ships themselves must now very soon part company, the *Scotia* to bear up for the green shores of our native land, the *Arrandoon* for regions as yet unknown

CHAPTER XXVII.

WORKING ALONG THE PACK EDGE—AMONG THE SEALS AGAIN—A BUMPER SHIP—ADVENTURES ON THE ICE—TED WILSON'S PROMOTION.

THE *Arrandoon* was steaming slowly along the pack edge, wind still westerly, the *Canny Scotia*, with all canvas exposed, a mile or more to leeward of her. Both were heading in the same direction, north and by east, for McBain and our heroes had determined not to desert Silas until he really had what he called a voyage—in other words, a full ship.

"We can spare the time, you know," the captain had said to Ralph; "a fortnight, will do it, and I dare say Rory here doesn't object to a little more sport before going away to the far north."

"That I don't," Rory had replied.

"If we fall among the old seals, a fortnight will do it."

"Ay," Allan had said; "and won't old Silas be happy!"

"Yes," from McBain; "and, after all, to be able to give happiness to others is certainly one of the greatest pleasures in this world."

Dear reader, just a word parenthetically. I am so sure that what McBain said is true, that I earnestly advise you to try the experiment suggested by his words, for great is the reward, even in this world, of those who can conquer self and endeavour to bring joy to others.

The *Arrandoon* steamed along the pack edge, but it must not be supposed that this was a straight line, or anything like it. Indeed it was very much like any ordinary coast-line, for here was a bay and yonder a cape, and yonder again, where the ice is heavier, a bold promontory. But Greenlandmen call a bay a " bight," and a cape they call a " point-end." Let us adopt their nomenclature.

The *Canny Scotia*, then, avoided these point-ends; she kept well out to sea, well away from the pack, for there was not over-much wind, and Silas Grig had no wish to be beset again. But the *Arrandoon*, on the other hand, steamed, as I have said, in a straight line. She scorned to double a point, but went steadily on her course, ploughing her way through the bergs. There was one advantage in this: she could the more easily discover the seals, for in the month of May these animals, having done their duty by their young, commence their return journey to the north, the polar regions being their home *par excellence*. They are in no hurry getting back, however. They like to enjoy themselves, and usually for every one day's progress they make, they lie two or three on the ice. The capes, or point-ends, are favourite positions with them, and on the bergs they may be seen lying in scores, nor if the sun be shining with any degree of strength are they at all easily disturbed. It is their summer, and they try to make the best of it. Hark now to that shout from the crow's-nest of the *Arrandoon*.

"A large patch of seals in sight, sir."

Our heroes pause in their walk, and gaze upwards; from the deck nothing is visible to windward save the great ice pack.

"Where away?" cries Stevenson.

"On the weather bow, sir, and a good mile in through the pack."

"What do you think, sir?" says Stevenson, addressing his commander. "Shall we risk taking the ice again?"

"Risk, Stevenson?" is the reply. "Why, man, yes; we'll risk anything to do old Silas a good turn. We'll risk more yet, mate, before the ship's head is turned homewards."

Then the ship is stopped, and signals are made to Silas, who instantly changes his course, and, after a vast deal if tacking and half-tacking, bears down upon them, and being nearly alongside, gets his main-yard aback, and presently lowers a boat and comes on board the *Arrandoon*.

Our heroes crowd around him.

"Why," they say, "you are a perfect stranger; it is a whole week since we've seen you."

"Ay," says Silas, "and a whole week without seeing a seal—isn't it astonishing?"

"Ah! but they're in sight now," says McBain. "I'm going to take the ice, and I'll tow you in, and if you're not a bumper ship before a week, then this isn't the *Arrandoon*, that's all."

Silas is all smiles; he rubs his hands, and finally laughs outright, then he claps his hand on his leg, and,

"I was sure of it," says Silas, "soon as ever I saw your signal. 'Matie,' says I, 'yonder is a signal from the *Arrandoon*. I'm wanted on board; seals is in sight, ye may be sure. Matie,' says I, 'luck's turned again;' and with that I gives him such a dig in the ribs that he nearly jumped out of the nest."

"Make the signal to the *Scotia*, Stevenson," says McBain, "to clew up, and to get all ready for being taken in tow. Come below, Captain Grig, lunch is on the table."

Fairly seated at the table, honest Silas rubbed his hands again and looked with a delighted smile at each of his friends in turn. There was a bluff heartiness about this old sailor which was very taking.

"I declare," he said, "I feel just like a schoolboy home for a holiday!"

Rory and Silas were specially friendly.

"Rory, lad," he remarked, after a pause, "we won't be long together now."

"No," replied Rory; "and it isn't sorry I am, but really downright *sad* at the thoughts of your going away and leaving us. I say, though—happy thought!—send Stevenson home with your ship and you stay with us in place of him."

Silas laughed. "What *would* my owners say, boy? and what about my little wife, eh?"

"Ah! true," said Rory; "I had forgotten." Then, after a pause, he added, more heartily, "But we'll meet again, won't we?"

"Please God!" said Silas, reverently.

"I think," Rory added, "I would know your house among a thousand, you have told me so much about it—the blue-grey walls, the bay windows, the garden, with its roses and—and——"

"The green paling," Silas put in.

"Ah, yes! the green paling, to be sure; how could I have forgotten that? Well, I'll come and see you; and won't you bring out the green ginger that day, Silas!"

"*And* the bun," added Silas.

"*And* the bun," repeated Rory after him.

"And won't my little wife make you welcome, too! you may bet your fiddle on that!"

Then these two sworn friends grasped hands over the table, and the conversation dropped for a time.

But there perhaps never was a much happier Greenland skipper than Silas Grig, when he found his ship lying secure among the ice, with thousands on thousands of old seals all around him. The weather continued extremely fine for a whole week. The little wind there had been, died all away, and the sun shone more warmly and brightly than it had done since the *Arrandoon* came to the country. The seals were so cosy that they really did not seem to mind being shot, and those that were scared off one piece of ice almost immediately scrambled on to another.

"Fire away!" they seemed to say; "we are so numerous

that we really won't miss a few of us. Only don't disturb us more than you can help."

So the seals hugged the ice, basking in the bright sunshine, either sleeping soundly or gazing dreamily around them with their splendid eyes, or scratching their woolly ribs with their flippers for want of something to do.

And bang, bang, bang! went the rifles; they never seemed to cease from the noon of night until mid-day, nor from mid-day until the noon of night again.

The draggers of skins went in pairs for safety, and thus many a poor fellow who tumbled into the sea between the bergs, escaped with a ducking when otherwise he would have lost his life.

Ralph—long-legged, brawny-chested Saxon Ralph—was among "the ducked," as Rory called the unfortunates. He came to a space of water which was too wide even for him. He would not be beaten, though, so he pitched his rifle over first by way of beginning the battle. Then he thought, by swinging his heavy cartridge-bag by its shoulder-strap the weight would help to carry him over. He called this jumping from a tangent. It was a miserable failure. But the best of the fun—so Rory said, though it could not have been fun to Ralph—was this : when he found himself floundering in the water he let go the bag of cartridges, which at once began to sink, but in sinking caught his heel, and pulled him for the moment under water. Poor Ralph! his feelings may be better imagined than described.

"I made sure a shark had me!" he said, quietly, when by the help of his friend Rory, he had been brought safely to bank.

It was not very often that Ralph had a mishap of any kind, but, having come to grief in this way, it was not likely that Rory would throw away so good a chance of chaffing him.

He suddenly burst out laughing at luncheon that day,

at a time when nobody was speaking, and when apparently there was nothing at all to laugh about.

"What now, Rory? what now, boy?" said McBain, with a smile of anticipation.

"Oh!" cried Rory, "if you had only seen my big English brother's face when he thought the shark had him!"

"Was it funny?" said Allan, egging him on.

"Funny!" said Rory. "Och! now, funny is no name for it. You should have seen the eyes of him!—and his jaw fall!—and that big chin of his. You know, Englishmen have a lot of chin, and——"

"And Irishmen have a lot of cheek," cried Ralph. "Just wait till I get you on deck, Row boy."

"I'd make him whustle," suggested the doctor.

"Troth," Rory went on, "it was very nearly the death o' me. And to see him kick and flounder! Sure I'd pity the shark that got one between the eyes from your foot, baby Ralph."

"Well," said Ralph, "it was nearly the death of me, anyhow, having to take off all my clothes and wring them on top of the snow."

"Oh! but," continued Rory, assuming seriousness, and addressing McBain, "you ought to have seen Ralph just then, sir. That was the time to see my baby brother to advantage. Neptune is nobody to him. Troth, Ray, if you'd lived in the good old times, it's a gladiator they'd have made of you entirely."

Here came a low derisive laugh from Cockie's cage, and Ralph pitched a crust of bread at the bird, and shook his fingers at Rory.

But Rory kept out of Ralph's way for a whole hour after this, and by that time the storm had blown clean away, so Rory was safe.

Allan had his turn next day. The danger in walking on the ice was chiefly owing to the fact that the edges of

"IT SEEMED MARVELLOUS THAT THE RIFLE DID NOT GO OFF."
[*Page* 253.

many of the bergs had been undermined by the waves and the recent swell, so that they were apt to break off and precipitate the unwary pedestrian into the water.

Here is Allan's little adventure, and it makes one shudder to think how nearly it led him to being an actor in a terrible tragedy. He was trudging on after the seals with rifle at full cock, for he expected a shot almost immediately, when, as he was about to leap, the snowy edge of the berg gave way, and down he went. Instinctively he held his rifle out to his friend, who grasped it with both hands, the muzzle against his breast, and thus pulled him out. It seemed marvellous that the rifle did not go off.*

When safe to bank, and when he noticed the manner in which he had been helped out, poor Allan felt sick, there is no other name for it.

"Oh, Ralph, Ralph!" he said, clutching his friend by the shoulder to keep himself from falling, "what if I had killed you?"

When told of the incident that evening after dinner, McBain, after a momentary silence, said quietly,

"I'm not sorry such a thing should have happened, boys; it ought to teach you caution; and it teaches us all that there is Some One in whose hands we are; Some One to look after us even in moments of extremest peril."

But I think Allan loved Ralph even better after this.

*   *   *   *   *

Two weeks' constant sealing; two weeks during which the crews of the *Arrandoon* and *Canny Scotia* never sat down to a regular meal, and never lay down for two consecutive hours of repose, only eating when hungry and sleeping when they could no longer keep moving; two weeks during which nobody knew what o'clock it was at any particular time, or which was east or west, or whether it were day or night. Two weeks, then the seals on the ice disappeared as if by magic, for the frost was coming.

* Both these adventures are sketched from the life.

"Let them go," said Silas, shaking McBain warmly by the hand. "Thanks to you, sir, I'm a bumper ship. Why, man, I'm full to the hatches. Low freeboard and all that sort of thing. Plimsoll wouldn't pass us out of any British harbour. But, with fair weather and God's help, sir, we'll get safely home."

"And now," McBain replied, "there isn't a moment to lose. We must get out of here, Captain Grig, or the frost will serve us a trick as it did before."

With some difficulty the ships were got about and headed once more for the open sea.

None too soon, though, for there came again that strange, ethereal blue into the sky, which, from their experiences of the last black frost, they had learned to dread. The thermometer sank, and sank, and sank, till far down below zero.

The *Arrandoon* took her "chummy ship" in tow.

"Go ahead at full speed," was the order.

No, none too soon, for in two hours' time the great steam-hammer had to be set to work to break the newly-formed bay ice at the bows of the *Arrandoon*, and fifty men were sent over the side to help her on. With iron-shod pikes they smashed the ice, with long poles they pushed the bergs, singing merrily as they worked, working merrily as they sang, laughing, joking, stamping, shouting, and cheering as ever and anon the great ship made another spurt, and tore along for fifty or a hundred yards. Handicapped though she was by having the *Scotia* in tow, the *Arrandoon* fought the ice as if she had been some mighty giant, and every minute the distance between her and the open water became less, till at last it could be seen even from the quarter-deck. But the frost seemed to grow momentarily more intense, and the bay-ice stronger and harder between the bergs. Never mind, that only stimulated the men to greater exertions. It was a battle for freedom, and they meant to win. With well-meaning though ridiculous doggerel, Ted Wilson led the music,

"Work and keep warm, boys; heave and keep hot,
Jack Frost thinks he's clever; we'll show him he's not,
    Beyond is the sea, boys;
    Let us fight and get free, boys;
One thing will keep boiling, and that is the pot.
    With a heave O!
    Push and she'll go.
To work and to fight is the bold sailor's lot.
    Heave O—O—O!

"Go fetch me the lubber who won't bear a hand,
We'll feed him on blubber, we'll stuff him with sand.
    But yonder our ships, boys,
    Ere they get in the nips, boys,
We'll wrestle and work, as long's we can stand,
    Then cheerily has it, men,
        Heave O—O—O!
    Merrily has it, men,
        Off we go, O—O—O!"

Yes, reader, and away they went, and in one more hour they were clear of the ice, the *Arrandoon* had cast the *Scotia* off, and banked her fires, for, together with her consort, she was to sail, not steam, down to the island of Jan Mayen, where they were to take on board the sleigh-dogs, and bid farewell to Captain Cobb, the bold Yankee astronomer.

There was but little wind, but they made the most of what there was. Silas dined on board that day, as usual. They were determined to have as much of the worthy old sailor as they could. But before dinner one good action was performed by McBain in Captain Grig's presence. First he called all hands, and ordered them aft; then he asked Ted Wilson to step forward, and addressed him briefly as follows:

"Mr. Wilson, I find I can do with another mate, and I appoint you to the post."

Ted was a little taken aback; a brighter light came into

his eyes; he muttered something—thanks, I suppose—but the men's cheering drowned his voice. Then our heroes shook hands with him all around, and McBain gave the order,

"Pipe down."

But as soon as Ted Wilson returned to his shipmates they shouldered him, and carried him high and dry right away forward, and so down below.

CHAPTER XXVIII.

A WONDERFUL YANKEE—"MAKING OFF" SKINS—PREPARING TO "BEAR UP"—THE SUMMER HOME OF THE GIANT WALRUS—THE SHIPS PART.

IN two days the ships sighted the island of Jan Mayen. As they neared it, they found the ice so closely packed around the shore that all approach even by boats was out of the question, so the sails were clewed, the ice-anchors got out, and both ships made fast to the floe.

It was not long ere Captain Cobb was on board the *Arrandoon*, to welcome our heroes back to "*his* island of Jan Mayen."

He was profuse in his thanks for what he called the clever kindness of Captain McBain, in saving his little yacht from a fatal accident among the ice; and, of course, they would do him the honour to come on shore and dine with him. He would take it as downright "mean" if they did not.

There was no resisting such an appeal as this, so, leaving their ships in charge of their respective mates, both McBain and Silas, in company with our heroes—Sandy McFlail, Seth, and all—they trudged off over the snowy bergs to take dinner in the hut of the bold Yankee astronomer. Very unprepossessing, indeed, was the building to behold from the outside, but no sooner had they entered, than they opened their eyes wide with astonishment.

When our young friends had visited it before, the hut looked neither more nor less than a big hall, or rather barn. But now—why, here were all the luxuries of civilised life. The place was divided into ante-room, saloon, and bed-chamber, and each apartment seemed more comfortable than another. The walls of the saloon were covered with rich tapestry, the floor with a soft thick carpet. There were couches and easy-chairs and skins *galore*, and books and musical instruments. A great stove, of American pattern, burned in the centre, giving out warmth and making the room look doubly cheerful, and overhead swung an immense lamp, which shed a soft, effulgent light everywhere, so that one did not miss the windows, of which the hut was *minus*. At one end of this apartment was a dining-table, as well laid and as prettily arranged as if it stood in the dining-hall of a club-room in Pall Mall, and beside the table were two sable waiters clad in white.

Captain Cobb seemed to thoroughly enjoy the looks of bewilderment and wonder exhibited on the faces of his guests.

"Why," said McBain at last, "pardon me, but you Yankees are about the most wonderful people on the face of the earth."

"Waal," said the Yankee, "I guess we like our little comforts, and don't see any harm in having them."

"So long's we deserve them," put in Seth, who, at that moment, really felt very proud of being a Yankee.

"Bravo! old man," cried his countryman; "let us shake your hand."

"And now, gentlemen," he continued, "sit in. I reckon the keen air and the walk have given ye all an appetite."

Soups, fish, *entrées*, joints—why I do not know what there was not in the bill-of-fare. It was a banquet fit for a king.

"I can't make out how you manage it," said McBain. "Do you keep a djin?"

Cobb laughed and summoned the cook. If he was not a djin, he was just as ugly. Four feet high—not an inch more—with long arms, black skin, flat face, and no nose at all worth mentioning. He was dressed as a *chef*, however, and very polite, for at a motion from his master, he salaamed very prettily and retired.

At dessert the host produced a zither, and, accompanying himself on this beautiful instrument, sang to them. He drawled while talking, but he sang most sweetly, and with a taste and feeling that quite charmed Rory, and held Silas and the doctor spellbound. He was indeed a wonderful Yankee.

"Do you know," said Rory, "I feel for all the world like being in an enchanted cave? Do sing again, if only one song."

It is needless to add that our friends spent the evening most enjoyably. It was a red-letter night, and one they often looked back to with pleasure, and talked about as they lay around their snuggery fire, during the long dreary time they spent in the regions round the Pole.

"I'm glad, anyhow," said Captain Cobb, as he bade them good-bye on the snow-clad beach, "that I've made it a kind o' pleasant for ye. Don't forget to call as you come back, and if Cobb be here, why, Cobb will bid you welcome. Farewell."

By eight bells in next morning watch everything was ready for a start. The dogs—twelve in number—were got on board and duly kennelled, and the old trapper was installed as whipper-in.

"But I guess," said Seth, "there won't be much whipping-in in the play. Trapper Seth is one of those rare old birds who know the difference between a dog and a door-knocker. Yes, Seth knows that there's more in a good bed and a biscuit, with a kind word whenever it is needed, than there is in all the cruel whips in existence."

The kennelling for the poor animals was got up under the supervision of Ap and Seth himself. It was built on what the trapper called "scientific principles."

There was a yard or run in common for the whole pack; but the large, roomy sleeping compartment had a bench, on which all twelve dogs could sleep or lie at once, yet nevertheless it was divided by boards about a foot high into six divisions. This was to prevent the dogs all tumbling into a heap when the ship rolled. The bedding was straw and shavings; of the former commodity McBain had not forgotten to lay in a plentiful supply before leaving Scotland. There was, besides, a whole tankful of Spratts' biscuits, so that what with these and the ship's scraps, it did not seem at all likely that the dogs would go hungry to bed for some time to come.

Seth was now much happier on board than ever he had been, because he had duties to perform and an office to fill, humble though it might be.

At half-past eight Silas came on board the *Arrandoon* to breakfast. Allan and Rory were tramping rapidly up and down the deck to keep themselves warm, for, though the wind was blowing west-south-west, it was bitterly cold, and the "barber" was blowing. The barber is a name given to a light vapoury mist that, when the frost is intense and the wind in certain directions, is seen rising off the sea in Greenland. I have called it a mist, but it in reality partakes more of the nature of steam, being due to the circumstance of the air being ever so much colder than the surface of the water.

Oh! but it is a cold steam—a bitter, biting, killing steam. Woe be to the man who exposes his ears to it, or who does not keep constantly rubbing his nose when walking or sailing in it, for want of precaution in this respect may result in the loss of ears or nose, and both appendages are useful, not to say ornamental.

"Good morning," cried Silas, jumping down on to the deck.

"The top of the morning to you, friend Silas," said Rory; "how do you feel after your blow-out at Captain Cobb's?"

"Fust-rate," said Silas—"just fust-rate; but where is Ralph and the captain?"

"Ralph!" said Rory; "why, I don't suppose there is a bit of him to be seen yet, except the extreme tip of his nose and maybe a morsel of his Saxon chin; and as for the captain, he is busy in his cabin. Breakfast all ready, is it, Peter? Thank you, Peter, we're coming down in a jiffy."

Just as they entered the saloon by one door, McBain came in by another.

"Ah! good morning, Captain Grig," he cried, extending his hand. "Sit down. Peter, the coffee. And now," he continued, "what think you of the prospect? It isn't exactly a fair wind for you to bear up, is it?"

"The wind would do," said Silas; "but I'm hardly what you might call tidy enough to bear up yet. It'll take us a week to make off our skins, and a day more to clean up. I'd like to go home not only a bumper ship, but a clean and wholesome sweet ship."

"Well, then," McBain said, "here is what I'll do for you."

"But you've done so much already," put in Silas, "that really——"

"Nonsense, man," cried McBain, interrupting him; "why, it has been all fun to us. But I was going to say that instead of lying here for a week, you had better sail north with us, Spitzbergen way, and my men will help you to make off and tidy up. Who knows but that after that you may get a fair wind to carry you right away south into summer weather in little over a week?"

"Bless your heart!" said Silas; "the suggestion is a grand one. I close with your offer at once. You see, sir, we Greenlandmen generally return to harbour all dirty, outside anyhow, with our sides scraped clean o' paint, and our masts and spars as black as a collier's."

"*You* shan't, though," said McBain. "We'll spend a bucket or two of paint over him, won't we, boys?"

"That will we," said Ralph and Allan, both in one breath.

"And I'll tell you what I'll do," added Rory.

"Something nice, I'm certain," said Silas.

"I'll paint and gild that Highland lassie of yours that you have for a figure-head."

"Glorious! glorious!" cried Silas Grig.

"Why, my own wife won't know the ship. And, poor wee body! she'll be down there looking anxiously enough out to sea when she hears I'm in the offing. Oh, it will be glorious! Won't my matie be pleased when he hears about it!"

"I say, though," said Rory, "I'll change the pattern of your Highland lassie's tartan. She came to the country a Gordon, she shall return a McGregor."

"Or a McFlail," suggested Sandy.

"Ha! ha! ha!" This was an impudent, derisive laugh from Cockie's cage, which made everybody else laugh, and caused Sandy to turn red in the face.

After breakfast the ice-anchors were cast off and got on board, and sail set. The *Arrandoon* led, keeping well clear of the ice, and taking a course of north-east and by north. When well off the ice, and everything working free and easy, McBain called all hands, and ordered the men to lay aft.

"Men," he said, "you all signed articles to complete the voyage with me to the Polar regions and back. Most of you knew, as you put your names to the paper, what you were about, because you had been here before, but some of you didn't. Now I am by no means short-handed, and if any of you thinks he has had enough of it already, and would like to return to his country, step forward and say so now, and I'll make arrangements with Captain Grig for your passage back."

Not a man stirred.

"I will take it as a favour," continued the captain, " if

any one who has any doubts on his mind will come forward now. I want only willing hands with me."

"We *are* willing, we *are* willing hands," the men shouted.

"Beg your pardon, sir," said bold Ted Wilson, stepping forward, "but I know the crew well. I'm sure they all feel thankful for your kind offer, but ne'er a man Jack o' them would go back, if you offered to pay him for doing so."

The captain bowed and thanked Ted, and the men gave one hearty cheer and retired.

Once fairly at sea, McBain sent two whalers on board the *Scotia*, their crews rigged out in working dress, and making off was at once commenced.

Upright boards were made fast here and there along the decks; the skins, with their two or three inches of blubber attached, were handed up from below, and the men set to work in this way—they stood at one side of the board and spread the skin in front of them on the other; then they leant over, and first cutting off all useless pieces of flesh, etc., they next cleaned the blubber from off the skin. This was by other hands cut into pieces about a foot square, carried away, and sent below to be deposited in the tanks. Other workmen removed the cleaned skins. These were dashed over with rough salt, rolled tightly and separately up, and cast into tanks by themselves. This latter duty devolved upon the mates, and old Silas himself stood, with book in hand, "taking tally," that is, counting the number of skins as they were passed one by one below. The refuse, or "orra bits," as Scotch sailors call them, were thrown overboard by bucketfuls, and over these thousands of screaming gulls fought on the surface of the water, and scores of sharks immediately beneath.

It was a busy scene, and one that can only be witnessed in Greenland north.

In three days all the skins were made off and stowed away. All this time the men had been as merry as sheepshearers, and only on the last day did Silas splice the mainbrace, even then diluting the rum with warm coffee.

Then came the cleaning up, and scouring of decks below and above, and white-washing and mast-scraping. After this McBain sent his painters on board, and in less than four-and-twenty hours she looked like a new ship.

And Rory was busy below on the 'tween decks. The Highland lassie had been unshipped, and taken below for him to paint and gild. Rory, mind you, did not wish it to be unshipped. He would have preferred being swung overboard. There would have been more fun in it, he said. But Silas would not hear of such a thing. The cold, he feared, would benumb him so that he might drop off into the sea, to the infinite joy and satisfaction of a gang of unprincipled sharks that kept up with the ship, but to the everlasting sorrow of him, Captain Silas Grig.

When the ship was all painted, and the masts scraped and varnished, and the Highland lassie—brightly arrayed in gold and McGregor tartan—re-shipped, why then, I do not think a prouder or happier man than Silas Grig ever trod a quarter-deck.

The day after this everybody on the *Arrandoon* was busy, busy, busy writing letters for home.

They were thus engaged, when a shout came from the crow's-nest,

"Heavy ice ahead!"

It was the ice-bound shores of the southernmost islands of Spitzbergen they had sighted. They passed between several of these, and grandly beautiful they looked, with their fantastically-shaped sides glittering green and blue and white in the sunshine. These islands seemed to be the northern home or summer retreat of the great bladder-nosed seal and the giant walrus. They basked on the smaller bergs that floated around them, while hundreds of strange sea-birds nodded half asleep on the snow-clad rocks.

It was here where the two ships parted, the *Canny Scotia* bearing up for the sunny south, the *Arrandoon* clewing sails and lighting fires to steam away to THE UNKNOWN LAND.

There were tears in poor Rory's eyes as he shook hands with Silas, and he could not trust himself to say much. Indeed, there was little said on either hand, but the farewell wishes were none the less heartfelt for all that. There is always somewhat of humour mixed up with the sad in life. It was not wanting on this occasion. Silas had brought a servant with him when he came to say adieu. This servant carried with him a mysterious-looking box. It was all he could do to lift it. Seeing McBain look inquiringly at it,

"It's just a drop of green ginger," said Silas. "When you tap it, boys, when far away from here, you won't forget Silas, I know. I won't forget you, anyhow," he continued; "and look here, boys, if a prayer from such a rough old salt as I am availeth, then Heaven will send you safely home again, and the first to welcome you will be Silas Grig. Good-bye, God be wi' ye."

"Good-bye, God be wi' ye."

CHAPTER XXIX.

NORTHWARD HO!— HOISTING BEACONS—THE **WHITE FOG** —THE GREAT SEA-SERPENT.

"GOOD-BYE, and God be with you."

It was a prayer as heartfelt and fervent as ever fell from the lips of an honest sailor.

The *Arrandoon* steamed away, and soon was hidden from view behind a lofty iceberg, and all that Silas Grig, as he stood on his own quarter-deck, could now hear, was the sad and mournful wail of Peter's bagpipes. Peter was playing that wild and plaintive melody which has drawn tears from so many eyes when our brave Highland regiments were departing for some far-off seat of war, to be

> "Borne on rough seas to a far distant shore,
> Maybe to return to Lochaber no more."

"Heigho! matie," sighed Silas, talking to his chief officer and giving orders all in one breath, "I don't think we'll—haul aft the jib-sheet—ever see them again. I don't think they can—take a pull on the main brace—ever get back from among that fearful—luff a little, lad, luff— ice, matie. And the poor boys, if any one had told Silas he could have loved them as much as he does in so short a time, he would have laughed in his face. Come below, matie, and we'll have a drop o' green ginger. Keep her close, Mortimer, but don't let her shiver."

"Ay, ay, sir," said the man at the wheel.

In a few hours the wind got more aft, and so, heading

now for more southern climes, away went the *Canny Scotia*, with stu'nsails up. I cannot say that she bounded over the waters like a thing of life. No; but she looked as happy and frisky as a plough-horse on a gala day, that has just been taken home from the miry fields, fed and groomed, and dressed with ribbons and started off in a light spring-van with a load of laughing children.

But eastwards and north steamed the *Arrandoon*. Indeed, she tried to do all the northing she could, with just as little easting as possible. She passed islands innumerable; islands that we fail to see in the chart, owing, no doubt, to the fact that they are usually covered entirely with ice and snow, and would be taken for immense icebergs. But this was a singularly open year, and there was no mistaking solid rocky land for floating ice.

The bearings of all these were carefully put down in the charts—I say charts, because not only the captain and mate, but our young heroes as well, took the daily reckoning, and kept a log, though I am bound in the interests of truth to say that Ralph very often did not write up his log for days and days, and then he impudently "fudged" it from Rory's.

"Are you done with my log?" Rory would sometimes modestly inquire of Ralph as he sat at the table busily "fudging."

"Not yet, youngster," Ralph would reply; "there, you go away and amuse yourself with your fiddle till I'm done with it, unless you specially want your ears pulled."

McBain landed at many of these islands, and hoisted beacons on them. These beacons were simply spare spars, with bunches of light wood lashed to their top ends, so that at some little distance they looked like tall brooms. He hoisted one on the highest peak of every island that lay in his route.

They came at length to what seemed the very nothernmost and most easterly of these islands, and on this

McBain determined to land provisions and store them. It would tend to lighten the ship; and "on the return voyage," said the captain, "if so be that Providence shall protect and spare us, they will be a welcome sight."

This done, the voyage was continued, and the sea becoming clearer of ice towards the west, the course was altered to almost due north.

The wind drawing round more to the south, the fires were banked, and the vessel put under easy sail. The water all round looked black and deep; but, with all the caution of your true sailor, McBain had two men constantly in the chains to heave the lead, with a watch continually in the crow's-nest to give warning of any sudden change in the colour of the water. More than once such a change was observed, the surface becoming of a yellowish ashen hue away ahead of them. Then the main or fore yard was hauled aback, and a boat despatched to investigate, and it was found that the strange appearance was caused by myriads of tiny shrimplets, what the northern sailor calls "whale's food." Whether this be whale food or not I cannot say for certain, but several times our heroes fell in with a shoal of bottle-noses, disporting themselves among these curious ashen-hued streams.

This formed a temptation too great to resist, for the oil would do instead of fuel when they wintered away up in the extreme north. So boats were lowered—not two but four, for these brutes are as wild as the winds and more wily than any old fox. No less than four were "bagged," as Rory called it. They were not large, but the blubber obtained from them was quite sufficient to fill one large tank. The best of it was, that Ralph—big, "plethoric" (another of Rory's pretty words), Saxon Ralph, made quite a hero of himself by manfully guiding his boat towards a floundering monster that was threatening destruction to the third whaler, which was fast to her, and skilfully spearing her at the very nick of time.

Rory was in the same boat, and drenched in blood from head to heels though both of them were, he must needs get up and shake his " baby brother " by the hand.

"Oh, sure!" said Rory, with tears in his eyes, "it's myself that is proud of the English race, after all. They haven't the fire of the Gael, but only just awaken them!—Dear Ray, you're a broth of a boy, entirely."

"What do you think," said McBain, one morning just after breakfast—"what do you think, Rory, I'm going to make to-day?"

"Sure, I don't know," said Rory, all interest.

"Why, fenders," said McBain.

"Fenders?" ejaculated Rory, with wider eyes. "Fenders? troth it'll be fire-irons you'll be making next, sir; but what do you want with fenders?"

"You don't take," said Ralph. "It is fenders to throw overboard when the ice is too obtrusive, isn't it, sir?"

"That's it," said the captain, laughing. "Sometimes the bergs may be a bit too pressing with their attentions, and then I'll hang these over. That's it."

It took nearly a fortnight to complete the manufacture of these fenders or trusses, for each of them was some twelve feet long by three in diameter composed of compressed straw and shielded by knitted ropework.

To the captain's foresight in making these fenders, they several times owed the safety of their gallant ship during the winter that followed.

A whole month passed away. The sun now set every night, and the still, long day began to get sensibly shorter.

The progress northward was hindered by dense white fogs,* which at times hugged the ship so closely that,

---

* The optical illusions caused among the ice by these fogs are well and humorously described in a book just to hand called "The Voyage of the *Vega*" (Macmillan and Co.) I myself wrote on the same subject *thirteen years ago*, in a series of articles on Greenland North.

standing by the bowsprit, you could not see the jibboom-end. The vessel, as Sandy McFlail expressed it, seemed enveloped in huge sheets of wet lint. Then the fog would lift partially off and away—in other words, it seemed to retire and station itself at some distance, with the ice looming through it in the most magical way. At these times the ship would be stopped, and our heroes were allowed to take boat exercise around the *Arrandoon*, with strict injunctions not to go beyond a certain distance of the vessel. Their laughing and talking and singing never failed to bring up a seal or two, or a round-eyed wondering walrus, or an inquisitive bladder-nose, but the appearance of these animals, as they loomed gigantic through the fog, was sometimes awful in the extreme. When a malley or gull came sweeping down towards them it looked as big as the fabulous Roc that carried away Sinbad the Sailor, and Rory would throw himself in the bottom of the boat and pretend to be in a terrible fright.

"Oh! Ray, boy, look at the Roc," he would cry. "I'm come for, sure enough. Do catch hold of me, big brother. Don't let the great baste carry me off. Sure, he'll fly up to the moon with me, as the eagle did with Daniel O'Rourke."

I think the fog must have caused delusions in sound as well as sight, else why the following.

They were pulling gently about, one day, in the first whaler, when, borne along on the slight breeze that was blowing, came a sound as of happy children engaged at play. The merry laughter and the occasional excited scream or shout were most distinctly audible.

"Whatever can it be?" cried Allan, looking very serious, his somewhat superstitious nature for a moment gaining the ascendency.

"Sure," said Rory, "you needn't pull so long a face, old man; it's only the childer just got out of school."

The "childer" in this instance were birds.

THE SEA SERPENT?

[*Page* 274.

"It's much clearer to-day," said Stevenson, one morning, as he made his usual report. "We can see the clouds, and they're all on the scud. I expect we'll have wind soon, sir."

"Very well, Mr. Stevenson," was the reply, "be ready for it, you know; have the fires lit and banked, and then stand by to get the ice-anchors and fenders on board" (the ship was fast to a berg).

"There is a line of ice to the westward, sir, about a quarter of a mile off, and clear water all between."

"Thank you, Mr. Stevenson."

But Stevenson did not retire. He stopped, hesitatingly.

"You've something to ask me, I think?" said McBain.

"I've something to tell you," replied the mate, with a kind of a forced laugh. "I dare say you will think me a fool for my pains, but as sure as you gentlemen are sitting there at breakfast this morning, about five bells in the middle watch I saw—and every man Jack of us saw——"

"Saw what?" said McBain. "Sit down, man; you are looking positively scared."

"We saw—*the great Sea-Serpent!*" *

McBain did not attempt to laugh him out of his story, but he made him describe over and over again what he had seen; then he called the watch, and examined them verbally man by man, and found they all told the self-same tale, talking soberly, earnestly, and truthfully, as men do who feel they are stating facts.

The terrible monster they averred came from the northwards, and was distinctly visible for nearly a minute, passing between the ship and the ice-line which Stevenson had mentioned. They described his length, which could not have been less than seventy or eighty yards, the undulations of his body as he swept along on the surface

---

* What is herein related really occurred as described. I myself was a witness to the event, being then in medical charge of the barque *Xanthus*, recently burned at sea.

of the water, the elevated head, the mane and—some added—the awful glaring eyes.

It did not come on to blow as the mate predicted, so the ship made no move from her position, but all day long there was but little else talked about, either fore or aft, save the visit of the great sea-serpent, and as night drew on the stories told around the galley fire would have been listened to with interest by any one at all fond of the mysterious and awful.

"I mean," said Rory, as he retired, "to turn out as soon as it is light, and watch; the brute is sure to return. I've told Peter to call me."

"So shall I," said Allan and the doctor.

"So shall I," said Ralph.

"Well, boys," said McBain, "I'll keep you company."

When they went on deck, about four bells in the middle watch, they were not surprised to find all hands on deck, eagerly gazing towards the spot where they had seen "the manëd monster of the deep"—as poet Rory termed him—disappear.

It was a cold, dull cheerless morning; the sun was up but his beams were sadly shorn—they failed to pierce the thick canopy of clouds and mist that overspread the sky, and brought the horizon within a quarter of a mile of them. They could, however, easily see the ice-line—long and low and white.

A whole hour passed, and McBain at all events was thinking of going below, when suddenly came a shout from the men around the forecastle.

"Look! look! Oh! look! Yonder he rips! There he goes!"

Gazing in the direction indicated, the hearts of more than one of our heroes seemed to stand still with a strange, mysterious fear, for there, rushing over the surface of the dark water, the undulated body well defined against the white ice-edge, was—what else could it be?—the great sea-serpent!

"I can see his mane and head and eyes," cried Rory. "Oh! it is too dreadful."

Then a shout from the masthead,

"He is coming this way."

It was true. The manëd monster had altered his course, and was bearing straight down upon the *Arrandoon*.

No one moved from his position, but there were pale, frightened faces and starting eyes; and though the men uttered no cry, a strange, frightened moan arose, a fearful quavering "Oh-h-h!"—a sound that once heard is never to be forgotten. Next moment, the great sea-serpent, with a wild and unearthly scream, bore down upon the devoted ship, then suddenly resolved itself *into a long flight of sea-birds* (Arctic divers)!

So there you have a true story of the great sea-serpent, but I am utterly at a loss to describe to you the jollity and fun and laughing that ensued, as soon as the ridiculous mistake was discovered.

And nothing would suit Ted Wilson but getting up on the top of the bowsprit and shouting,

"Men of the *Arrandoon*, bold sailors all, three cheers for the great sea-serpent. Hip! hip! hip! Hurrah!!!"

Down below dived Ralph, followed by all the others. "Peter! Peter! Peter!" he cried.

"Ay, ay, sir," from Peter.

"Peter, I'm precious hungry."

"And so am I," said everybody.

Peter wasn't long in laying the cloth and bringing out the cold meat and the pickles, and it wasn't long either before Freezing Powders brought hot coffee. Oh! didn't they do justice to the good things, too!

"I dare say," said the doctor, "this is our breakfast."

"Ridiculous!" cried Ralph, "ridiculous! It's only a late supper, doctor. We'll have breakfast just the same."

"A vera judeecious arrangement," said Sandy.

CHAPTER XXX.

LAND HO! THE ISLE OF DESOLATION—THE LAST BLINK OF SUNSHINE—THE AURORA BOREALIS—STRANGE ADVENTURE WITH A BEAR.

"WELL, Magnus," said Captain McBain one day to his old friend, "what think you of our prospects of gaining the North Pole, or your mysterious island of Alba?"

Magnus was seated at the table in the captain's own room, with an old yellow, much-worn chart spread out before him, the only other person in the cabin, save these two, being Rory, who, with his chin resting on his hands and his elbows on the table, was listening with great interest to the conversation.

"Think of it?" replied the weird wee man, looking up and glaring at McBain through his fierce grey eyebrows. "Think of it, sir? Why we are nearly as far north now as *we* were in 1843. We'll reach the Isle of Alba, sir, if——"

"If what, good Magnus?" asked McBain, as the old man paused. "If what?"

"If that be all you want," answered Magnus.

"Nay, nay, my faithful friend," cried the captain, "that isn't all. We want to reach the Pole, to plant the British flag thereon, and return safely to our native shores again."

"So you will, so you will," said Magnus, "if——"

"What, another 'if,' Magnus?" said McBain. "What does this new 'if' refer to?"

"If," continued Magnus, "Providence gives us just such another autumn as that we have had this year. If not——"

"Well, Magnus, well?"

"We will leave our bones to lie among the eternal snows until the last trump shall sound."

After a pause, during which McBain seemed in deep and earnest thought.

"Magnus," he said, "my brave boys and I have determined to push on as far as ever we can. We have counted all the chances, we mean to do our utmost, and we leave the rest to Providence."

Allan had entered while he was speaking, and he said, as the captain finished,

"Whatever a man dares he can do."

"Brave words, my foster-son," replied McBain, grasping Allan's hand, "and the spirit of these words gained for the English nation the victory in a thousand fights."

"Besides, you know," added Rory, looking unusually serious, "it is sure to come right in the end."

The *Arrandoon*, wonderful to relate, had now gained the extreme altitude of 86° north latitude, and although winter was rapidly approaching, the sea was still a comparatively open one. Nor was the cold very intense; the frosts that had fled away during the short Arctic summer had not yet returned. The sea between the bergs and floes was everywhere calm; they had passed beyond the region of fogs, and, it would almost seem, beyond the storm regions as well, for the air was windless.

So on they steamed steadily though slowly, never relaxing their vigilance; so careful, indeed, in this respect was McBain, that the man in the chains as well as the "nest hand' were changed every hour, and only old and tried sailors were permitted to go on duty on these posts.

"Land ahead!" was the shout one day from the nest. The day, be it remembered, was now barely an hour long.

"Land ahead on the port bow!"

"What does it look like, Mr. Stevenson?" cried the captain.

The mate had run up at the first hail.

"I can just see the tops of a few hills, sir," was the reply, "towering high over the icebergs."

The *Arrandoon* bore away for this strange land. In three hours' time they were lying off one of the dreariest and most desolate-looking islands it has ever been the lot of mariners to behold. It looked like an island of some worn-out planet, whose internal fires have gone for ever out, from which life has long since fled, which possesses no future save the everlasting night of silence and death.

Some slight repairs were required in the engine-room, so the *Arrandoon* lay here for a week.

"To think," said McBain, as he stood on the bridge one day with our heroes, "that in the far-distant past that lonely isle of gloom was once clad in all the bright colour of tropical vegetation, with wild beasts roaming in its jungles and forests, and wild birds filling its groves with music,—an island of sunshine, flowers, and beauty! And now behold it."

An expedition was got up to explore the isle, and to climb its highest peak to make observations.

McBain himself accompanied it, so did Allan, Rory, and Seth. It was no easy task, climbing that snowy cone by the light of stars and Aurora. But they gained the summit ere the short, short day broke.

To the north and west they saw land and mountains, stretching away and away as far as eye could follow them. To the east and north water studded with ugly icebergs that looked as if they had broken away from the shores of the western land.

"But what is that in the middle of yonder ice floe to the south and west?" cried Rory.

"As I live," exclaimed McBain, as he eyed the object through the glass, "it is a ship of some kind, evidently deserted; and it is quite as evident that we are not the only explorers that have reached as far north as this island."

The mystery was explained next day, and a sad story brought to light. McBain and party landed on the floe and walked towards the derelict. She was sloop-rigged, with sails all clewed, and her hull half hidden in snow. After a deal of difficulty they succeeded in opening one of the companion hatches, and making their way down below.

No less than five unburied corpses lay huddled together in the little cabin. From their surroundings it was plain they had been walrus-hunters, and it was not difficult to perceive that the poor fellows had died from cold and hunger *many, many years before*.

Frozen in, too far up in this northern sea, they had been unable to regain the open water, and so had miserably perished.

Next day they returned and laid the mortal remains of these unfortunate men in graves in the snow, and even Rory was much more silent and thoughtful than usual as they returned to the ship.

Was it not possible that they might meet with a similar fate? The poor fellows they had just buried had doubtless possessed many home ties; their wives and mothers had waited and wished a weary time, till at long last the heart had grown sick with hope deferred, and maybe the grave had long since closed over them.

Such were some of Rory's thoughts, but after dinner McBain "brought him up with a round turn," as he phrased it.

"Rory," he cried, "go and play to us. Freezing Powders, you young rascal, bring that cockatoo of yours up on the table and make us laugh."

Rory brightened up and got hold of his fiddle; and "All right, sal.," cried Freezing Powders. "I bring de old cockatoo plenty quick. Come along, Cockie, you catchee my arm and pull yourse'f up. Dat's it."

"Come on," cried Cockie, hopping on the table and at once commencing to waltz and polka round. "Come on; play up, play up."

A queer bird was Cockie. He cared for nobody except his master and Rory. Rory he loved solely on account of the fiddle, but his affection for Freezing Powders was very genuine. When his master was glad, so was Cockie; when the little nigger boy felt tired, and threw himself down beside the cage to rest, then Cockie would open his cage door and back tail foremost under the boy's arm, heaving as he did so a deep, delighted sigh, as much as to say, "Oh, what joy it is to nestle in here!"

Cockie was not a pretty bird; his bill was worn and all twisted awry, and his eyes looked terribly old-fashioned, and the blue, wrinkled skin around them gave him quite an antediluvian look. He was white in colour—or, more correctly speaking, he had been white once; but time, that steals the roses from the softest cheeks, had long since toned him down to a kind of yellow lilac, so he did not look a very respectable bird on the whole.

"You ought to wash him," McBain said, one day.

"Wash him, sah?" said Freezing Powders; "is dat de 'xpression you make use of, sah? Bless you, sah! I have tried dat plenty much often; I have tried to wash myself, too; No good in eeder case, sah; I'ssure you I speak de truf."

"Come on! come on!" cried Cockie. "Play up! play up! La de lal, de lal, de lal!"

And round spun the bird, keeping time to the merry air, and every now and then giving a "whoop!" such as could only be emitted by Cockie himself, a Connemara Irishman, or a Cuscarora Indian.

But this is a remarkable thing, Cockie danced and whirled in one direction till he found his head getting light, then he reversed the action, and whirled round the other way!

* This description of the wonderful bird is in no way overdrawn.

It really seemed as if he would tire Rory out. "Lal de dal!" he sung; "our days are short—whoop!—our lives are merry—lal de dal, de dal, de *whoop!*"

But Rory changed his tactics; he began to play *The Last Rose of Summer*, leaning down towards the table. Cockie stopped at once, and backed, tail foremost, in under the musician's hands, crouching down with a sigh to listen.

But Rory went off again into the *Sprig of Shillelagh*, and off went Cockie, too, dancing more madly than ever with a small flag in his mouth that Freezing Powders had handed him. Then he stopped at last, and walked about gasping, pitching penholders and pencils in all directions.

"Here's a pretty to-do!" he said; and when somebody laughed, Cockie simply shrieked with laughter till he had everybody joining him and holding their sides, and feeling sore all over. Verily, Cockie was a cure! No wonder his, master loved him.

In a few days the *Arrandoon* left the desolate island which Rory had named "Walrus Isle."

Everybody was on deck as the vessel slowly steamed away.

Most of the land was already shrouded in gloom, only in the far distance a tall mountain-cone was all ablaze with a crimson glory, borrowed from the last blink of sunshine. Yes, the god of day had sunk to rest, and they would bask no more in his cheering beams for many a long and weary month to come.

"Give us a bass, Ray, old boy!" cried Rory; "and you, doctor, a tenor."

And he started,—

"Shades of evening, close not o'er us,
Leave our lonely bark awhile,
Morn, alas! will not restore us
Yonder dim and distant isle."

Ah, reader! what a glorious thing music is; I tell you, honestly and truthfully, that I do not believe I could have come through half the trials and troubles and griefs and worries I have had in life, if I had not at times been able to seek solace and comfort from my old cremona.

Our heroes thought at first they would greatly miss the light of the sun, but they soon got quite used to the strange electric light emitted by the splendid Aurora, combined with that which gleamed more steadily downwards from the brilliant stars. These stars were seen to best advantage in the south; they seemed very large and very near, and whether it was the reflection of the Aurora, or whether it was real, I never could tell, but they seemed to shine with differently coloured lights. There were pure white stars, mostly low on the horizon; there were crimson and green changing stars, and yellow and rose-coloured changing stars, and some of a pale-golden hue, the soft light of which was inexpressibly lovely. But any effort of mine to paint in words the extreme beauty of the heavens on clear nights would prove but a painful failure, so I leave it alone. The chief bow of the Aurora is, I may just mention, composed apparently of spears of ever-changing rainbow-coloured light continually falling back into masses and phalanxes, and anon advancing and clashing, as it were. While walking on the ice-fields, if you listen, you can hear a strange whispering, hissing sound emitted from these clashing, mixing spears. The following letters, whispered rapidly, give some faint idea of this mysterious sound,—

"Ush—sh—sh—sh—sh—sh—sh."

You can also produce a somewhat similar noise by rubbing your fingers swiftly backwards and forwards on a sheet of paper.

But indeed the whole firmament, when the sky was clear, was precisely as Rory described it—"one beautiful poem."

Many bears were now seen, and nearly all that were seen were killed. They were enormously large and fierce, foolishly fierce indeed, for they seldom thought of taking to flight.

There were unicorns (narwhals) in the sea in scores, and walruses on the flat ice by the dozen. It was after these latter that Master Bruin came prowling.

A nice juicy walrus-steak a Greenland bear will tell you is the best thing in the world for keeping the cold out.

Old trapper Seth had strange ways of hunting at times. One example must suffice.

Our heroes had been out after a walrus which they had succeeded in killing. A bear or two had been seen an hour or two before that, evidently on the prowl, and probably very hungry. Now, nothing will fetch these kings of the northern ice more surely than the scent of blood.

"Young gentlemen," said Seth, "there's a b'ar about somewheres, and I reckon he ain't far off either. Now, we'll just whip this old walrus out o' his skin, and Seth will creep in, and you'll see what you'll see."

He was very busy with his knife as he spoke, and in a few minutes the crang was got out and thrown into the water, the head being left on. Into the skin crept the trapper, lying down at full length with his rifle close by his side, and by his directions away pulled the boat.

It was not two hundred yards off, when up out of the sea scrambled a huge bear.

"Hullo," says Bruin, shaking himself like a dozen great Newfoundland dogs rolled into one—"hullo! they've killed the wallie and left him. Now won't I have a blow-out just!" and he licked his great chops in anticipation.

"Dear me!" continued Bruin, as the walrus turned right round and confronted him; "why, they haven't quite killed you! Never mind, wallie, I'll put you out of pain, and I'll do it ever so gently. Then I'll just have one leetle bite out of your loin, you know."

"I guess you won't this journey," said Seth, bringing his rifle into position as the bear prepared to spring. "I reckon it'll be the other way on, and b'ar's steak ain't to be sneezed at when it's nicely cooked."

Bang!

It was very soon over with that poor bear; he never even changed the position into which he had thrown himself, but lay there dead, with his great head on his paws like a gigantic dog asleep.

CHAPTER XXXI.

A COUNCIL—PREPARING FOR WINTER QUARTERS—THE ISLE OF ALBA AND ITS MAMMOTH CAVES—MAGNUS'S TALE—AT HIS BOY'S GRAVE.

THE word "canny" is often applied to Scotchmen in a somewhat disparaging sense by those who do not know the meaning of the word, nor the true character of the people on whom they choose to fix the epithet. The word is derived from "can," signifying knowledge, ability, skill, etc., and probably a corruption of the Gaelic "caen" (head). The Scotch are pre-eminently a thinking nation, and, as a rule, they are individually skilful in their undertakings; they like to look before they leap, they like to know what they have to do before they begin, but having begun, they work or fight with all their life and power. It was "canniness" that won for Robert Bruce the Battle of Bannockburn, it was the canniness of Prince Charles Stuart that enabled him to defeat Sir John Cope at the Battle of Dunbar. There is no nation in the world possesses more "can" than the Scotch, although they are pretty well matched by the Germans. Prince Bismarck is the canniest man of the century.

"À Berlin! À Berlin!" was the somewhat childish cry of the volatile Gaul, when war broke out betwixt his sturdy neighbour and him.

Yes, fair France, go to Berlin if you choose, only first and foremost you have to overthrow—what? Oh! only one man. A very old one, too. Yonder he is, in that tent in the corner of a field, seated at a table, quietly solving, one would almost think, a chess problem. And so it is, but he is playing the game with living men, and every move he makes is carefully studied. That old man in the tent, to which the wires converge from the field of battle, is General von Moltke, the best soldier that the world has ever known since the days of Bonaparte and Wellington, and the *canniest*.

But the word "canny" never implies overfrugality or meanness, and I believe my readers will go a long way through the world, without meeting a Scotchman who would not gladly share the last sixpence he had in the world to benefit a friend.

Our Captain McBain was canny in the true sense of the word, and it was this canniness of his that induced him to call his officers, and every one who could think and give an opinion, into the saloon two days after the events described in the last chapter.

After making a short speech, in which he stated his own ideas freely, he called upon them to express theirs.

"If," he concluded, "you think we have gone far enough north with the ship, here, or near here, we will anchor; if you think we ought to push on, I will take that barrier of ice to the north-east, and push and bore and forge and blast my way for many miles farther, and it may be we will strike the open water around the Pole, if such open water exists."

"We are now," said Stevenson, after consulting for a short time with the second mate, with Magnus, and De Vere the aëronaut—"we are now nearly 88° north and 76° west from the meridian; the season has been a wonderful one, but will we have an open summer to find our way back again if we push on farther?"

"No," cried old Magnus, with some vehemence; "no such seasons as these come but once in ten years."

"I see how the land lies," said McBain, smiling, "and I am glad that we are all of the same way of thinking.

Well, gentlemen, this decides me; we shall winter where we are."

"Hurrah!" cried Stevenson; "we wouldn't have gone contrary to your wishes for the world, captain, but I'm sure we will be all delighted to go into winter quarters."

After this the *Arrandoon* was kept away more to the west, where the water was clearer of bergs, and where mountainous land was seen to lie.

They steamed along this land or shore for many miles, although lighted only by the bright silvery stars and the gleaming Aurora. They came at length to a small landlocked bay or gulf, entirely filled with flat ice. The ship was stopped, and all hands ordered away to a clear a passage by means of ice-saws and torpedoes. After many hours of hard work this was successfully accomplished, and the vessel was warped in till she lay close under the lee of the brae-land, that rose steeply up from the surface of the sea. Those braes were to the north and west of them, and would help to shelter the ship from at least one of the coldest winds.

"Well, boys," said McBain that day as they sat down to dinner, and he spoke more cheerfully than he had done since the departure of the *Scotia*,—"well, boys, here we are safe and snug in winter quarters. How do you like the prospect of living here for three months without ever catching a blink of the sun?"

"I for one don't mind it a bit," said Allan. "It'll do us all good; but won't we be glad to see the jolly visage of old Sol again, when he peeps over the hills to see whether we are dead or alive!"

"I'm sure," said Rory, "that I will enjoy the fun immensely."

"What fun?" asked Ralph.

"Why, the new sensation," replied Rory; "a winter at the Pole."

"You're not quite there yet," said Ralph; "but as for

me, I think I'll enjoy it too, though of course winter in London would be more lively. Why, what is that green-looking stuff in those glasses, doctor?"

"That's your dram," said Sandy.

"Why it's lime-juice," cried Rory, tasting his glass and making a face.

"So it is," said Ralph. "Where are the sugar-plums, doctor?"

"Yes," cried Rory: "where are the plums? Oh!" he continued, "I have it—a drop of Silas Grig's green ginger, steward, quick."

And every day throughout the winter, when our heroes swallowed their dose of lime-juice, they were allowed a tiny drop of green ginger to put away the taste, and as they sipped it, they never failed to think and talk of honest Silas.

And lime-juice was served out by the surgeon to all hands. They knew well it was to keep scurvy at bay, so they quietly took their dose and said nothing

The sea remained open for about a week longer, and scores of bears* were bagged. This seemed, indeed, to be the autumn home of the King of the Ice. Then the winter began to close in in earnest, and all saving the noon-day twilight deserted them. The sky, however, remained clear and starry, and many wonderful meteors were seen almost nightly shooting across the firmament, and for a time lighting up the strange and desolate scene with a brightness like the noon of day. The Aurora was clearer and more dazzling after the frost came, so that as far as light was concerned the sun was not so much missed.

On going on deck one morning our heroes were astonished to find a light gleaming down upon them from the maintop, of such dazzling whiteness that they were fain, for the moment, to press their hands against their eyes.

---

* These animals are said to bury themselves in the snow during winter, and sleep soundly for two or three months. This, however, is doubtful.

It was an electric candle, means for erecting which McBain had provided himself with before leaving the Clyde. So successful was he with his experiment that the sea of ice on the one hand, and the brae-land on the other, seemed enshrouded in gloom. Rory gazed in ecstasy, then he must needs walk up to McBain and shake him enthusiastically by the hand, laughing as he remarked,

"'Deed, indeed, captain, you're a wonderful man. Whatever made you think of this? What a glorious surprise. Have you any more in store for us? Really! sir, I don't know what your boys would do without you at all at all."

Thus spoke impulsive young Rory, as McBain laughingly returned his hand-shake, while high overhead the new light eclipsed the radiance of the brightest stars. But what is that strange, mournful cry that is heard among the hills far up above them? It comes nearer and still more near, and then out from the gloom swoops a gigantic bird. Attracted by the light, it has come from afar, and now keeps wheeling round and round it. Previously there had not been a bird visible for many days, but now, curious to relate, they come in hundreds, and even alight close by the ship to feed on the refuse that has been thrown overboard.

"It is strange, isn't it, sir?" said Rory.

"It is, indeed," replied McBain, adding, after a pause, "Rory, boy, I've got an idea."

"Well," said Rory, "I know before you mention it that it is a good one."

"Ah! but," said McBain, "I'm not going to mention it yet awhile."

"I vill vager," said the aëronaut, who stood beside them, gazing upwards at the bright light and the circling birds—"I vill vager my big balloon dat de same idea has struck me myself."

"Whisper," said the captain.

The aëronaut did so, and McBain burst out laughing.

"How funny!" he remarked; "but you are perfectly right, De Vere; only keep it dark for a bit."

"Oh yes," said De Vere, laughing in turn; "very dark; as dark as———"

"Hush!" cried McBain, clapping a hand on his mouth.

"How tantalising!" said Rory.

"You'll know all about it in good time," McBain said; "and now, boys, we've got to prepare for winter in right good earnest. Duty before pleasure, you know. Now here is what I propose."

What he did propose was set about without loss of time. Little Ap was summoned aft.

"Can you build barrows?" asked McBain.

Little Ap took an immense pinch of snuff before he replied.

"I have built many a boat," he said, "but never a barrow. But look, you see, with the help of the cooper and the carpenters I can build barrows by the dozen. Yes, yes, sir."

"Bravo, Ap!" cried McBain; "then set about it at once, for we are all going to turn navvies. We are going," he added, "to excavate a cave half-way up that brae yonder on the starboard quarter. It will be big enough, Ap, to hold the whole ship's crew, officers and all. It will be a glorious shelter from the cold, and it will———"

"Stop," cried Sandy McFlail. "Beg your pardon, sir, but let me finish the sentence: it will give the men employment and keep sickness away."

"That's it, my worthy surgeon," said McBain.

"Bravo!" said Sandy. "I look upon that now as———"

Sandy paused and reddened a little.

"As a vera judeecious arrangement," said Rory, laughing. "Out with it, Sandy, man."

Rory edged off towards the door of the saloon as he

spoke; the doctor kicked over his chair and made a dart after him, but Rory had fled. Hardly, however, was the surgeon re-seated ere his tormentor keeked in again.

"Eh! mon, Sandy McFlail," he cried; "you'll want to take a lot more salt in your porridge, mon, before ye can catch Rory Elphinston."

On the hillside, fifty feet above the sea level, they commenced operations, and in a fortnight's time the cave was almost completed; and not only that, but a beautiful staircase leading up to it. The soil was not hard after the outer crust was tapped, although some veins of quartz were alighted upon which required to be blasted. Several times they came across the trunks of huge trees that seemed to have been scorched by fire, the remains, doubtless, of the primeval forest that had once clad these hills with a sea of living green. Nor were bones wanting; some of immense size were turned up and carefully preserved.

Rory made a careful study of the remains of the animal and vegetable life which were found, and the result of this was his painting two pictures representing the Past and Present of the strange land where their vessel now lay. The one represented the *Arrandoon* lying under bare poles and yards in the ice-locked bay, with the wild mountainous land beyond, peak rising o'er peak, and crag o'er crag, all clad in the garments of eternal winter, and asleep in the uncertain light of the countless stars and the radiant Aurora. But the other picture! Who but Rory—who but an artist-poet could have painted that? There are the same formations of hill and dale, the same towering peaks and bold bluffs, but neither ice nor snow is there; the glens and valleys are clad in waving forests; flowers and ferns are there; lichens, crimson and white, creep and hang over the brown rocks; happy birds are in the sky; bright-winged butterflies seem flitting in the noonday sunshine, and strange animals of monstrous size are basking on the sea-shore.

Rory's pictures were admired by all hands, but the artist had his private view to begin with, and, among others like privileged, aft came weird old Magnus. First he was shown the picture of the Past.

He gazed at it long and earnestly, muttering to himself, "Strange, strange, strange."

But no sooner was the companion picture placed before him, than he started from the chair on which he had been sitting.

"I was right! I was right!" he cried. "Oh! bless you, boy Rory; bless you, Captain McBain. This—this is the Isle of Alba. Yonder are the dear hills. I thought I could not be mistaken, and not far off are the mammoth caves. I can guide you, gentlemen, to the place where lies wealth untold. This is the happiest day of old Magnus's life."

"Sit down, Magnus," said McBain, kindly; "sit down, my old sea-dad. Gentlemen, gather round us; Magnus has something to tell us I know. Magnus," he continued, taking the old man's thin and withered hand in his, "I have often thought you knew more about this Isle of Alba than you cared to tell. What is the mystery? You have spoken so often about these mammoth caves. How know you there is wealth of ivory lying there?"

"I have no story to relate," said Magnus, talking apparently to himself; "only a sad reminiscence of a voyage I took years and years ago to these same dreary latitudes. I had a son with me, a son I loved for his dead mother's sake and his own. I commanded a sloop—'twas but a sloop—and we sailed away from Norwegian shores in search of the ivory mines. We reached this very island. The year was an open one, just like this; myself and my brave fellows found ivory in abundance; in such abundance that our sloop would not carry a thousandth part of it, for, gentlemen, in ages long gone by, this island and those around it were the homes of the mammoth and the mastodon. We collected all the ivory and placed it in one cave. How I used to gloat over my treasure! It was all for my boy. He would be the richest man in Northern Europe. My boy, my dear boy, with his mother's eyes! I had only to go back to Norway with my sloop and charter a large vessel, and return to the Isle of Alba for my buried treasure."

Here poor old Magnus threw his body forward and covered his face with his skinny hands, and the tears welled through his fingers, while his whole form was convulsed with sobs.

"My boy—died!" was all he could utter. "He sleeps yonder—yonder at the cave's mouth. Yonder—yonder. To-morrow I will guide you to the cave, and we will see my boy."

The old man seemed wandering a little.

"I would sleep now," he added. "To-morrow—to-morrow."

There was a strange light in Magnus's eye next day when he joined the search party on deck, and a strange flush on his cheek that seemed to bode no good.

"I'll see my boy," he kept repeating to himself, as he led the way on shore. "I'll see my boy."

He walked so fast that his younger companions could hardly keep pace with him.

Along the shore and upwards through a glen, round hills and rocks, by many a devious path, he led them on and on, till they stood at last at the foot of a tall perpendicular cliff, with, close beside it, a spar or flag-staff.

They knew now that Magnus had not been raving, that they were no old man's dream, these mammoth caves, but a glorious reality.

"Quick, quick," cried Magnus, pointing to a spot at the foot of the spar. "Clear away the snow."

Our heroes were hardly prepared for the sight that met their eyes, as soon as Magnus had been obeyed, for there, encased in a block of crystal ice, lay the form of a youth of probably sixteen summers, dressed in the blue uniform of a Norwegian sailor, with long fair hair floating over his shoulders. Time had wrought no change on the face; this lad, though buried for twenty years, seemed even now only in a gentle slumber, from which a word or touch might awake him.

"My boy! my boy!" was the cry of the old man, as he knelt beside the grave, kissed the cold ice, and bedewed it with his tears. "Look up, look up; 'tis your father that is bending over you. But no, no, no; he'll never speak nor smile again. Oh! my boy, my boy!"

Rory was in tears, and not he alone, for the roughest sailor that stood beside the grave could not witness the grief of that old man unmoved.

McBain stepped forward and placed his hand kindly on his shoulder.

Magnus turned his streaming eyes just once upwards to his captain's face, then he gave vent to one long, sobbing sigh, threw out his arms, and dropped.

Magnus was no more.

They made his grave close to that of his boy's, and there, side by side, these twain will sleep till the sea gives up its dead.

CHAPTER XXXII.

THE TERRIBLE SNOWSTORM — SOMETHING LIKE AN AQUARIUM—THE MAMMOTH CAVES AND THEIR STARTLING TREASURES—THE JOURNEY POLEWARDS—COLLAPSE OF THE BALLOON—"GOD SAVE THE QUEEN."

FOUR long months have passed away since poor old Magnus dropped dead on the grave of his son. The sun has once more appeared above the horizon, bringing joy to the hearts of the officers and crew of the *Arrandoon*. Despite every effort to keep their spirits up, the past winter has been a weary one. Had the stars always shone, had the glorious Aurora always flickered above them, it might have been different; but shortly after the cave was finished and furnished, divided into compartments, and made comfortable with chairs and sofas, and carpets and skins, a terrible storm came on them from the north-west. Never had our young heroes, never had McBain himself, known such cold, or such fierce winds and depth of snow. For three whole weeks did this Arctic storm rage, and during this time it would have been certain death for any one to have ventured ten yards from the mouth of the cavern.

But the wind fell at last, the clouds dispersed, and once more the goodly stars shone forth, and the bright Aurora. Then they ventured to creep out from their friendly shelter. The Arctic night seemed now as bright as day; they could hardly believe that the sun was not hidden behind some of those quartz-like clouds, that were still banked up on the south-eastern horizon. But where was the ship? where was their lordly *Arrandoon?* For a moment it seemed as if the ice had opened and swallowed her up. They rubbed their wondering eyes and looked again. Three silver streaks glimmering against the dark blue of the sky represented her topmasts; all the rest of her was buried beneath the snow.

And as far as they could see seaward it was all a waste of smooth dazzling white, with here and there only the points and peaks of the icebergs appearing above it.

As soon as the snow had sunk, which it soon did many feet, McBain had got his crew ready to start for the mammoth mines. The weather had continued fine, only there were whole weeks during which the wind blew so cuttingly fierce that no work or walking either could be attempted.

The troglodytes—an expression of Rory's—were, therefore, a good deal confined to their cave, and it was well for them then that they had books to read and the wherewithal to amuse themselves in many other ways. The following is a remark that Rory had made to Ralph and Allan one day, after nearly three months of the winter had passed away.

"Which of you troglodytes is going with me to-morrow to see the sun rise?"

"Not I, thanks," said Ralph. "Pass the ham, old man; that bit of bear-steak was a treat."

"I'll go," said Allan.

"Hurrah!" cried Rory. "It is you that's the brave boy after all. We'll have friend Seth, too, and the dogs. It's the first time they've been out; it will do us all good."

This sledging-party had been a merry one, but they were obliged to leave the dogs at the foot of the mountain, and climb, as best they could, to the top, where, sure enough, they were soon rewarded by a glimpse, just one thrilling glimpse, of the king of day. They could not refrain from shouting aloud with joy. They shouted and cheered, and though well-nigh three miles from the cave, the troglodytes there heard it, so intense was the silence, and gave them back shout for shout and cheer for cheer.

They had seen something, though, from the hill-top that had very much astonished them. In the centre of this curious island, and entirely surrounded by mountains, was a lake of open water, as black as ink it looked in contrast with the snow-clad braeland around it, and right in the centre thereof played an enormous geyser, or natural fountain. It was evidently of volcanic origin.

The days got longer and longer, and in five months from the time they had entered the cave day and night were about equal.

But I must not omit telling you of the strange experiment that had suggested itself to McBain while gazing upwards at the birds—lured from afar—circling round the electric light. It was nothing more nor less than that of paying a visit, by means of a diving-bell and the electric light, to the denizens of the deep—the creatures that lived in the ocean under the ice.

Everything was got ready under the supervision of the aëronaut, ably assisted by the carpenter and crew and little Ap. The bell itself was an immense one, and most carefully constructed to float or sink at will. Inside it was quite as comfortable as the room in the lift of some of our large hotels.

Ralph seldom went far out of his way in search of adventure, but this new and wonderful experiment seemed to possess an irresistible charm even for him.

As for Rory, he was, as Sandy McFlail said, "half daft" over the idea.

McBain was most careful in seeing that everything was in working order; and the bell was sunk and re-sunk empty a dozen times in the water before he would allow any one to venture down in it. The snow had been previously cleared away all from and around the ship, and an immense ice-hole made for the purpose of conducting the experiment.

When all seemed safe, and it was found that the bell, sunk to a depth of forty feet, was acted on by no current, but rose straight to the surface of the ice-hole when wanted, then the captain himself and De Vere ventured down. They remained beneath for fully twenty minutes—and anxious minutes they were to those on the surface; then the signal to hoist was given, and presently up bobbed the bell, and was raised to the level by the derrick, when out stepped De Vere and McBain.

"Smiling all over, sure!" said Rory, "and looking as clean and sweet and pretty as if they'd just popped out of a band-box."

The diving-bell was called "the band-box" after this.

But it was after dark that the real experiment was to take place.

"Troth!" said Rory at dinner that day, "will you fellows never have done eating? It's myself that is longing to get away down to the bottom of the sea."

The four of them entered the band-box—Allan, Ralph, the doctor, and Rory; then they were slowly lowered down—down—down amid a darkness that could be felt. But presently a green glimmer of light shone in through the strong window of the bell; they could see each other's faces. The light got stronger and stronger as the electric ball came nearer and nearer, till at last it stopped stationary about twelve yards from their window, making the sea all round, beneath, and above it as bright as noon.

"Yonder is the stage, boys," cried Rory; "but where are the performers?"

They had not long to wait for these. Fish, first of the smaller kinds, came sailing round the light; presently these fled in all directions, and a monster shark took up the room. He soon had company, for dozens of others came floating around, and not sharks only, but creatures of more hideous forms than anything even Rory could have imagined in his wildest dreams.

"Oh!" cried the young poet, "if Gustave Doré were only here to see this terrible sight!"

"It beats," said Sandy, "the Brighton Aquarium all to pieces. Oh!" he screamed, shrinking into a corner of the band-box, as a huge hammer-headed shark sidled up to the window, crooked his awful eyes, and stared in. "Oh, Rory, man, signal quick! I want to get up out o' here. No more divin'-bells for me, lad."

For nearly six weeks it became the regular custom to visit this submarine vivarium every night after dinner.

"It was just as good," Ralph and Allan said, "as going to a show."

"And a deal better," added Rory.

Even the mates and the crew begged for a peep at the wonders displayed in the depths of the illuminated sea.

"Well," said Ted Wilson, when he ascended after his first view, "I'm a sadder and a wiser man, and I'll dream of what I've seen this night as long as ever I live."

They found the mouth of the mammoth cave, near which lay all that was mortal of poor old Magnus and his son, after days and days of digging; but when at long last they succeeded in forcing an entrance, one glance around them proved that they had indeed fallen upon riches and wealth untold. Those vast tusks and teeth of the mighty monsters of an age long past and gone were of the purest ivory, more white and hard than any they had ever seen before.

"Why, sure," said Rory, "the cave of Aladdin was nothing to this!"

"The next thing, gentlemen," said the captain, "is to transport our treasure to the good ship *Arrandoon*. Seth, old friend, your dogs will be wanted now in good earnest."

"I reckon," replied Seth, "they're all ready, sir, and just mad enough to eat each other's collars, 'cause they don't get anything to do."

What a change it was to have sunshine and a comparative degree of warmth again. Rough and toilsome enough was the road between the ship and the mammoth cave, but the snow was crisp and hard. The dogs were wild with delight, and so were our heroes, and so hard did everybody work all day that no one thought any more about the diving-bell and the denizens of the deep. After dinner they needed rest. Rory took his boat, or canoe, with him once or twice, and, all alone, he embarked on the volcanic lake and paddled round the geyser.

In three weeks from the day they had found the entrance to the cave they had transported all the ivory to the *Arrandoon*. They were now what Silas would have called a "bumper ship." If they should succeed in regaining their own country, Rory would be able to live all his days in peace and comfort, independent of the whims of his Irish tenantry, and Allan—ah, yes, poor Allan!—began to dream of home now. Already, in imagination, he saw Glentruim a fair and smiling valley, every acre of it tilled, comfortable cottages sending their blue smoke heavenwards from the green birchen woods, a new and beautiful church, and the castle restored, himself once more resuming his rights of chief of his clan, and his dear mother and sister honoured and respected by all.

"I'll roast an ox whole, boys!" he cried, one evening, jumping up from the sofa in the snuggery, where he had been lying thinking and dreaming of the future. "A whole ox; nothing less!"

Rory and Ralph burst out laughing.

"A vera judeecious arrangement!" cried Sandy. "But where will ye get the ox? I'm getting tired o' bear-beef, and wouldn't mind a slice out of a juicy stot's rump."

"Oh, dear!" said Allan, smiling; "I forgot you hadn't been following the train of my thoughts. I was back again in Arrandoon."

"Hurrah!" cried Rory. "Gather round the fire, boys;

sit in, captain; sit in, Sandy; let us talk about home and what we all will do when we get there."

Little, little did they know then the hardships that were in store for them.

Summer had fairly set in, but as yet there were not the slightest signs of the ice breaking up. Several balloon flights were made, the aëronaut always making most careful calculations for days before starting, and generally succeeding in catching a favourable time.

Then the principal adventure of the whole cr'se was undertaken—a great sledging journey towards the Pole itself.

The sledges, specially prepared for the purpose, were got out and carefully loaded with everything that would be found necessary.

For a time the *Arrandoon* was to be left with but a few hands, or "ship-keepers," as they are called, on her.

The great snowstorm of the previous winter McBain judged, and rightly too, would be in favour of the expedition; it smoothed the roughness of the ice, and made sledging even pleasurable. De Vere had two sledges, devoted to carrying his balloon and the means wherewith to inflate it.

Ted Wilson was left in charge of the ship, with little Ap, the cook, and carpenter's crew, to say nothing of little Freezing Powders and Cockie.

"If you do find the North Pole," cried Ted Wilson, as a parting salutation to one of his companions, "do fair Johnick, Bill, fair Johnick—bring us a bit."

I have to tell of no terrible hardships or sufferings experienced by our heroes during this memorable sledge journey. They accomplished on an average about twelve miles a day, or seventy miles a week, and they invariably rested on the Sabbath, merely taking exercise on that day to keep up the warmth of their bodies.

They suffered but little from the cold, but it must be remembered that by this time they had become thoroughly inured to the rigours of the Arctic regions. It was easy to keep warm trudging along over the snow, and helping to drag the sledge by day.

The dogs they found were a great acquisition. Under the wise and judicious management of Trapper Seth they were most tractable, and their strength seemed something marvellous. They were fat and sleek, and comfortable-looking, too, and had entirely lost the gaunt, hungry, wolfish appearance they presented when Captain Cobb first sent them on board. Well did they work for, and richly did they deserve, the four Spratts' biscuits given to each of them daily; that, followed by a mouthful of snow, was all they cared for and all they needed to make them the happiest of the happy.

A short halt was made for luncheon every noon, and at six o'clock they stopped for the night, and dinner was cooked. This was Seth's duty, and, considering the limited means at his command, he succeeded wonderfully. The tent was erected over a large pit in the snow, the sledges being drawn up to protect it against the prevailing wind. But of this there was but little.

After dinner they gathered around a great spirit-lamp stove, wrapped in skins and blankets, and generally talked themselves to sleep. But Seth always slept with the dogs.

"I like to curl up," he explained, "with the animiles. They keeps me warm, they do; and, gentlemen, Seth's bones ain't quite so young as they used to be."

For weeks our heroes journeyed on towards the Pole, but they came to the end of what McBain called the snowfields at last, and all farther progress by sledge was practically at an end. Before them stretched away to the utmost limits of the horizon

THE SEA OF ANCIENT ICE,

a chaos of boulders, over which it would take a week at least to drag the sledges even a distance of ten miles.

Now came the balloon to the rescue, but who were to go in it? Its car would, big as it was, contain but four. The four were finally selected; they were McBain, the aëronaut himself, Allan, and Rory.

Upwards mounted the great balloon, upwards but sailing southwards; yet well had De Vere counted his chances. Ballast was thrown out, and they rose into the air with inconceivable rapidity, and McBain soon perceived that the direction had now changed, and that the balloon was going rapidly northwards.

*   *   *   *   *

To those left behind on the snowfields the time dragged on very slowly indeed, and when four-and-twenty hours had gone by, and still there was no sign of the return of the aëronauts, Ralph's anxiety knew no bounds. He seemed to spend most of his time on the top of a large iceberg, gazing northwards and skywards in hopes of catching a glimpse of the balloon. But all in vain, and so passed six-and-thirty hours, and so passed forty-eight and fifty. Something must have happened. Grief began to weigh like lead on poor Ralph's heart. A hundred times in an hour he reproached himself for not having gone in the balloon instead of Rory. He was strong, Rory was not, and if anything had happened to his more than brother, he felt he could never forget it and never forgive himself. Despair was slowly taking the place of grief; he was walking up and down rapidly on the snow, for he could not rest,—he had taken neither food nor sleep since the balloon departed,—when there was a shout from the man on the outlook.

"Something black on the northern horizon, sir, but no signs of the balloon."

"Hurrah!" cried Ralph. "Now, men, to the rescue. Let us go and meet them, and help them over this sea of boulders."

In three hours more McBain and party were back in

camp, safe and sound, terribly tired, but able to tell all their story.

"We've planted the dear old flag as far north as we could get," said McBain, "and left it there."

"Ay," said Rory, "and kissed and blessed it a hundred times over."

"And but for the accident to the balloon, which we were obliged to abandon, we would have been back long ere now."

"But we have not seen de open sea around de Pole," said De Vere.

"No," said McBain; "there is no such sea; that is all a myth; only the sea of ancient ice, and land, with tall, cone-shaped mountains on it, evidently the remains of extinct volcanoes. Oh! it was a dreary, dreary scene. No signs of life, never a bird or bear, and a silence like the silence of death."

"It was on one of those hills," added Rory, "we planted the flag—'the flag that braved a thousand years the battle and the breeze.' It was a glorious moment, dear Ralph, when we saw that bit of bunting unfurled. How Allan and myself wished you'd been with us. It was so funny, too, because, you see, there was no north, no east, and no west; everything was south of us. The whole world lay down beneath us, as it were, all to the south'ard, and we could walk round the world, so to speak, a dozen times in a minute."

"Yes, it is curious," replied Ralph, musing in silence for a moment. Then he stretched out his hand and grasped Rory's. He did not speak. There was no need, Rory knew well what he meant.

"Now, boys and men," cried the captain, "we have to return thanks to Him who has safely guided us through all perils into these distant regions, and pray that He may permit us to return in safety to our native land. Let us pray."

A more heartfelt prayer than that of those hardy sailors probably never ascended on high. Afterwards a psalm was sung, to a beautiful old melody, and this closed the service; but next morning, ere they started to return to the *Arrandoon*, another spar was erected on the top of the biggest and highest iceberg. On this the English colours were *nailed*, and around it the crew assembled, and cheer after cheer rent the air, and, as Sandy McFlail afterwards observed, hats and bonnets were pitched on high, till they positively darkened the air, like a flock o' craws.

Then "Give us a good bass and tenor, boys," cried Rory, and he burst into the grand old National Anthem,

> "God save our Gracious Queen,
> Long may Victoria reign,
> God save the Queen."

CHAPTER XXXIII.

ANOTHER WINTER AT THE POLE—CHRISTMAS DAY—THE CURTAIN RISES ON THE LAST ACT—SICKNESS—DEATH—DESPAIR.

THE summer was far advanced before Captain McBain and his crew returned to where their vessel lay off the island of Alba. They had fully expected to see some signs of the ice breaking up, so as to allow them to get clear and bear up for home, but the chance of this taking place seemed as far off as ever. If the truth must be told, the captain had counted upon a break-up of the sea of ice shortly after midsummer at the very latest. But midsummer went past, the sun each midnight began to decline nearer and nearer to the northern horizon, and it already seemed sadly probable that another winter would have to be passed in these desolate regions. McBain could not help recalling the words of old Magnus, "Open seasons do not come oftener than once in ten years." If this indeed were true, then he, his boys and his crew, were doomed to sufferings more terrible than tongue could tell or pen relate—sufferings from which there could be no escape save through the jaws of death. Provisions would hardly last throughout another winter, and until the ice broke up and they were again free, there could be no chance of getting those that had been stored on the northernmost isle of Spitzbergen.

The sky remained clear and hard, and McBain soon began to think he would give all he possessed in life for the sight of one little cloud not bigger than a man's hand. But that cloud never came, and the sun commenced to set and the summer waned away. The captain kept his sorrow very much to himself; at all events he tried to talk cheerfully and hopefully when in the company of any of our young heroes; but they could mark a change, and well they knew the cause.

The ice-hole was opened, but, strange to say, although they captured sharks and other great fish innumerable, neither seal nor walrus ever showed head above the water.

Bears were pretty numerous on the ice, and now Mc-Bain gave orders to preserve not only the skins but even the flesh of those monsters. It was cut in pieces and buried in the ice and snow, well up the braeland near to the mouth of the cave, in which they had found shelter during all the dark months of the former winter.

The fact that no seals appeared at the ice-hole proved beyond a doubt that the open water was very far indeed to the southward of them.

How they had rejoiced to see the sun rise for the first time in the previous spring; how their hearts sank now to see him set!

"Boys," said McBain one day, after he had remained silent for some time, as if in deep thought—"boys, I fear we won't get out of this place for many months to come. How do you like the prospect?"

He smiled as he spoke; but they could see the smile was a simulated one.

"Never mind," said Ralph and Allan; "we'll keep our hearts up, never fear; don't you be unhappy on our account."

"I'll try not to be," said McBain, "and I'm sure I shall not be so on my own."

"Besides, captain dear," added Rory, "it's sure to come right in the end."

McBain laid his hand on boy Rory's head, and smiled somewhat sadly.

"You're always hopeful, Rory," he said. "We must pray that your words may come true."

And, indeed, besides waiting with a hopeful trust in that all-seeing Providence who had never yet deserted them in their direst need, there was little now to be done.

As the days got shorter and shorter, and escape from another winter's imprisonment seemed impossible, the crew of the *Arrandoon* was set to work overhauling stores. It was found that with strict economy the provisions would last until spring, but, with the addition of the flesh of sharks and bears, for a month or two longer. It was determined, therefore, that the men should not be put upon short allowance, for semi-starvation—McBain was doctor enough to know—only opened the door for disease to step in, in the shape perhaps of that scourge called scurvy, or even the black death itself.

When the sun at last sank to rise no more for three long months, so far from letting down their hearts, or losing hope, the officers and crew of our gallant ship once more settled down to their "old winter ways," as Seth called them. They betook themselves to the cave in the hill-side, which, for sake of giving the men exercise, McBain had made double the size, the mould taken therefrom and the rocks being used to erect a terrace near the entrance. This was surrounded by a balustrade or bulwark, with a flagstaff erected at one end, and on this was unfurled the Union Jack. Watches were kept, and meals cooked and served, with as much regularity as if they had been at sea, while the evenings were devoted to reading, music, and story-telling round the many great fires that were lighted to keep the cave warm.

Where, it may be asked, did the fuel come from? Certainly not from the ship. The coals were most carefully stored, and retained for future service; but tons on tons of great pine-logs were dug from the hill-sides. And glorious fires they made, too. It was, as Rory said, raking up the ashes of a long-past age to find fuel for a new one.

Once more the electric light was got under way, and twice a week at least the diving-bell was sunk. This was a source of amusement that never failed to give pleasure; but so intense was the frost at times that it was a matter of no small difficulty to break the ice on the water.

The captain was untiring in his efforts to keep his men employed, and in as happy a frame of mind as circumstances would admit of.

There was no snowstorm this winter, and very seldom any wind; the sky was nearly always clear, and the stars and Aurora brighter than ever they had seen them.

Christmas—the second they had spent together since leaving the Clyde—passed pleasantly enough, though there was no boisterous merriment. Songs and story-telling were in far greater request than dancing. Never, perhaps, was Rory in better spirits for solo-playing. He appeared to know intuitively the class of music the listeners would delight in, and his rendering of some of the old Scottish airs seemed simply to hold them spell-bound. As the wild, weird, plaintive notes of the violin, touched by the master fingers of the young poet, fell on their ears, they were no longer ice-bound in the dreary regions of the pole. It was no longer winter; it was no longer night. They were home once more in their native land; home in dear auld Scotland. The sun was shining brightly in the summer sky, the purple of the heather was on the moorland, the glens and valleys were green, and the music of merle and mavis, mingling with the soft croodle of the amorous cushat, resounded from the groves. No wonder that a few sighs were heard when Rory ceased to play; he had touched a chord in their inmost hearts, and for the time being had rendered them inexpressibly happy.

* * * *

It is well to let the curtain fall here for a short time; it rises again on the first-scene of the last act of this Arctic drama of ours.

Three months have elapsed since that Christmas evening in the cave when we beheld the crew of the *Arrandoon* listening with happy, hopeful, upturned faces to the sweet music that Rory discoursed from his darling instrument. Only three months, but what a change has come over the prospects of all on board that seemingly doomed ship! Often and often had our heroes been face to face with death in storms and tempests at sea, in fighting with wild beasts, and even with wild men, but never before had they met the grim king of terrors in the form he now assumed. For several weeks the men had been falling ill, and dying one by one, and already no less than nine graves had been dug and filled under the snow on the mountain's side.

The disease, whatever it was, resisted all kinds of treatment, and, indeed, though the symptoms in every case were similar at the commencement, no two men died in precisely the same way. At first there was an intense longing for home; this would be succeeded in a few days by loss of all appetite, by distaste for food or exertion of any kind, and by fits of extreme melancholy and depression. The doctor did his best. Alas! there are diseases against which all the might of medical skill is unavailing.

Brandy and other stimulants were tried; but these only kept the deadly ailment at bay for a very short time; it returned with double force, and poor sufferers were doubly prostrated in consequence.

There was no bodily pain, except from a strange hollow cough that in all cases accompanied the complaint, but there was rapid emaciation, hot, burning brow, and hands and feet that scorched like fire, and while some fell into a kind of gentle slumber from which they awoke no more in this world, others died from sheer debility, the mind being clear to the last—nay, even brighter as they neared the bourne from which no traveller ever returns.

As the time went on—the days were now getting long again, for spring had returned—matters got even worse. It was strange, too, that the very best and brightest of the crew were the first to be attacked and to die. I do not think there was a dry eye in the ship when the little procession wound its way round the hillside bearing in its unpretending coffin the mortal remains of poor Ted Wilson. All this long cruise he had been the life and soul of the whole crew. No wonder that the words of the beautiful old song *Tom Bowling* rose to the mind of more than one of the crew of the *Arrandoon* when Ted was laid to rest:

> "His form was of the manliest beauty,
> His heart was warm and soft,
> Faithful below he did his duty,
> And now he's gone aloft."

Just one week after the burial of Ted Wilson, De Vere, the French aëronaut, was attacked, and in three days' time he was dead. He had never been really well since the journey to the vicinity of the Pole, and the loss of his great balloon was one which he never seemed to be able to get over. He was quite an enthusiast in his profession, and, as he remarked to McBain one day, "I have mooch grief for de loss of my balloon. I had give myself over to de thoughts of mooch pleasant voyaging away up in de regions of de upper air. I s'all soar not again until I reach England."

It was sad to hear him, as he lay half delirious on the bed of his last illness, muttering, muttering to himself and constantly talking about the home far away in sunny France that he would never see again. Either the doctor or one or other of our young heroes was constantly in the cabin with him. About an hour before his demise he sent for Ralph.

"I vould not," he said, "send for Rory nor for Allan, dey vill both follow me soon. Oh! do not you look sad.

Ralph, dere is nothing but joy vere ve are going. Nothing but joy, and sunshine, and happiness."

He took a locket from his breast. It contained the portrait of a grey-haired mother.

" Bury dis locket in my grave," he said.

He took two rings from off his thin white fingers.

" For my sister and my mother," he said.

He never spoke again, but died with those dear names on his lips.

Ralph showed himself a very hero in these sad times of trouble and death. He was here, there, and everywhere, by night and by day assisting the surgeon and helping Seth to attend upon the wants of the sick and dying; and many a pillow he soothed, and many a word of comfort he gave to those who needed it. The true Saxon character was now beautifully exemplified in our English hero. He possessed that noble courage which never makes itself uselessly obtrusive, which fritters not itself away on trifles, and which seems at most times to lie dormant or latent, but is ever ready to show forth and burn most brightly in the hour of direst need.

Sorrows seldom come singly, and one day Stevenson, in making his usual morning report, had the sad tidings to add that cask after cask of provisions had been opened and found bad, utterly useless for human food.

McBain got up from his chair and accompanied the mate on deck.

" I would not," he said, " express in words what I feel, Mr. Stevenson, before our boys; but this, indeed, is terrible tidings."

" It can only hasten the end," said Stevenson.

" You think, then, that that end is inevitable?"

" Inevitable," said Stevenson, solemnly but emphatically. " We are doomed to perish here among this ice. There can be no rescue for us but through the grave."

" We are in the hands of a merciful and an all-powerful

Providence, Mr. Stevenson," said McBain; "we must trust, and wait, and hope, and do our duty."

"That we will, sir, at all events," said the mate; "but see, sir, what is that yonder?"

He pointed, as he spoke, skywards, and there, just a little way above the hightest mountain-tops, was a cloud. It kept increasing almost momentarily, and got darker and darker. Both watched it until the sun itself was overcast, then the mate ran below to look at the glass. It was "tumbling" down.

For three days a gale and storm, accompanied with soft, half-wet snow, raged. Then terrible noises and reports were heard all over the pack of ice seaward, and the grinding and din that never fails to announce the break-up of the sea of ice.

"Heaven has not forgotten us," cried McBain, hopefully; "this change will assuredly check the sickness, and perhaps in a week's time we will be sailing southwards through the blue, open sea, bound for our native shores."

McBain was right; the hopes raised in the hearts of the men did check the progress of the sickness. When at last the wind fell, they were glad to see that the clouds still remained, and that there were no signs of the frost coming on again.

The pieces of ice, too, were loose, and all hands were set to work to warp the ship southwards through the bergs. The work was hard, and the progress made scarcely a mile a day at first. But they were men working for their lives, with new-born hope in their hearts, so they heeded not the fatigue, and after a fortnight's toil they found the water so much more open that by going ahead at full speed in every clear space, a fair day's distance was got over. For a week more they strove and struggled onwards; the men, however, were getting weaker and weaker for want of sufficient food. How great was their joy, then, when one morning the island was sighted on which McBain had left the store of provisions!

Boats were sent away as soon as they came within a mile of the place.

Sad, indeed, was the news with which Stevenson, who was in charge, returned. The bears had made an attack on the buried stores. They had clawed the great cask open, and had devoured or destroyed everything.

Hope itself now seemed for a time to fly from all on board. With a crew weak from want, and with fearful ice to work their way through, what chance was there that they would ever succeed in reaching the open water, or in proceeding on their homeward voyage even as far as the island of Jan Mayen, or until they should fall in with and obtain relief from some friendly ship? They were far to the northward of the sealing grounds, and just as far to the east. McBain, however, determined still to do his utmost, and, though on short allowance, to try to forge ahead. For one week more they toiled and struggled onwards, then came the frost again and all chance of proceeding was at an end.

It was no wonder that sickness returned. No wonder that McBain himself, and Allan and Rory, began to feel dejected, listless, weary, and ill.

Then came a day when the doctor and Ralph sat down alone to eat their meagre and hurried breakfast.

"What prospects?" said Ralph.

"Moribund!" was all the doctor said just then.

Presently he added—

"There, in the corner, lies poor wee Freezing Powders, and, my dear Ralph, one hour will see it all over with him. The captain and Allan and Rory can hardly last much longer."

"God help us, then," said Ralph, wringing his hands, and giving way to a momentary anguish.

The unhappy negro boy was stretched, to all appearance lifeless, close by the side of his favourite's cage.

Despite his own grief, Ralph could not help feeling for

that poor bird. His distress was painful to witness. If his great round eyes could have run over with tears, I am sure they would have done so. I have said before that Cockie was not a pretty bird, but somehow his very ugliness made Ralph pity him now all the more. Nor was the grief of the bird any the less sad to see because it was exhibited in a kind of half ludicrous way. He was not a moment at rest, but he seemed really not to know what he was doing, and his anxious eye was hardly ever withdrawn from the face of the dying boy:—jumping up and down from his perch to his seed-tin and back again, grabbing great mouthfuls of hemp, which he never even broke or tried to swallow, and blowing great sighs over his thick blue tongue. And the occasional sentence, too, the bird every now and then began but never finished,

"Here's a——"

"Did you——"

"Come——"

all spoke of the anguish in poor Cockie's breast.

A faint moaning was heard in the adjoining cabin, and Ralph hurried away from the table, and Sandy was left alone.

CHAPTER XXXIV.

A SAILOR'S COTTAGE—THE TELEGRAM—"SOMETHING'S IN THE WIND"—THE GOOD YACHT "POLAR STAR"—HOPE FOR THE WANDERERS.

A COTTAGE on a cliff. A cliff whose black, beetling sides rose sheer up out of the water three hundred feet and over; a cliff around which sea-birds whirled in dizzy flight; a cliff in which the cormorant had her home; a cliff against which all the might of the German Ocean had dashed and chafed and foamed for ages. Some fifty yards back from the edge of this cliff the cottage was built, of hard blue granite, with sturdy bay windows—a cottage that seemed as independent of any storm that could blow as the cliff itself was. In front was a neat wee garden, with nicely gravelled walks and edging of box, and all round it a natty railing painted an emerald green. At the back of the cottage were more gravelled walks and more flower garden, with a summer-house and a smooth lawn, from the centre of which rose a tall ship's mast by way of flagstaff, with ratlines and rigging and stays and top complete.

Not far off was a pigeon-house on a pole, and not far from that still another pole surmounted by a weather-vane, and two little wooden blue-jackets, that whenever the wind blew, went whirling round and round, clashing swords and engaging in a kind of fanatic duel, which seemed terribly real and terribly deadly for the time being.

It was a morning in early spring, and up and down the walk behind the cottage stepped a sturdy, weather-beaten old sailor, with hair and beard of iron-grey, and a face as red as the newest brick that ever was fashioned.

He stood for a moment gazing upwards at the strutting fantails.

"Curr-a-coo—curr-a-coo," said the pigeons.

"Curr-a-coo—curr-a-coo," replied the sailor. "I dare say you're very happy, and I'm sure you think the sun was made for you and you only. Ah! my bonnie birdies, you don't know what the world is doing. You don't—hullo!"

"Yes, my dear, you may say hullo," said a cheerful little woman, with a bright, pleasant face, walking up to him, and placing an arm in his. Didn't you hear me tapping on the pane for you?"

"Not I, little wife, not I," said Silas Grig. "I've been thinking, lass, thinking——"

"Well, then," interrupted his wife, "don't you think any more; you've made your hair all white with thinking. Just come in and have breakfast. That haddock smells delicious, and I've made some nice toast, and tried the new tea. Come, Silas, come."

Away went the two together, he with his arm around her waist, looking as happy, the pair of them, as though their united ages didn't make a deal over a hundred.

"Come next month," said Silas, as soon as he had finished his first cup of tea—"come next month, little wife, it will just be two years since I first met the *Arrandoon*. Heigho!"

"You needn't sigh, Silas," his wife remarked. "They may return. Wonders never cease."

"Return?" repeated Silas, with a broken-hearted kind of a laugh, "Nay, nay, nay, we'll meet them no more in this world. Poor Rory! He was my favourite. Dear boy, I think I see him yet, with his fair, laughing face, and that rogue of an eye of his."

Rat—tat.

Silas started.

"The postman?" he said; "no, it can't be. That's right, little woman, run to the door and see. What! a telegram for me!"

Silas took the missive, and turned it over and over in his hand half a dozen times at least.

"Why, my dear, who *can* it be from?" he asked with a puzzled look, "and what *can* it be about? *Can* you guess, little wife? Eh? can you?"

"If I were you, Silas," said his wife, quietly, "I'd open it and see."

"Dear me! to be sure," cried Silas. "I didn't think of that. Why, I declare," he continued, as soon as he had read it, "it is from Arrandoon Castle, and the poor widow, Allan's mother, wants to see me at once. I'm off, little woman, at once. Get out my best things. The blue pilots, you know. Quick, little woman—quick! Bear a hand! Hurrah!"

Silas Grig didn't finish that second cup of tea. He was dressed in less than ten minutes, had kissed his wife, and was hurrying away to the station. Indeed, Silas had never in his life felt in such a hurry before.

"It'll be like my luck," he muttered, "if I miss this train."

But he did not miss it, and it was a fast one, too, a flying train, that every day went tearing along through Scotland, and was warranted to land him at Inverness six hours after he first stepped on board.

No sooner was Silas seated than he pulled out the telegram again, and read it over and over at least a dozen times. Then he looked at the back of it, as if it were just possible that some further information might be found there. Then he read the address, and as he could not get anything more out of it he folded it up and replaced it in his pocket, merely remarking, "I'll vow something's in the wind."

Silas had bought a newspaper. He had meant to read;

he tried to read as hard as ever he had tried to do anything, but it was all in vain. His mind was in too great a ferment, so he threw down the paper and devoted himself to gazing out of the window at the glorious panorama that was passing before him; but if anybody else had been in the same compartment, he or she would have heard this ancient mariner frequently muttering to himself, and the burden of all his remarks was, "Something's in the wind, I'm sure of that!"

A fast train? A flying train? Yes, a deal too much so, many would have thought, but she could not fly a bit too fast for Silas. Yet how she did rattle and rush and roar along the lines, to be sure! The din she made only deepening for a moment as she dived under a bridge or brushed past a wayside station, too insignificant by far to waste a thought upon! Now she passes a country village, with rows of trim-built cottages and tidy gardens, with lines for clothes to dry, and fences where children hang or perch and wave their caps at the flying train. Now she shaves past rows of platelayers, who stand at attention or extend their grimy arms like signal yards, while a blue-coated jack-in-a-box waves a white flag from his window to show that all is safe. Now she ploughs through some larger junction, over a whole field of rails that seems to run in every conceivable direction; but she makes her way in safety in a whirl of dust, and next she shrieks as she plunges into the darkness of a long, dreary tunnel. Ah! but she is out again into the glare of the day, and again the telegraph posts go popping past as fast as one could wink. Five miles now on a stretch of level country as straight as crow could fly, through fields and woods and past thriving farms, with far beyond on the horizon hills, hills, hills.

'Tis spring-time, spring changing into summer, summer coming six good weeks before its time. Look, Silas, look! crimson flowers are already peeping red through the greenery of cornfields, drowsy-looking cows are wading knee-deep in grass and buttercups, the braelands are snowed over with the gowan's bloom. Birds are singing in meadow and copse, the yellow furze is blossoming on heathy moorlands. Great black spruces raise their tall heads skywards, and their every branch is tipped with a tassel of tender green; rowan-trees seem studded with roses of a pearly hue, and the feathery larches are hung round with a fringe-work of darkest crimson. Is it not glorious, Silas? is it not all beautiful? Did ever you see a sky more blue before, or cloudlets more fleecy and light?

"I'll stake my word," replies Silas, "that something's in the wind."

Wilder scenery now, dark, frowning mountains, lonely glens, heathlands, highlands, cañons, and tarns, then a long and fertile flat, every sod of which marks a Scottish warrior's grave.

Inverness at last!

"Boat gone, is it?" cried Silas. "Like my luck. But why didn't she wait for the train? Tell me that, eh?"

"Yes, sir; dare say I could, sir." This from an ostler in answer to another query of friend Silas. "Five-and-twenty mile, sir. I've just the horse that'll suit. Three hours to a tick, sir, rough though the road is, sir. I'll be ready in twenty minutes. Thank'ee, sir, much obliged. Now then, Donald, bustle about, will you? Get out the bay mare. Look sharp, gentleman's only got five minutes to feed."

* * * * *

"It can't be Captain Grig already," said Mrs. McGregor.

"And yet who else can it be?" said Helen Edith.

"I'll run out and see," said Ralph's father, who had been spending some weeks at the castle.

"Ha! welcome, honest Silas Grig," he cried, rushing up and literally receiving Silas with open arms as he jumped from the high-wheeled dog-cart. "A thousand welcomes. Well, I do declare you haven't let the grass grow under your feet. How your horse steams! Take him round, driver, and see to his comfort, then go to the kitchen and see to your own. Old Janet is there. Now, Silas," continued Mr. Leigh, "before you go to talk to the ladies, I'll tell you what we have arranged. We have thought well over all you said when you were here in the autumn, and I've chartered a German Arctic cruiser, and we're going to put you in command. She is lying at Peterhead, everything ready, crew and all, stores and all. Our prayers will follow you, dear Captain Grig, and if you find our poor boys, or even bring us tidings of their fate, we will be ever grateful. Nay, nay, but 'grateful' poorly expresses my meaning. We will——"

"Not another word," cried Silas, "not one single word more, sir, or as sure as my name is Silas Grig I'll clap my fingers in my ears."

He shook Mr. Leigh's hand as he spoke.

"I'll find the boys if they be alive," he said. "I knew, sir, when I got the telegram there was something in the wind. I told my little wife I was quite sure of it. Ha! ha! ha!"

Silas was laughing, but it was only to hide the tears with which his eyes were swimming.

"When can you start, my dear Silas?"

"To-night. At once. Give me a fresh horse and five minutes for a mouthful of refreshment, and off I start; and I'll take command to-morrow before the sun is over the foreyard."

"To-night?" cried Mr. Leigh, smiling. "No, no, no."

"But I say 'yo, yo, yo,'" said Silas, "and 'yo heave, O,' and what Silas says he means. There! Ah, ladies, how are you? Nay, never cry, Miss McGregor. I'm going straight away to the Arctic Sea, and I'm sure to bring your brother back, and Rory as well, to say nothing of honest Ralph and Peter the piper. So cheer ye up, my little lass,

If Silas Grig doesn't come back in company with the bonnie *Arrandoon*, may he never chew cheese again!"

There was no getting over the impetuosity of this honest old sailor, but there was withal a freshness and happiness about him, which made every one he talked with feel as hopeful as he was himself. Before dinner was done both Mrs. McGregor and her lovely daughter were smiling and laughing as they had not smiled or laughed for months before, and when Silas asked for a song, the latter went quite joyfully to the harp.

You see it appeared quite a foregone conclusion with everybody that night, that Silas would find the lost explorers and bring them safely home.

The moon rose in all its majesty as nine tolled forth from the clock-tower of the ancient castle. Then Silas said "good-bye," and, followed by many a blessing and many a prayer, the dogcart wound away up through the solemn pine forest, and was soon lost to view.

He was just as good as his word. He took command of his new ship—a splendid sea-going yacht—before noon next day. Almost immediately afterwards he summoned both officers and men and mustered them all aft, and somewhat startled them by the following curt speech: "Gentlemen and men of the *Polar Star*, we'll sail to-morrow morning. We touch nowhere until we enter harbour here again. Any one that isn't ready to go can step on shore and stop there. All ready, eh? Bravo, men! You'll find your skipper isn't a bad fellow to deal with, but he means to crack on! No ship that ever sailed 'twixt Pekin and London, no clipper that ever left Aberdeen, or yacht from New York city, ever did such cracking on as I mean to do. Go to your duty. Pipe down."

Then Silas Grig inspected the ship. He was pleased with her get-up and her rig-out, only he ordered extra spars and extra sails, and these were all on board ere sundown.

"The old man means business," said the first mate to the second.

"That he does!" replied the inferior officer.

The *Polar Star* sailed away from Peterhead on the very day that poor Ted Wilson was laid in his grave beneath the eternal snows of Alba. Could Silas have seen the desperate position of the *Arrandoon* just then, how little hopes he would have entertained of ever reaching her in time to save the precious lives on board!

* * * * *

The doctor was left alone in the saloon of the great ship.

The silence that reigned both fore and aft was oppressive even to dismalness.

For a moment or two Sandy buried his face in his hands, and tears welled through his fingers. "Oh," he whispered, "it is terrible! The silence of death is all about us! Our men dying forward, our captain doomed, and Allan and Rory. Ay, and poor Ralph will be next; I can see that in his face. Not one of us can ever reach his native land again! I envy—yes, I envy the dead in their quiet graves, and even wish it were all past—all, all over!"

"Doctor!" a kindly hand was laid on his shoulder. Sandy started to his feet, he cared not who saw his face, wet though it was with tears. "Doctor, don't you take on so," said Stevenson.

"Speak, man! speak quick! There is hope in your face!" cried the doctor.

"There is hope in my heart, too," said the mate—"only a glint, only a gleam; but it is there. The frost is gone; the ice is open again."

"Then quick," cried the surgeon, "get up steam! that alone can save the dying. Energy, energy, and something to do. *I* can do nothing more to save my patients while this hopeless silence lies pall-like around us. Break it, dear mate, with the roar of steam and the rattle of the engine's screw!"

"Listen," said the mate. "There goes the steam. Our chief has not been long."

Round went the screw once more, and away moved the ship.

Poor McBain came staggering from his cabin. Ghastly pale he looked. He had the appearance of one risen from the grave.

He clutched Sandy by the shoulder.

"We are—under—way?" he gasped.

"Yes, yes," said the surgeon. "Homeward bound, captain."

"Homeward—bound," muttered the captain, pressing his hand on his brow, as if to recall his memory, which for a time had been unseated from her throne.

For a minute or two the surgeon feared for his captain's life or reason.

"Drink this, dear sir," he said; "be seated, too, you are not over well, and there is much to be done."

"Much to be done?" cried McBain, as soon as he had quaffed the medicine. "I'm better. Thank you, good doctor; thank you, Sandy. There is much to be done. Those words have saved your captain's life."

Sandy gave a big sigh of relief and hastened away to Rory's cabin.

Rory had been lying like a dead thing for hours, but now a new light seemed to come into his eye. He extended his hand to Sandy and smiled.

"We are positively under steam again, Sandy?" he said.

Sandy, like a wise surgeon, did not tell him the frost was quite gone. Joy kills, and Sandy knew it.

"Yes," he said, carelessly, "we'll get down south a few miles farther, I dare say. It is nice, though, isn't it, to hear the old screw rattling round again?"

"Why, it is music, it is life!" said Rory. "Sandy, I'm going to be well again soon. I know and feel I am."

Then Ralph burst into the cabin.

"I say, Sandy," he said, "run and see dear old Allan; he says he is going to get up, and I know he is far, far too weak."

Sandy had to pass through the saloon. Freezing Powders was sitting bolt upright in the corner, and Cockie was apparently mad with joy. The bird couldn't speak fast enough, and he seemed bent on choking himself with hemp.

"Peter, Peter, Peter, Peter," he was saying, "here's a pretty, pretty, pretty to-do. Call the steward, call the steward. Come on, come on, come on."

"Oh, Cockie," Freezing Powders said, "I'se drefful, drefful cold, Cockie. 'Spects I'se gwine to die, Cockie. 'Spects I is—Oh! de-ah, what my ole mudder say den?"

"Come, come," cried Sandy, "take this, you young sprout, and don't let me catch you talking about dying. There now, pull yourself together."

"I'll try," said the poor boy, "but I 'spects I'se as pale as deaf (death)."

CHAPTER XXXV.

THE RESCUE—HOMEWARD BOUND—ALL'S WELL THAT ENDS WELL.

I NEVER have been able to learn with a sufficient degree of exactitude whether it was the *Polar Star* that first sighted the *Arrandoon*, or whether the *Arrandoon* was the first to catch a glimpse of the *Polar Star*. And with such conflicting evidence before me, I do not see very well how I could.

What evidence have I before me, do you ask? Why the logs of the two ships, written by their two captains respectively. I give below a portion of two extracts, both relating to the joyful event. Extract first from the log of the good yacht *Polar Star*:—" June 21st, 18—. At seven bells in the forenoon watch—ice heavy and wind about a S.S.W.—caught sight of the *Arrandoon's* topmasts bearing about a N. and by E. Praise God for all His goodness." Extract second, from the log of the *Arrandoon*:—" June 21st, 18—. Seven bells in the forenoon watch—a hail from the crow's-nest, 'A schooner among the ice to the south'ard and west of us, can just raise her topmasts, think she is bearing this way.' Heaven be praised, we are saved."

Yes, dear reader, the *Arrandoon* was saved. The news that a vessel was in sight spread through the ship like wildfire; those that were hale and well rushed on deck, the sick tottered up, and all was bustle and excitement, and the cheer that arose from stem to stern reminded McBain of the good old times, a year ago, when every man Jack of his crew was alive and well.

It had been a very narrow escape for them, for, although not far from the open water where the *Polar Star* lay with foreyard aback, they were unable to reach it, being once more frozen in, and had not good Silas appeared at the time he did, probably in a few weeks at most there would not have been a single human being living on board the lordly *Arrandoon*.

No sooner had Silas satisfied himself with his own eyes that it was the *Arrandoon* that lay icebound to the nor'ard of him, than he called away the boats and gave orders to load them with the best of everything, and to follow his whaler.

His whaler took the ice just as eight bells were struck on the *Polar Star*, and next moment, guided by the fan in the crow's-nest of the yacht, he was hastening over the rough ice towards the *Arrandoon*.

McBain and his boys, and the doctor as well, were all on deck, when who should heave round the corner of an iceberg but Captain Silas Grig himself, looking as rosy and ten times more happy than they had last seen him.

He was still about fifty yards away, and for a moment or two he stood undecided; it seemed, indeed, that he wished not to walk but to jump or fly the remaining fifty intervening yards. Then he took off his cap, and—Scotch fashion —tossed it as high into the air as he possibly could.

"*Arrandoon*, ahoy!" he shouted. "*Arrandoon*, ahoy! Hurrah!"

There was not a soul on board that did not run aft to meet Silas as he sprang up the side. Even Freezing Powders, with Cockie on his shoulder, came wondering up, and Peter must needs get out his bag-pipes and strike into *The Campbells are coming*.

And when Silas found himself once more among his boys, and shaking hands with them all round; when he noticed the pale faces of Allan and Rory, and the pinched visage of the once strong and powerful McBain, and read in their weak and tottering gait the tale of all their sufferings, then it must be confessed that the bluff old mariner had to turn hastily about and address himself to others in order to hide a tear.

"Indeed, gentlemen all," said Silas, many, many months after this, "when I saw you all looking so peaky and pale, as I first jumped down on to your quarter-deck, I never felt so near making an old ass o' myself in all my born days!"

For three weeks longer the *Arrandoon* lay among the ice before she got fairly clear, and, consorted by the *Polar Star*, bore up for home. Three weeks—but they were not badly spent—three weeks, and all that time was needed to restore our invalids to robust health. And that only shows how near to death's door they must have been, because to make them well they had the best medicine this world can supply, and Silas Grig was the physician.

"Silas Grig! Silas Grig!" cried Rory, one morning at breakfast, about a fortnight after the reunion, "sure you're the best doctor that ever stepped in shoe-leather! No wonder we are all getting fat and rosy again! First you gave us a dose of hope—we got that before you jumped on board; then you gave us joy—a shake of your own honest hand, the sound of your own honest voice, and letters from home. What care I that my tenantry—'the foinest pisintry in the world'—haven't paid up? I've had letters from Arrandoon. What, Ray boy! more salmon and another egg? Just look at the effects of your physic, Dr. Silas Grig!"

Silas laughed. "But," he said, "there is one thing you haven't mentioned."

"Tell us," said Rory: "troth, it's a treat to hear ye talking!"

"The drop o' green ginger," said Silas.

* * * * *

Nor were these three weeks spent in idleness, for during that time the whole ship, from stem to stern, was redecorated; and when at last she was once more clear of the ice, once more out in the blue, she looked as bran new and as span new as on the day when she steamed down the wide, romantic Clyde.

I do not know any greater pleasure in life than that of being homeward bound after a long, long cruise at sea,

> "Good news from home, good news for me,
> Has come across the deep blue sea."

So runs the song. Good news from home, is certainly one of the rover's joys, but how much more joyous it is to be "rolling home, rolling home" to get that good news, eye to eye and lip to lip!

Once fairly under way, the weather seemed to get warmer every day. They reached Jan Mayen in a week; they found the rude village deserted, and Captain Cobb they would never be likely to meet again. So they left the island, and on the wings of a favouring breeze bore away for Iceland. Here Sandy McFlail, Doctor of Medicine of the University of Aberdeen, and surgeon of the good ship *Arrandoon*, begged to be left. Ah! poor Sandy was sadly in love with that blue-eyed, fair-haired Danish maiden. He fairly confessed to Rory, who had previously promised not to laugh at him, "that he had never seen a Scotch lassie to equal her, and that if she weren't a 'doctor's leddy' before six months were over it would not be his, Sandy McFlail's, fault."

"You are quite right, Sandy," said Rory in reply—"quite right; and do you know what it will be, Sandy?."

"What?" asked Sandy.

"A vera judeecious arrangement," cried Rory, running off before Sandy had a chance of catching him by the ear and making him "whustle."

But right fervent were the wishes for the doctor's welfare when he bade his friends adieu. And,

"You'll be sure to send us a piece o' the bride-cake," said Ralph.

"I'm no vera sure," said Sandy, "if it will ever come the length o' bride-cake. But," he added, bravely, "a body can only just try."

"Bravo!" cried Allan; "whatever a true man honestly dares he can do."

"And it's sure to come right in the end," said Rory.

So away went Sandy's boat, and away went the *Arrandoon*, firing the farewell guns, and as gaily bedecked in flags as if it had been Sandy's wedding morning.

The *Arrandoon* sailed nearly all the way home, for a favouring breeze was blowing, and with stunsails set, low and aloft, she looked like some gigantic sea-bird; and bravely, too, the little *Polar Star* kept her in sight. As for Silas, he did not live on board his own ship at all, but on board the *Arrandoon*. There was so much to be said and to say that they could not spare him.

The inhabitants of Glentruim turned out *en masse* to welcome the wanderers home. It was a day long to be remembered in that part of the Highlands of Scotland. The young chief, Allan McGregor, was not allowed to walk across one inch of his own grounds towards his castle of Arrandoon—no, nor to ride nor to drive; he must even be carried shoulder high, while slogans rent the air, and blue bonnets darkened it, and claymores were drawn and waved aloft, and the dogs all went daft, and danced about, barking at everybody, plainly showing that they had taken leave of their senses for one day, and weren't a bit ashamed of having done so.

Behind the procession marched Freezing Powders, with Cockie on his shoulder. The poor bird did not know what to make of all this Highland din, all this wild rejoicing. But he evidently enjoyed it.

"Keep it up, keep it up, keep it up!" he cried; "here's a pretty, pretty, pretty to-do! Go on, go on! Come on, come on—ha! ha! ha! ha! Lal de dal de dal lel al!"

And off went Cockie into the maddest dance that ever legs of bird performed. And Freezing Powders got frightened at last, and tried to lecture the bird into a quieter state of mind.

"I 'ssure you, Cockie," said Freezing Powders, "you is overdoin' it. Try to 'llay your feelin's, Cockie—try to 'llay your feelin's. As sure as nuffin' at all, Cockie, you'll have a drefful headache in de mornin'."

But Cockie only bowed and becked and danced and laughed the more, till at last Freezing Powders, looking upon the case as one of desperation, extracted from his pocket a red cotton handkerchief—the same he carried Cockie in when Captain McBain first met him on the Broomielaw—and in this he rolled Cockie as in the days of yore; but even then all the way to the castle Cockie was constantly finding corners to pop his head through, and let every one within hearing know that, though captured, he was as far from being subdued as ever.

Poor old Janet was beside herself with joy. She had been preparing pastry and getting ready puddings for days and days. She was fain to wipe her eyes with very joy when she shook hands once more with Ralph and Allan, and her old favourite, Rory. She was a little subdued when she looked at old Seth; she was just a trifle afraid of him, I believe. But she soon became herself again, and finished off by catching up Freezing Powders, Cockie and all, and bearing them off in triumph to the cosiest corner of the kitchen.

That same night fires were lit on every hill around Glentruim, and the reflection of them was seen southwards over all the wilds of Badenoch, and northward to the borders of Ross.

A few weeks after the return home Rory paid his promised visit to Silas at his little cottage by the sea, his cottage on the cliff-tops. Silas's flag fluttered right gaily in the wind that day, the summer flowers were all in bloom in the garden, and the green paling looked brighter, probably, than ever it had done, for the sun shone as it seldom shines—shone as if it had been paid to shine for the occasion, and the clouds lay low on the horizon, as if they had been paid to keep out of the way for once. The flag fluttered gaily, and the two little blue-jackets on the top of the pole ever and anon made such terrible onslaughts upon each other, that the only wonder was there was a bit of them left, that they did not demolish each other entirely, like the traditional cats of Kilkenny.

Silas had gone to the station to meet Rory. Silas was dressed, as he thought, like a landsman. Silas really thought that nobody could tell he was a sailor, because he wore a blue frock-coat and a tall beaver hat.

And Silas's little wife was all bustle and nervousness; but Rory had not been in the house half an hour ere all this was gone, and she was quietly happy, with a kind of feeling at her heart that she had known Rory all his life, and had even nursed him when he was quite a little mite.

Day and dinner and all passed off right cheerily, and of course with dessert Silas nodded to his little wife, and his little wife opened a bottle of fresh green ginger, and produced the bun—the wonderful bun, which was a pudding one day and a cake the next.

Silas kept smirking and nodding so long at Rory over his first drop of green ginger, that Rory knew he was going to say something, and so, by way of encouragement,

"Out with it, Silas," says Rory.

"Only this," says Silas: "Success to the wooing."

Well, who else in all the wide world could Rory have taken advice from except from Silas, in one little matter that deeply concerned his future welfare?

"Go in and win," had been Silas's advice. "Go in and

win, like the man you are. Faint heart never gained fair lady."

It is pleasant for me to be able to state that Rory took his old friend's advice to the letter. Now we know that the course of true love never did run smooth, and the course of Rory's wooing proved no exception to the proverb, but everything came right in the end, as Rory himself was fond of observing, and all is well that ends well. Just one year after this visit to Silas, Rory led Helen Edith McGregor to the altar. What a beautiful bride she made—more modest and bonnie than the rose just newly blown, or gowans tipped with dew!

Rory and Allan were not greater friends after the wedding than they had been before—that were impossible; but they were now brothers, and Allan made a vow that Rory should make his home in Glentruim.

There is a mansion there now as well as a castle, and in it dwell Rory and his wife.

Years have passed since the days of which I have been writing; they have not made very much change in our Irish hero. He is still the painter, still the poet, only there is not one only, but two little listeners now, that gaze up round-eyed and wonderingly at their father, whenever he takes up his magical instrument, the violin! Old Ap teaches these little ones to cut boats out of scraps of wood, and to rig small yachts in the summer evenings. The glen and castle both are wonderfully improved. There is some good after all in ambition, if it is an honest one, and some truth, too, in the motto of the Camerons, "Whatever a man dares he can do."

Every year Ralph, brave English Ralph, comes to the castle on *the* twelfth, and always spends a month; and every year Allan and Rory go southwards to Leigh Hall to return the visit. And they never go without taking Silas and McBain with them, so you may be sure these are very happy, very pleasant seasons.

. What about Seth? Oh, merely this, Ralph offered to take him back to his own country, and to reinstal him as an Arctic Crusoe in his far northern home.

"Gentlemen," said Seth, "I'm right sensible of all your kindness, but I guess I'm getting old, and if my young friend here wouldn't mind, I'd prefer leaving my bones in the glen here. Civilisation has kind o' spoiled the old trapper, and he'd feel sort o' lonely now in his old farm. There ain't many b'ars in the glen, I reckon; but never mind, old Seth can still draw a bead on a rabbit."

"And so you shall," said Allan. "I'll make you my warren-master, and head of all my keepers."

So Seth has settled down to end his days in peace. He dwells in one of the prettiest little Highland cottages that ever you saw. It gets snowed over in winter sometimes, it is true, and that might be looked upon as a drawback; but oh, to see it in summer, when the feathery birches nod green around it and the heather is all in bloom!

Peter played a little trick on poor old Seth, which I cannot help recording.

"It will never do, you know," Peter told him, "for a Highland keeper on the estate of Glentruim not to wear the kilt."

"Guess you're a kind o' right," said Seth, "but, bless you, Peter, my legs ain't o' no consequence, they ain't a bit thicker than old Bran the deerhound's, and I reckon they're just about the same shape."

"Well," replied Peter, "I grant you that is a kind of an objection, but then custom is everything, you know."

So, lo and behold! one fine summer morning, who should stalk into the castle yard but old trapper Seth arrayed in full Highland costume. No wonder the dogs barked and ran away! no wonder Allan and Rory laughed till their sides ached and they could hardly hold their guns! no wonder old Janet shouted and screamed with merriment, and Cockie whistled shrill, and Freezing Powders nearlk went into a fit! No, Seth's legs were but little thicker than Bran's. Seth arrayed in skins from head to heel was passable, but Seth in a kilt!!!

Poor Seth! it was somewhat unkind of Peter. However, the trapper never wore a kilt again.

THE END.

www.ingramcontent.com/pod-product-compliance
Lightning Source LLC
Chambersburg PA
CBHW020244240426
43672CB00006B/638